Graphic
Design
school

ALBUM COVERS

Although our label knew me photojournalists, I very soon became interested in developing ideas the album covers. Bands like Deep Purple and Uriah Heep were very encouraging when I was working my novel example that would reflect the music within.

I: Banana-like the ideas was a fascinating and rewarding experience. When we started work on Ozzy Osbourne's 'Bark at the Moon' we looked at everything we could find in literature and on film that related to werewolves. We also went to Shepperton film theatre and sent O.C. Gillman set-ups to find we would have a wide choice for the actor and the related promotional material. Ozzy was to make-up for ten hours and we shot right through the night. Exhausting chef for everyone involved. A look of photographs taken in China in the 1950's by the Magnum photographer Marc Riboud initially inspired the cover of The Drum for Japan. We started to keep the far Eastern connection applied to the band's name without giving Japanese. It won several design and photography awards and we recently moved to a lemon repackaging.

JAPAN TIN DRUM

I kind of grew up surrounded by black culture. I went to an all-black school. It is this culture I identify with. I can identify with other cultures too; we all have a lot of people inside of us, and one of the ones inside of me is black. Don't let the pigmentation fool you; it is a state of mind. It has affected me a lot in my work. To try to point out would be kind of be beside the point. You just see it. It is there. In the case of Jackie Brown, it really enabled me to write truthfully, heartfeltly and realistically, and to become the characters of Jackie Brown and Ordell.

You have heard of method acting I am a method writer. I become the characters as I am writing them. That is how I am able to get them to talk to each other, and I am everybody. I am Louis. I am Melanie. The way I write my dialogue is to get them to talk to each other, and then they are doing it so it is all coming from me. I know some of the people in my life I have admired and trust were older black women. I have a lot of respect for them, so I was able to bring all of that into Jackie Brown. As far as Ordell, I was a little crazy for around a year I just walked around as Ordell. It was a spell I was under and I could not break it because I did not want the work to suffer.

"He creates that kind of atmosphere where what you do is suddenly part of life, the moment you are doing it."

London Film Festival

A world of amusement presented by the British Film Institute in association with American Express.

THE FULL CUPBOARD OF LIFE

FROM THE AUTHOR OF THE NO.1 LADIES' DETECTIVE AGENCY

The Full Cupboard of Life

Winner of the Saga Award for Wit

Alexander McCall Smith

Graphic
Design
school

A FOUNDATION COURSE IN THE PRINCIPLES AND PRACTICES OF GRAPHIC DESIGN

Third Edition | **David Dabner**

WILEY

A QUARTO BOOK

Copyright ©2005 Quarto Publishing Inc.

Published by John Wiley & Sons Inc., Hoboken, New Jersey
Published simultaneously in Canada

Library of Congress Cataloging-in-Publication Number
20540-4320

ISBN 0-471-68683-2
10 9 8 7 6 5 4 3 2 1

Manufactured by Provision Pte Ltd in Singapore
Printed by SNP Leefung Printers Pte Ltd in China

Contents

Introduction

Whether your goal is to become a whizz at web design, create memorable ads, or develop the look of a trail-blazing magazine, this book will give you a thorough grounding in the principles that underlie all good graphic design. Rooted in practice rather than theory, the text has been constructed to mirror how the subject is taught in design colleges today, and the illustrations—a mixture of student and professional work—have been carefully chosen to illuminate specific teaching points. Many units, moreover, contain step-by-step exercises for students to work through and solutions to real-life problems.

The process of looking, and translating what you see, is a key fundamental of Section 1, but learning how to control the different media at your disposal—many of them digital—should go hand in hand with the joy of creating images and a delight in visual freedom. As you are introduced to the basics of photography, type, color, and composition, you will learn how to become visually aware and culturally literate, a sure prerequisite for generating graphic ideas that get noticed.

In the middle section, the solving of particular design problems moves center stage, and we see how visual ideas evolve from loose sketches to more finished pieces. You will learn how type, the primary graphic medium of communication, can be used to create myriad different effects, depending on context, and you'll be shown the importance of grids and layouts, commissioning and sourcing images, and understanding how production issues should come into play early on. Above all, you'll learn that successful work requires careful planning and research before ideas can be carried forward.

Finally, with the help of some seasoned professionals, you will acquire a unique insight into the five main areas of graphic design and be able to test what you've learned through some in-depth commercial assignments. In the process we hope to spark your imagination and help you reach a decision about your future direction.

⬇ **Strong use of diagonals,** even within the photograph, creates dynamism within the rectilinear format.

AEROSMITH
DAVID DIMBLEBY
DURAN DURAN
PETER GABRIEL
ROY HATTERSLEY
JAPAN
ALED JONES
LEMMY
ANTHONY MINGHELLA

FIN COSTELLO photographs

FIN COSTELLO has photographed many of the best known faces in the public arena. Iconic pictures of Mick Jagger, Steven Tyler and Pete Townsend sit alongside more intimate portraits of Will Self, Sir Malcolm Arnold and Roy Hattersley in a portfolio of work that covers three decades of photographic portraiture. He has achieved worldwide recognition for his images of artists including Ozzy Osbourne, Peter Gabriel, Michael Jackson and Fleetwood Mac; and for album covers including Kiss 'Alive' and Japan's 'Tin Drum'. These covers and others have achieved recognition today as some of the genre-defining record sleeves of the last thirty years. In recent times he has maintained his high profile in the music and publishing industries as well as pursuing more personal projects in rural Spain and Ireland. He is based in east London and is currently working on a book that collects images from every area of an illustrious photographic career.

OZZY OSBOURNE
ROBERT PLANT
ROLLING STONES
SIR MALCOLM ARNOLD
WILL SELF
STING
PETE TOWNSEND

⬆ **Rhythm** The black space, and the full-page photo opposite, act as counterweights to the busy layout.

⊕ Color associations Red equates symbolically to danger and anger, a principle exploited to full effect in this stylish poster.

⊕ Overlapping type is the visual equivalent to clamoring voices and can create a feeling of panic and mental distress.

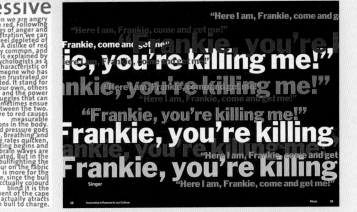

⊕ Conversation piece
Colloquial phrases snake through this poster, a witty rendering of the London Underground map that encapsulates the diversity of the capital's population.

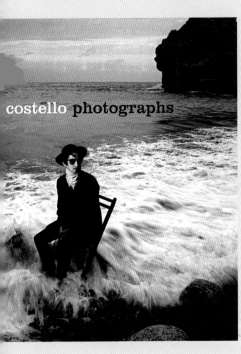

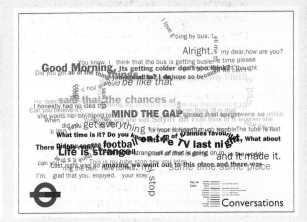

⊕ Type as object In this poster characters are juxtaposed with simple images to playful effect.

the Language of Design

What is meant by the language of design? Just as a child learns a language in order to communicate with the world, a design student needs to learn a different type of language in order to enter the world of graphic design. This language is a visual one, which starts with a heightened awareness of the way the world looks. It is a way of seeing that is different from what is just physically there. The artist Henri Matisse said that when he ate a tomato he just looked at it. But, he added, when he painted a tomato he saw it differently.

There are many strategies for teaching a child to learn and use language; the same applies to teaching students the language of design. The language has three basic parts: form, color, and concept.

Form is the composition of the fundamental elements in a design. It is the way a thing looks—the shape, proportion, balance, and harmony of the constituent parts. Understanding form comes from developing the ability to see the intrinsic qualities of elements and the relationships between them.

Color plays an important part in graphic-design decision-making, adding variety and mood, as well as a spatial dimension. The colors you choose for your designs will not only provoke psychological and emotional responses, but should also support and enhance the formal aspects.

The word "concept" refers to the idea or thought behind a design. The thought processes that designers go through when they absorb and develop a client's brief are a vital part of finding a graphic solution to a particular problem. Unless you get the thinking right, form and color are of little value. But, as with form and color, you can employ strategies for helping to develop concepts. Edward de Bono has written extensively about how we think and the type of thinking necessary for designers. His work is worth investigating for this reason. When the concept and use of form and color are well integrated you have a good chance of the design achieving its objectives. These components are what constitutes the language of design.

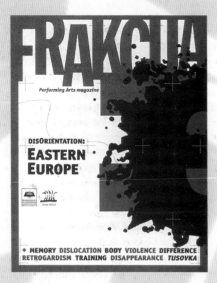

Butting letters By butting the letters at varying distances from the border, they become abstract shapes as much as letters. The movement that is created by the negative background shapes is entirely in keeping with this performing-art magazine.

Drop in The title and author panels were sized and placed very specifically to create a symmetric design within the background space. The surrounding negative space uses similarly tinted large and small type in a subtle way.

SECTION 1	THE LANGUAGE OF DESIGN
MODULE 1	Fundamentals
UNIT 1	**Form and Space**

Seeing is such a commonplace experience that we pay it little attention. For the graphic designer the process of perception (the way our eyes and brains make sense of what we see) is of the greatest interest and importance. Whether consciously or not, our eyes are constantly supplying information to our brains, which processes and makes sense of that visual input.

SEE ALSO: Negative and Positive Space *p12*

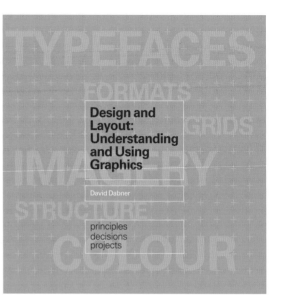

Design and Layout: Understanding and Using Graphics

David Dabner

principles
decisions
projects

Two-dimensional space

Graphic design is mostly carried out within the confines of two dimensions (height and width). A sheet of white paper is a flat surface until we place a mark on it, then it becomes the scene of visual forces, which become more complex as the number of elements is increased. These forces are the underlying dynamics of visual stimulus and should be explored by a number of simple experiments.

Figure and ground

A form is always experienced in relation to the space in which it is placed and to other forms that may be present in the format. Every form is seen in context and cannot be totally isolated. Generally speaking, a form is considered to be "positive" and the space around it "negative." The space within a format—sometimes described as "the ground"—is an important element of any design and not just something left over once a form is placed on it.

Space should be organized and controlled, for it provides important information about the form, which, of course, in turn must have a non-form around it in order to exist at all. Badly arranged space is a bit like mis-timed pauses in speech; they can disrupt meaning and emphasis. Similarly, space should not be allowed to spread about aimlessly, because it can weaken the structure of the design.

Form relationships

To appreciate the primary visual experience of form and space it is a good idea to try a number of experiments yourself. This can be done by drawing up on a sheet of paper a 5-in (12.5-cm) square with a firm pencil line, and cutting out from a piece of black paper a number of ½-in (1.25-cm) squares.

Symmetry and asymmetry

Placing one black square in the middle of your pencil format, you will notice that your drawn square has the appearance of a different surface from the paper outside the square. Your pencil line and the presences of the black square have changed your understanding of the flat surface in front of you. The square created by pencil seems to come forward. However, the central positioning of the black square means that the space around it is the same on all four sides; each pencil-drawn border echoes a side of the black square. The result is a visual sensation that can be described as still, peaceful, passive, or even boring. It is also an example of symmetry. If a line is drawn down the center of the format, the two half squares will be a mirror image of their opposites (perfect balance).

To continue this experiment, you can glue the black square in place and draw more 5-in (12.5-cm) squares. In the second square, position the black square exactly as the first, but now, place between the left border and the black square a second black square so that it is in the middle of the space and aligned with the first black square. These two squares now seem to enter the pencil format from the left, this impression coming from our convention of reading from left to right. In another 5-in (12.5-cm) square, position a second black square between the central black square and the right-hand border. Now we experience a sense of the two as moving to the right, as if leaving the pencil square. If a second black square is positioned between the top border and the central black square, the two appear to be dropping into the format. All these designs are asymmetric, that is, they do not balance perfectly.

One can create the same series of arrangements, but with the black squares set at 45 degrees to the pencil border so that they no longer echo the border. The effect will be a stronger sense of dynamic movement.

The above experiments can be extended by adding more elements, but do look carefully and be aware of the visual effects of each arrangement.

Three-dimensional form

We can now continue with these simple explorations by moving into three dimensions, or at least the illusion thereof. The illusion of depth and volume in space came to us through perspective, a device developed at the start of the Italian Renaissance.

Return to your 5-in (12.5-cm) pencil line square and centered ½-in (1.25-cm) black square. Add to this a 2-in (5-cm) black square. Position the new square in the top left-hand corner of the format, so that it is in the center of the space and the bottom edge aligns with the top edge of the original centered square. The larger square appears to be closer to you than the centered square, as it might be in the physical world. As it is in the top part of the format it also appears above your eye level and the centered square in the middle distance. The larger square also demands more of your attention.

⊕ Figure and ground The centered square is still or passive, as the space around the square is equal on all sides.

⊗ Entering left When a second square is introduced, visual forces develop. There is a sense that the squares are entering from the left.

⊕ Moving right The position of the two squares suggests movement to the right.

⊕ Going down The position of the two squares hints at movement downward.

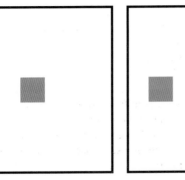

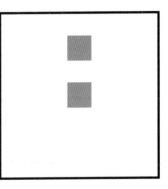

UNIT 2 | **Negative and Positive Space**

You should consider the effective use of positive and negative space. The positive space is that which occupies the image area, while the negative space is the background, otherwise known as the ground or picture plane. It is important here to recognize that, generally speaking, negative space works in supporting the image area and so cannot be left to develop as an active space in its own right.

⬅ ➡ **Face front**
Does Rubin's Vase show a drawing of an elegant vase or the profiles of two people facing each other?

It is worthwhile exploring the effects that this "unused" space has on the overall feel of an image by deliberately altering the ratio of positive to negative space. Sometimes you can actively encourage ambiguity between the picture elements and the background. Situations can occur when a particular group of forms come together to support each other and compete in such a way that the (normally negative) space is given form by the positive elements. In such cases, our eyes have trouble working out what is form and what is ground. This creates ambiguity, which can be intriguing and stimulate visual excitement. Form can be used to "capture," or enclose, space in such a way that an image emerges that can be read as positive even though elsewhere in the design it retains its usual role.

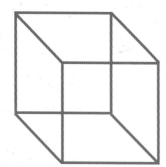

➡ **Problems of perception** The Necker cube shows how the eye can come to two conclusions. Are you looking at a cube seen from above and facing to the left or a cube seen from below and facing to the right?

EXERCISE

Finding the component shapes
Using tracing paper and an interesting, but not over-complicated photograph, break down the image to its major component shapes. This will reveal the underlying compositional structure, how the picture surface has been divided up effectively, and how positive and negative space play their respective parts.

Using line to build up internal forms

Highlighting the positive space

Masking the negative space

SEE ALSO: Form and Space *p10*
Pace and Contrast *p106*

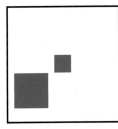

Relative scale and importance The large square appears to be closer. This effect creates an illusion of depth or three-dimensional space.

Negative and positive space The black elements in these two arrangements can be experienced as a ground that throws the white forward as positive form.

Making a viewing device is a simple way of isolating the area to be drawn. It can be cut from stiff gray or black board in various shapes and sizes.

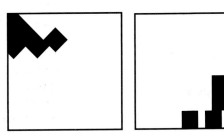

EXERCISE

Black and white forms
This is a project that continues exploring the principles of form and space, but in a more complex way. Using scissors, cut out two or three letter forms of varying sizes from white paper, and their counter forms from black paper. These should be used as the basic elements to explore the dynamics of form and space. The letters are not intended to have a specific meaning, but as familiar forms they avoid becoming pure abstractions and maintain a basic sense of meaning as to whether they are upright, tilted or upside-down, which adds to the sense of dynamics within the composition.

A OK The letter A and its reversed-out version, which appears abstract against the black tint.

White on black These three designs make use of black-and-white letterforms to create a sense of ambiguity between form and space, or figure and ground.

Introducing color
Introducing color into a design, changes the dynamic completely, and allows the designer to differentiate information.

UNIT 3 | **Composition**

Composition refers to the structure and organization of subject matter, and a practical understanding and exploration of this topic is crucial for effective visual communication. Composition should be seen as equally important as the elements that are used to construct the image itself.

Exploring composition
These three designs show various compositional options for the same visual ingredients. The "grid" background gives structure to the scattered leaves. Although the solutions are very different, each is balanced and successful.

⬆ The main elements of the design fall roughly on or within the golden section lines.

➡ A more formal composition with the main image central and the other leaves balancing or acting as a frame in each corner.

⬅ A more random approach, working with diagonals against the background square grid.

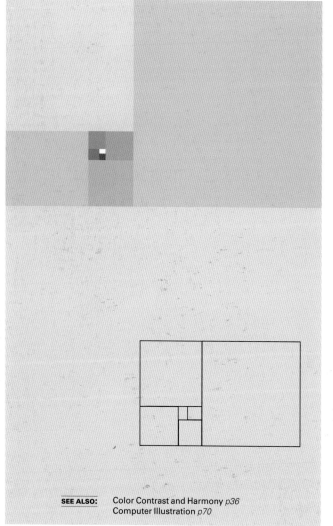

⬅ **The Golden Section**
Each time a square is taken from the section, a smaller rectangle remains with the same proportions as the original.

Throughout the history of the visual arts different theories of composition have been advanced. Vitruvius, the Roman architect and engineer, devised a mathematical formula for the division of space within a picture. His solution, known as the Golden Section and sometimes as the Golden Mean, was based on a set ratio between the longer and shorter sides of a rectangle. The French painter Henri Matisse (1869–1954) put greater emphasis on inspiration, maintaining that composition is the art of arranging the various elements so as to express feelings in a decorative fashion.

SEE ALSO: Color Contrast and Harmony p36
Computer Illustration p70

The key notion here is that elements are capable of expressing feelings when they derive from effective compositional studies. A good starting-point is to use abstract shapes and textures, which are capable of suggesting and evoking feeling just as much as figurative work but which allow you to focus purely on how those elements are arranged. Immediately questions arise. How should the picture surface be divided up? In what way should the subject matter occupy the surface space? The elements chosen do not simply have to sit in a central position on the paper but can appear to protrude out of or enter in from the edges. A symmetrical composition makes for a calmer, more peaceful work, while something more dynamic can be achieved if the elements are arranged asymmetrically.

Exploring the physical idea of space and the illusion of depth of field on a two-dimensional surface will create interesting relationships. This can be achieved by varying the size (and color) of shapes or through the use of perspective, in which the subject appears to recede into the distance at one or more vanishing points.

Observation

When working from direct observation on a still-life composition, you need either to rearrange the objects within the space or to find the right perspective in which to see them. The first option is easier because you can arrange the objects to create any shape, form, or mood. The second approach requires you to move around the object or objects to find a position that has the potential to make an interesting composition. A series of quick preliminary studies can be carried out to discover this best position, or you could also use a viewfinder made from cutting two L-shapes from black card and placing them together to create a movable frame.

This is also an ideal way to begin exercising your understanding and feel for interesting composition. To explore this you can use any type of picture, although it can be particularly advantageous with photographic work. By cropping into the image and eliminating a proportion, you emphasize a specific area, creating a new visual tension.

EXERCISE

Opposites

From a dictionary or thesaurus find a good pair of descriptive but contrasting words, such as remote/close or immense/tiny. Use simple abstract shapes, marks, and textures to create a composition that illustrates the meaning of these words. Experiment with how the paper surface can be divided up and how the shapes can occupy the surface area. Chosen shapes need not lie within the picture plane itself but can intrude from a surface edge. Any media can be used to achieve this, including collage. Once the composition has been completed it can be developed further, by incorporating a figurative element or elements that echo your chosen words.

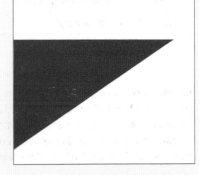

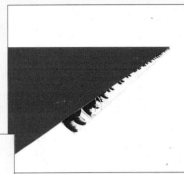

↑ Near/far The designer first divided the picture plane diagonally, creating the potential for deep perspectival space. She uses a mixture of watercolor base and receding lines of people to illustrate the opposite "near" and "far".

UNIT 4 | **Basic Principles of Layout**

The term "layout" refers to the way in which we organize the disparate material that makes up the content of a design. Your aim is both to present information in a logical, coherent way, and to make the important elements stand out. Use of a grid and consistently styled elements also helps the reader to absorb information in a visually pleasant way.

Urban life
the fumes, **the future, the facts**

Left: Duis autem vel eum iriure dolor in hendrerit in vulputate velit esse molestie consequat, vel illum dolore

Korem ipsum dolor sit amet, consectetuer adipiscing elit, sed diam nonummy nibh euismod tincidunt ut laoreet dolore magna aliquam erat volutpat. Ut wisi enim ad minim veniam, quis nostrud exerci tation ullamcorper suscipit lobortis nisl ut aliquip ex ea commodo consequat.

Duis autem vel eum iriure dolor in hendrerit in vulputate velit esse molestie consequat, vel illum dolore eu feugiat nulla facilisis at vero eros et accumsan et iusto odio dignissim qui blandit praesent luptatum zzril delenit augue duis dolore te feugait nulla facilisi. Lorem ipsum dolor sit amet, consectetuer adipiscing elit,

sed diam nonummy nibh euismod tincidunt ut laoreet dolore magna aliquam erat volutpat.

Ut wisi enim ad minim veniam, quis nostrud exerci tation ullamcorper suscipit lobortis nisl ut aliquip ex ea commodo consequat. Duis autem vel eum iriure dolor in hendrerit in vulputate velit esse molestie consequat, vel illum dolore eu feugiat nulla facilisis at vero eros et accumsan et iusto odio dignissim qui blandit praesent luptatum zzril delenit augue duis dolore te feugait nulla facilisi. Nam liber tempor cum soluta nobis eleifend option congue nihil imperdiet doming id quod mazim

urban life
the fumes, the future, the facts

Korem ipsum dolor sit amet, consectetuer adipiscing elit, sed diam nonummy nibh euismod tincidunt ut laoreet dolore magna aliquam erat volutpat. Ut wisi enim ad minim veniam, quis nostrud exerci tation ullamcorper suscipit lobortis nisl ut aliquip ex ea commodo consequat.

Duis autem vel eum iriure dolor in hendrerit in vulputate velit esse molestie consequat, vel illum dolore eu feugiat nulla facilisis at vero eros et accumsan et iusto odio dignissim qui blandit praesent luptatum zzril delenit augue duis dolore te feugait nulla facilisi. Lorem ipsum dolor sit amet, consectetuer adipiscing elit, sed diam nonummy nibh euismod tincidunt ut laoreet dolore magna aliquam erat volutpat.

Right: Duis autem vel eum iriure dolor in hendrerit in vulputate velit esse molestie consequat, vel illum dolore

Nam liber tempor cum soluta nobis eleifend option congue nihil imperdiet doming id quod mazim placerat facer possim assum. Lorem ipsum dolor sit amet, consectetuer adipiscing elit, sed diam nonummy nibh euismod tincidunt ut laoreet dolore magna aliquam erat volutpat. Ut wisi enim ad minim veniam, quis nostrud exerci tation ullamcorper suscipit lobortis nisl ut aliquip ex ea commodo consequat.

⬇ **Clean and structured**
White space around all the text boxes makes it easy for the eye to navigate the information, and the bled image across the top of the spread adds a touch of dynamism.

⬆ **Authoritative** With its full-page picture, classic serif face for the header, and consistent caption column, this is the classic opener. The justified text makes the information appear more serious.

⬅ **Funky** The cutting-edge heading type, the complex grid, and the varied type measures makes for a "hard-working" layout that is aimed at a young, committed audience.

Above: Duis autem vel eum iriure dolor in hendrerit in vulputate velit esse molestie consequat, vel illum dolore

Urban life
the fumes, **the future, the facts**

Korem ipsum dolor sit amet, consectetuer adipiscing elit, sed diam nonummy nibh euismod tincidunt ut laoreet dolore magna aliquam erat volutpat. Ut wisi enim ad minim veniam, quis nostrud exerci tation ullamcorper suscipit lobortis nisl ut aliquip ex ea commodo consequat.

Duis autem vel eum iriure dolor in hendrerit in vulputate velit esse molestie consequat, vel illum dolore eu feugiat nulla facilisis at vero eros et accumsan et iusto odio dignissim qui blandit praesent luptatum zzril delenit augue duis dolore magna. aliquam erat volutpat.

Ut wisi enim ad minim veniam, quis nostrud exerci tation ullamcorper suscipit lobortis nisl ut aliquip.

• Duis autem vel eum iriure dolor in vulputate velit esse molestie consequat, vel illum dolore eu feugiat nulla facilisis.
• Duis autem vel eum iriure dolor in hendrerit in vulputate velit esse molestie consequat, vel illum dolore eu feugiat nulla facilisis at vero eros et accumsan et iusto odio dignissim qui blandit praesent luptatum zzril delenit augue duis dolore te feugait nulla facilisi.
• Duis autem vel eum iriure dolor in hendrerit in vulputate velit esse molestie consequat, vel illum dolore eu feugiat nulla facilisis.
• Nam liber tempor cum soluta nobis eleifend option congue nihil imperdiet doming id quod ipsum dolor sit amet, consectetuer adipiscing elit, sed diam nonummy nibh euismod tincidunt ut laoreet dolore magna aliquam erat volutpat.
• Duis autem vel eum iriure dolor in hendrerit in vulputate velit esse molestie consequat, vel illum dolore eu feugiat nulla facilisis.

Duis autem vel eum iriure dolor in hendrerit in vulputate velit esse molestie consequat, vel illum dolore eu feugiat nulla facilisis at vero eros et accumsan et iusto odio dignissim qui blandit praesent luptatum zzril delenit augue duis dolore te feugait nulla facilisi. Lorem ipsum dolor sit amet, consectetuer adipiscing elit, sed diam nonummy nibh euismod tincidunt ut laoreet dolore magna aliquam erat eros et volutpat.

Ut wisi enim ad minim veniam, quis nostrud exerci tation ullamcorper suscipit lobortis nisl ut aliquip.

Ipsum dolor sit amet, consectetuer adipiscing elit, sed diam nonummy nibh euismod tincidunt ut laoreet dolore magna aliquam erat volutpat. Ut wisi enim ad minim veniam, quis nostrud exerci tation ullamcorper suscipit lobortis nisl blandit praesent luptatum zzril delenit augue duis.

Ipsum dolor sit amet, consectetuer adipiscing elit, sed diam nonummy nibh euismod tincidunt ut laoreet dolore magna aliquam erat volutpat. Ut wisi enim ad minim veniam, quis nostrud exerci tation ullamcorper suscipit lobortis nisl blandit praesent luptatum zzril delenit augue duis.

Duis autem vel eum iriure dolor in hendrerit in vulputate velit esse molestie consequat, vel illum dolore eu feugiat nulla facilisis at vero eros et accumsan et iusto odio dignissim qui blandit praesent luptatum zzril delenit augue duis dolore magna. aliquam erat eros et volutpat.

Ut wisi enim ad minim veniam, quis nostrud exerci tation ullamcorper suscipit lobortis nisl ut aliquip.

The brief

There are three basic stages in producing layouts. First, the designer receives a brief in which the client establishes what material should be used. This will normally include a combination of text—main text, display copy (headings), boxes or sidebars, and captions—and images, such as photographs, illustrations, maps, or diagrams. The brief should also cover the desired look or "feel" of the work, which in turn will depend on the target audience. Should the layout look authoritative and packed with information? Clean and structured, with lots of white space? Or funky and cutting-edge?

SEE ALSO: Type Size *p48* • Emphasis and Hierarchy *p88*
Size and Format *p98* • Grids and Margins *p100*
Styles of Layout *p102* • Pace and Contrast *p106*

A head — Urban life

B head — the fumes, the future, the facts

Text — Korem ipsum dolor sit amet, consectetuer adipiscing elit, sed diam nonummy nibh euismod tincidunt u aliquam erat volutpa minim veniam, quis ullamcorper suscipi ex ea commodo cor

Duis autem vel eu hendrerit in vulputat consequat, vel illum facilisis at vero eros odio dignissim qui b luptatum zzril deleni feugait nulla facilisi. amet, consectetuer diam nonummy nibh laoreet dolore magn

Ut wisi enim ad minim veniam, quis nostrud exerci tation ullamcor suscipit lobortis nisl ut aliquip.

Bullet points
- Duis autem vel eum iriure dolor in hendrerit in vulputate velit esse molestie consequat, vel illum dolore eu feugiat nulla facilisis.

- Duis autem vel eum iriure dolor in hendrerit in vulputate velit esse molestie consequat, vel illum dolore eu feugiat nulla facilisis at vero eros et accumsan et iusto odio dignissim qui blandit praesent luptatum zzril delenit augue duis dolore te feugait nulla facilisi.

Editorial mark-up Once typesetters would have interpreted an editor's mark-up; these days the task typically falls to the designer.

Scamps offer a rough guide to the overall look of the page; at this stage, the lack of detail is a bonus.

The grid serves as an invisible framework for all the page elements—a visual anchor for text, headings, and pictures.

Urban life

Above: **Duis autem vel eum iriure dolor in hendrerit in vulputate velit esse molestie consequat, vel illum dolore**

Korem ipsum dolor sit amet, consectetuer adipiscing elit, sed diam nonummy nibh euismod tincidunt ut laoreet dolore magna aliquam erat volutpat. Ut wisi enim ad minim veniam, quis nostrud exerci tation ullamcorper suscipit lobortis nisl ut aliquip ex ea commodo consequat.

Duis autem vel eum iriure dolor in hendrerit in vulputate velit esse molestie consequat, vel illum dolore eu feugiat nulla facilisis at vero eros et accumsan et iusto odio dignissim qui blandit praesent luptatum zzril delenit augue duis dolore te feugait nulla facilisi. Lorem ipsum dolor sit amet, consectetuer adipiscing elit, sed diam nonummy nibh euismod tincidunt ut laoreet dolore magna aliquam erat volutpat.

Ut wisi enim ad minim veniam, quis nostrud exerci tation ullamcor suscipit lobortis nisl ut aliquip.

- Duis autem vel eum iriure dolor in hendrerit in vulputate velit esse molestie consequat, vel illum dolore eu feugiat nulla facilisis.

- Duis autem vel eum iriure dolor in hendrerit in vulputate velit esse molestie consequat, vel illum dolore eu feugiat nulla facilisis at vero eros et accumsan et iusto odio dignissim qui blandit praesent luptatum zzril delenit augue duis dolore te feugait nulla facilisi.

- Duis autem vel eum iriure dolor in hendrerit in vulputate velit esse molestie consequat, vel illum dolore eu feugiat nulla facilisis.

- Nam liber tempor cum soluta nobis eleifend option congue nihil imperdiet doming id quod ipsum dolor sit amet, consectetuer adipiscing elit, sed diam nonummy nibh euismod tincidunt ut laoreet dolore magna aliquam erat volutpat.

- Duis autem vel eum iriure dolor in hendrerit in vulputate velit esse molestie consequat, vel illum dolore eu feugiat nulla facilisis.

12

Practical factors

Next, the designer needs to start thinking about how various practical factors, such as format and available colors, will influence his or her approach. If there are many pictures and extensive copy to be fitted into a relatively short extent, this will affect the look of the layout, too. At this stage agreement should be reached as to the establishment of hierarchies within the copy, or the main points of emphasis. In some cases, an editor may have labeled headings A, B, C, and so on to indicate their relative importance. These and other elements can be treated typographically to enhance their meaning through differences in type size, weight, form, and even color.

checklist of questions before layout commences

- What text material will be used?
- Will there be photographs, illustrations, diagrams?
- How many colors can be used?
- What is the format and size of the job?
- What parts of the text need emphasizing?
- Who is the target audience?
- Is the client looking for a particular style?

The grid

The third stage is getting down to business. Do not rush to the computer straight away. Assuming the job has a number of pages you should draw up a double-page spread to actual size. This gives you a first chance of seeing the area in which you have to work. To aid the organization of the material, it is best to devise a grid, in which the overall structure of the page is divided into units of space. The grid will show the layout of columns, margins, and areas for main text, captions and images, and will also show the position of repeating headlines, or running heads, and the page numbers. After drawing out your double-page spread you can prepare some "roughs" of your layouts. These may be small "thumbnails" or half-sized visuals known as "scamps" in which first ideas are sketched out. This

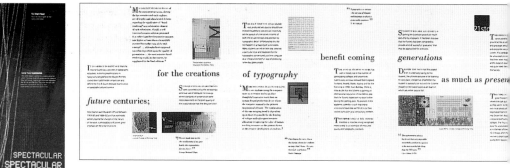

Format mirrors content The long format chosen here reflects the content of a poster listing events for Chinese New Year. Inspiration for format often emanates from subject matter.

Picture power Here the main point of emphasis is the photograph, which dominates the spread. The image is supported by several lines of display copy, and the small amount of text copy creates minimal clutter.

Easy on the eye Type, small pictures, and white space combine to create a calm but attractive feel.

No clutter The designer has met the challenge of incorporating many elements— display and text copy, photographs and a large diagrammatic chart—while maintaining a clean, easy-to-grasp appearance.

Elements working together Photograph and type work innovatively in tandem to create maximum impact. The page's graphic power draws in the reader to tackle what is otherwise a dense block of text.

thinking time is important in the overall layout process to help make decisions about the composition and uses of the material. Time spent at this initial stage will give several variants that can be taken to the computer and quickly produced. The time it takes to draw out ideas is infinitely faster than trying to create designs directly onto the computer. It cannot be emphasized enough that the computer is simply a tool; it cannot do the thinking for you. This is where the imaginative designer can fully extend their abilities before any production takes place.

White space is often a feature of books about art, architecture, and design. Images and text are given equal emphasis in this nicely structured approach.

Typography is the content of these four different layouts. Display type is exploited to reinforce the subject matter.

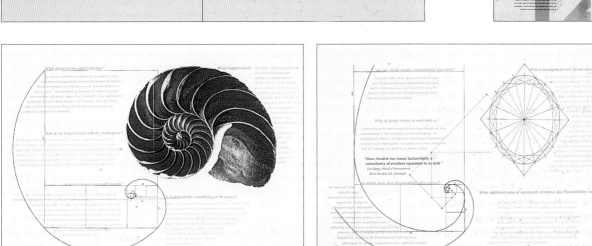

Overlapping of illustration with text copy makes these layouts visually stimulating.

UNIT 5 | **Exploratory Drawing**

The purpose of exploratory drawing for the future graphic designer is to explore ideas; it is a means of translating the outside world and of giving concrete form to abstract ideas. Even bearing in mind modern computer technology (itself just another tool to be utilized), you should find that drawing becomes the basis of expression and underpins all your design decisions.

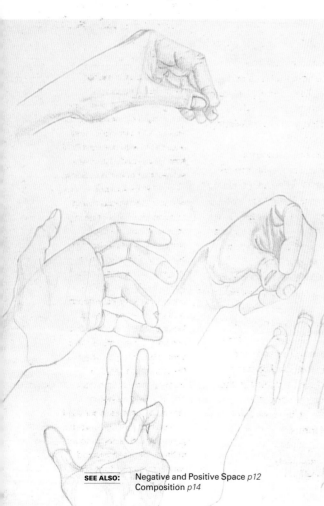

SEE ALSO: Negative and Positive Space *p12*
Composition *p14*

🔙 **Life drawing** Detailed monochromatic pencil studies of the drawer's own hand. Here form is used to create the illusion of depth of space.

🔽 **Drawing your environment** Imaginative and energetic drawing of a street scene, based on direct observation. If a camera is used to record the scene, off-site drawings can later incorporate more detail.

Observation

Drawing is relevant to graphic design because it makes you see the subject as a shape or shapes, and color as tones; it teaches you to understand and manipulate perspective, to create the illusion of space and depth of field; and it shows you how to convey texture and density. Students should in any event experiment beyond their own territory, attempting to understand fully as many kinds of visual image-making as possible and the methods by which they are created. Regardless of how good you are at drawing, it is essential to start at the beginning. Even though you may already be able to interpret objects and structures in a skilful way, your vision is probably too narrow. Continual practice is the key.

In establishing the essential elements of drawing, you must train your eye to see the subject matter of all kinds of diverse structures in detail. A still life represents a good start, as it enables you easily to explore your chosen subject matter from different angles, by moving around and taking up fresh positions, and by spending time sitting and viewing what is front of you. You are then able to work at your own pace. But equally you should not be daunted by working from life itself. Going out and visually researching the environment around offers a stimulating array of moving and static subject matter. You can work directly in a sketchbook or perhaps use a camera so that you can do more finished drawings at a

Line A strong use of line is used to describe almost every blade of densely textured hair. This is in contrast with the sparseness of horizontal lines and soft shadows on the face.

A direct response This picture of buildings has been achieved by working directly in watercolor and not relying on an underlying drawn structure. This kind of approach enables you to engage immediately with the subject matter.

later date. It is important to familiarize yourself with as diverse aspects of form as possible and to allow for energetic mark-making.

For all these drawings experiment with different media, as the image you create will be conditioned by the medium used. Whether charcoal or pencil, crayon or brush, each instrument you use requires some understanding, as each has specific effects. For example, pencils, with grades ranging from hard to soft, allow tonal control, detailed modeling, and a strong line. Do not limit yourself to conventional media as other implements, such as a toothbrush, piece of string, or even a sewing machine, can create interesting and valid marks. The aim is not merely to interpret the objects pictorially, although of course this is useful for assessing the various complexities of the form.

Understanding form

There are no lines around objects. They consist of their own form and the light that falls upon them. It is tone that defines them. The normal procedure for understanding form is to create black-and-white drawings. Abstracting from real life, you are translating the language of color into tone, substituting monochromatic tones for a wide range of colors.

Remember, too, that the media themselves are an abstraction, for while you may be drawing, say, a plastic bowl in charcoal, this medium has nothing to do with plastic per se. And if charcoal can be used to represent a plastic object, then why not try representing that same object in a non-conventional material, anything that enables you to express visually what you see. Experimentation should be made with a mix of media, so that you can explore both the linear and tonal nature of your subject matter.

Try to be as direct and spontaneous as possible. For the sake of immediacy, do several studies in a short space of time. Use materials to describe form and mass as areas of color, replacing a monochromatic scheme, while only using an outline as a guide to the subsequent layers applied. Here you should be concerned not with an end product, but with the process of a rich description of forms.

Tonal form Part of an energetic portrait study, using broken brushmarks to create tonal form without an outline.

EXERCISE

Taking a line for a walk
Linear drawing can be achieved in many ways. One such way is by the idea of "taking a line for walk," first associated with the artist Paul Klee (1879–1940). Choose a subject that offers variation in form. Pick a visual point from which to start your drawing and continue without taking your pencil off the paper surface until your drawing is complete. Complete up to four such drawings. Once you're familiar with this process, start to experiment with the time you expend looking at the paper surface and your subject matter. You should be aiming to observe the subject matter for a longer period of time than that of your developing drawing. Complete a series of four studies, giving yourself a gradually increasing amount of time—between five and twenty minutes—to execute each one.

UNIT 6 | Photography Basics

Although it is still considered a modern form of graphic representation, photography is now entering its third century. Its influence has been enormous in many areas of human life: as social documentary and historical evidence; in the advertising, fashion, and art worlds; and as a marker of time for all those ordinary people that have documented their own lives at births and weddings, at parties, and on holiday.

For the graphic designer, though, perhaps the key question is, Why does the photo hold so much power over our judgments? A magazine will sell thousands more copies if the choice of cover picture is right and fits in with the aims of the title. More prosaically, your designs will be more powerful if you learn how to spot an effective, well-composed picture, with a good tonal range, which combines effectively with typography, tints, and other illustrations.

There are several reasons why every designer should be able to take a simple photograph: to help him or her work out rough proportions, to understand composition, and as a support for drawing.

Few professional graphic designers become involved in this specialized image-making process. Their role, as yours will be, is to commission or select photographs to solve design problems rather than to produce the finished pictures, which is the job of the professional photographer. However, it is important for the designer to have a basic understanding of how to operate a camera, take a photograph, and create an image with that photograph.

SEE ALSO: Digital Photography *p64*
Photography or Illustration? *p122*

⬆️ ➡️ **Using lines** helps to create a visual pathway for the viewer connecting foreground and mid-ground to background. Diagonals created by tilting the camera can transform mundane subjects into something fabulous. They are also a great way of symbolizing movement or activity.

What makes a good photo?

There are many reasons why one image will capture your imagination and another will make you turn the page without stopping to look. Let us see if we can find some common reasons. Technique is always important. It helps if an image is in focus, correctly exposed, placed in a part of the page where it is shown off at its best (pictures going down the gutter of a magazine always suffer), and has some content that is of interest. But that is not all. For an image to work well it must give you some information, and it will make you stop and think by confounding your expectations, forcing you to reassess the familiar.

⬆ **Unusual image shapes** are a great way of attracting attention. Just because your camera makes rectangular images, there's no reason why you can't stretch them into panoramic shots or crop them to a square format.

⬆ **Symmetrical compositions** tend to evoke feelings of calm, serenity, and harmony.

⬇ **Asymmetrical compositions** are inherently edgier and more mysterious.

⬇ **Striking light and shadow** offers powerful emotional impact and a sense of impending danger.

⬆ **Abstraction** You easily forget you're looking at a skyscraper through a domed glass roof. Instead, you get lost in a pleasing aesthetic of radial lines on a background of receding rectangles.

We all recognize the "snapshots" that surround us in our daily life. But a photograph that is used in a commercial context should carry more weight than one of these informal pictures. For example, most snaps are taken at a shutter speed of around a 60th of a second, an exposure time that will freeze most movements. But why should an image not have movement in it? When the wind is blowing the branches of a tree, an exposure time of 60th/s will make the tree look calm and still; in other words, none of the drama will be captured. The same picture shot at 15th/s will look very different, although more technical skill is required to make such a photograph look good.

Composition

This is an area of vital importance. Bad composition can ruin a good picture. Too few items of interest in a picture and things can look a little bare, too many and your shot will look cluttered. When shooting a portrait it is not always necessary to show all of your subject's face, one side of their face may be enough. Either by lighting on one side or by going in close you will still get a good picture. You do not always need to see everything in a shot: leave something to the imagination of the viewer. Good composition can help you avoid cropping later. In fact, try to do your cropping in the camera: that is composition.

⬆ **Diagonals** add drama to any photograph by creating a tension with the standard rectilinear format.

↑ ⊙ **Cropping** Some landscape photos look better when cropped to portrait format.

↑ ⊙ **Dramatic effects** can be achieved by cropping and zooming in. The somewhat static image of a vase of flowers is transformed so that one feels among the foliage.

Cropping an image

To crop an image is to select a part of the shot. Often cropping is used to take out an unwanted part of the picture (the side of a stranger's head, etc), but it also a very useful tool to get rid of superfluous information and leave the image strengthened.

What camera? What film?

To take a good picture you will need a decent camera. This needn't cost a fortune but you need good equipment to make good images. A 35mm Single Lens Reflex (SLR) camera will allow you to shoot exactly what you see through the viewfinder. This is important as you will be able to choose where you focus the image and exactly how you compose it. A digital camera will also be fine but you will need one that has a viewer on the back so that you can see exactly what you are getting.

You must also choose the right film for the job. Film is rated from fast to slow (sensitive to not so sensitive); this is called the ASA. A high ASA (800) will allow you to get fast exposures in good light or reasonable exposures under dim conditions. A low ASA (50) will mean that you have to have bright conditions to get a

EXERCISE

Taking some images and using two L shapes made of black card, try to see how much of an image you can lose without the essence of the image disappearing.

good image (plenty of sun or bright snow). There are lots of different films on the market and you will need to experiment with some of them to see which ones give you the best results. When starting out, buy your film from a camera shop and ask the assistant in the shop to help you with making your choice.

A side-effect of these different films is the differing results they will give you. A high-rated film of 800/3200 will give your pictures high contrast and a grainy finish. A low-rated film of 50/100 will give you full mid-range tones and a smooth finish. As a rule, most studio photography is done on low-rated films, because they provide the most detail.

Darkroom effects

Having developed your roll of film, you can now judge whether the exposures are correct by checking the density of the gray tones on your contacts with a magnifying glass. Contacts are made by exposing negatives on to printing paper, resulting in a sheet of images the same size as your negatives. Look for good contrast and any frames that are out of focus. Once you have picked the shots suitable for your purpose from the contact sheets, you are ready to make

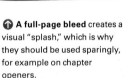 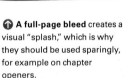 **A non-bleed image**, even one used fairly large, allows other elements of a spread to compete visually.

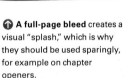 **A full-page bleed** creates a visual "splash," which is why they should be used sparingly, for example on chapter openers.

prints, and the way in which you make that print will have a direct effect on the finished result.

Simply put, a print is made by shining light through a negative on to light-sensitive paper. The more intense the light that strikes the paper, the darker the image, so that, for example, a dark jacket would appear clear on the negative. This would allow a high degree of light to pass through it and hit the paper to form a dark image. After exposure to light, the development, and fixing of the image on the paper are achieved chemically.

Preparing for a photoshoot

The type of work and the scale of the commission will play a great part in your decision-making. Here are some general and specific pointers:

- Draw up a list of all the photographs required and categorize them into different types (interior shots, model shots, location shots, and so on).
- Consider the style of photography you want. Select a photographer (possibly more than one), talk to him/her about what you want, and send him/her some rough designs with your ideas. At this point, decide if you want color or black and white or both.
- Once you know how many shots you need you should discuss the fee and the copyright on the pictures. The photographer will either charge a daily rate (generally negotiable), or you could offer a flat fee, making sure you ask what extras will be charged. Check that the costs fit your budget.
- Start a shoot diary and work with the photographer to pencil in which shot will be done when and where—in the photographer's studio or on location.
- Draw up a list of props required, anything from a car to a mouse. The client might well supply all props, or you might have to buy or hire from a prop house. It makes sense to do a mini drawing of a complex shot to check that there are no "holes."
- Consider the background: On location, check if you need to get permission or if anything unsightly is showing. In the studio, do you need to paint a backdrop? If the floor is in the shot, what is it like?

- If it is a large shot you might hire a stylist who will go out and get all the props, and if it is a really complex interior, say for a catalog, you might have to commission a set builder to re-create an interior room.
- If you are shooting in someone's home, check that the room is big enough to achieve the shots needed.
- In the studio, the photographer will have control over the lighting, power points, and so on, but on location you or they will have to check these out.
- If you are using models, you will need to "cast them," either by selecting them from an agency, or by arranging for candidates to call in to the studio. Clothing? Sometimes they will be the model's own but you should always discuss it. Make-up and hair all need to be decided—the model can do it or you could hire a make-up artist.
- If you are doing a cookery shoot, you will need the services of a home economist and a food stylist, to cook the food and arrange it attractively.
- Computers help the logistics of some photos: a complex car ad can now be achieved be combining two shots (but you still need to get both shots!).

 Thumbnails Specially commissioned photography is expensive. Preplan each shot before you go into the studio.

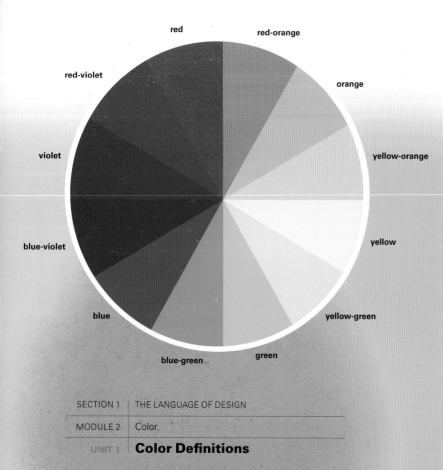

red   red-orange

red-violet

orange

violet

yellow-orange

blue-violet

yellow

blue

yellow-green

blue-green   green

This color wheel shows primary, secondary, and tertiary colors of pigment. The primary colors are red, yellow, and blue. Secondary colors are made by mixing any two primary colors together, producing orange, green, and violet. A tertiary color is produced by mixing a primary color with the secondary color nearest to it on the wheel. The tertiary colors here are red-orange, yellow-orange, yellow-green, blue-green, blue-violet, and red-violet.

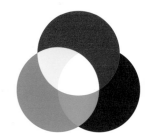

Subtractive primaries
These are the primaries used in printing; magenta, yellow, and cyan. Unlike the additives, which produce white light when combined, subtractives make black.

Additive primaries are red, green, and blue, and are used to create colors on computers, televisions, and so on—anything related to the projection of light. Combined, the additive primaries result in white light.

SECTION 1	THE LANGUAGE OF DESIGN
MODULE 2	Color
UNIT 1	**Color Definitions**

There are literally tens of thousands of colors at the designer's disposal, and almost infinite ways of combining them. The designer must get to grips with the ways in which colors are classified and the terms used to describe them. Color can be said to differ in three significant ways.

Hue, tone, saturation

A pure color, such as a red or blue, is known as the hue. It is the generic name of the color. A single hue will have many variations of its pure color, ranging from light to dark. The term describing this is "tone." On computers, the tonal range is given as a percentage, so that 10 percent would be a very pale version of a hue and 90 percent almost the full value. When a hue is used without any tonal percentage it is known as a "solid." Finally, a single hue will vary according to its brightness. This is known as "saturation," also called chroma or intensity. The saturation of a hue ranges from full intensity to low intensity or from brightness to grayness. Other significant terms used in design vocabulary are associated with how colors are used in combination. An excellent aid is a color wheel that shows the full spectrum of colors from red through to violet.

SEE ALSO: Print Media *p126*

Hue is what distinguishes one color from another. In effect it is the generic name of the color—red, say, as opposed to blue.

Tone (or value) is the relative lightness or darkness of a color. A color with added white is called a tint; a color with added black is called a shade.

The subtractive primaries

The system for viewing colors on a screen—additive color—is discussed on p30. But in the case of printed matter you will be working with subtractive color (because each color printed on to a stock subtracts from white and if the three primaries overlap black will result). A color wheel shows "primary" colors. The subtractive primaries are red, yellow, and blue. Secondaries are a mix of any two primaries resulting in orange, green, and violet, and tertiaries are a mix of any two secondaries. The term "full color" refers to four-color printing and in order to achieve a full range of colors, printers use cyan, yellow, magenta, and black (known on the computer as CMYK; K = black = key color). An additional color used as a design element in a layout is called a "flat color" or sometimes a "spot color." When selecting colors for this, you should use a universal color-matching system known as Pantone.

"Complementary colors," such as red and green, lie opposite each other on the color wheel, whereas "analogous colors," like green and blue, lie adjacent to each other. The former are associated with contrast, while the latter are linked to harmony.

While the above terms are linked to the visual appearance of color, we analyze now how colors affect each other when combined in a color scheme.

tone

Bravo
Bravo
Bravo
Bravo
Bravo
Bravo

saturation

Saturation (or chroma) is roughly equivalent to brightness. A line of high intensity is a bright color, while one of low intensity is a dull color. Two colors can be of the same line but have different intensities.

Temperature Colors appear hotter as yellow diminishes and red increases. Blue is very cold. Green is slightly warmer because of the addition of yellow.

advance　　advance

recede　　recede

⬆ **Advancing/receding** Some colors appear to advance, while others seem to recede. If you want to make something come toward the viewer, choose warm colors, such as red or orange. Blues and greens seem to recede when set next to red.

⬆ ⬈ **Simultaneous contrast** The word "Bravo" is set against two different background hues. Although the word is the same color in both images, we perceive it to be darker in the left picture, than in the right picture.

Other color terms

●Advancing and receding
If a man was asked to put a box on either of two workbenches, one red, and one blue, he would probably place it on the red because it appeared nearer to him (advancing) than the blue (receding).
●Simultaneous contrast
The human eye tends to differentiate between two neighboring colors by emphasizing their differences—the background colors affect the foreground colors (the image).

●Vibration
Complementary colors of equal lightness and high saturation tend to make each other appear more brilliant.
●Weight
Colors differ in "weight." For example, if a man was to move two large boxes equal in size but one pale green, and the other dark brown, he would probably pick up the green one because it appeared lighter. It is generally assumed that blue-greens look lighter while reds appear stronger, and therefore heavier.

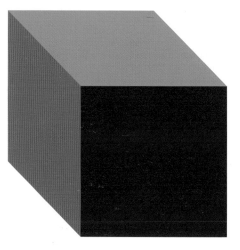

⬋ ⬇ **Weight** Blue-greens appear lighter; reds appear stronger and heavier.

⬆ **Vibration** When complementary colors are juxtaposed, as here, viewers can experience an optical vibration.

Defining colors

This exercise needs to be tackled on computer. Working to a landscape format, set the word "super" in lower case in a sans serif bold type. The size should be such that it occupies at least two-thirds of the width of the format. Center the word visually.

Now, using the word "super" in each instance, do the following experiments, each one on a new page:

Advancing color Select two different hues, one for the image (the word "super") and one for the background in such a way that the image advances.

Receding color Repeat the above but alter the colors so that the image recedes.

Tints Choosing two different tints of a hue, use one for the image and one for the background. Do two variations, one showing good legibility and one poor legibility.

Simultaneous contrast Using the same hue for the image, alter the background hue and note how the appearance of the image changes.

Analogous Select two hues to demonstrate this term.

Complementary Select two hues to demonstrate this term.

super

Advancing

Receding

Legibility of tints

Simultaneous contrast

Analogous

Complementary

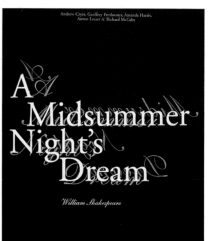

←**Contrast problems**
Though a very strong
graphic design, the
legibility suffers
because magenta is
printed over a dark
background. Selecting
colors to overprint
images that have strong
contrast between dark
and light areas always
presents problems. Very
often a compromise has
to be reached between
the contrast of color and
the legibility.

↑**Recession** The green and
violet recede against the white
type, which is what the designer
intends to reinforce the concept.

SECTION 1	THE LANGUAGE OF DESIGN
MODULE 2	Color
UNIT 2	**Color Differences and Legibility**

Fundamental to using color in graphic design is knowing the context in which the finished work will be viewed. How the same color is perceived—and how legible it is—will vary depending on whether it is viewed on a screen or in a print-based medium.

Screen- or print-based color?

On screen you will be working with additive color, made up of red, green, and blue lights, which when combined (added) produce white light. Print-based color, known as subtractive, consists of pigments placed on a paper surface, which when combined subtract from white to make black.

This phenomenon creates two kinds of problems for designers and clients: First, colors on screen will always appear brighter than those printed. Both client and designer can be misled if they expect printed colors to have the same saturation and tonal range as those they have approved on screen. Second, when a designer works color into his design and produces a computer printout for presentation, the client can falsely assume that this is how the printed version will look. Again, unfortunately, color printers cannot produce the same range of colors as a conventional printing press, and so sometimes clients reject presentation visuals as being either too garish or too insipid. To pre-empt this problem, the designer can, when presenting, subtly amend the color values to approximate more closely

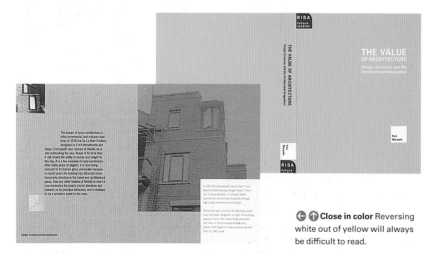

←↑**Close in color** Reversing
white out of yellow will always
be difficult to read.

SEE ALSO: Readability and Legibility *p84*
Emphasis and Hierarchy *p88*

Legible Although a serif typeface is used in this poster (sometimes a problem with colored display type), the overall legibility is acceptable. The dark ground provides a strong contrast.

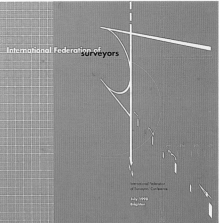

Monochrome mood The proximity of gray to black reduces the legibility. Obviously, designers sometimes break the rules to create particular moods.

Reversing-out type can create problems. If the background color is dark, a printed black may advance less than a type reversed-out in white.

EXERCISE

Construct a scale of legibility

Working on the computer, typeset the word "legibility" in a landscape format with a white background. Then do the following exercises:

• Make the word "legibility" violet, so that it stands out strongly against the white background. Now change its color, gradually moving through the color wheel from blue, green, red, orange, and finally to yellow. You will see that this is the most difficult color to read against white.

• Now show "legibility" against a background of contrasting colors. Change the word to yellow on a violet ground, then orange on a blue ground. Continue with increasingly similar colors until you finish with a red/orange word on a red ground—the least legible combination of colors.

the finished look of the printed piece—readjusting them before sending material to the printer. Reproduction is also bedeviled by the fact that colors can differ between inkjet and laser printers. Software programs, such as Photoshop and QuarkXPress, will also produce variable results in the color produced, even when the same percentages have been given. Finally, the paper on which a color is printed will have an effect. A coated (shiny) stock will give a richer feel to a color than an off-white matt one.

The best advice for a designer is to make sure the client understands these difficulties and is aware of how carefully selected color schemes can go awry if the problems of color reproduction are not carefully considered.

Color legibility

Legibility refers to how clearly something can be read. Many factors influence how a color is perceived; most fundamentally it will be the physical context in which the color is viewed. For example, lighting conditions in the reading environment will have a clear effect on the legibility of both print- and screen-based color work. Compare looking at a computer monitor in a darkened room to viewing it when sunlight is directly shining on it. Looking at a poster in a dingy unlit area is very different from a back-lit version in a well-appointed main street.

In addition to the viewing conditions, legibility will be affected by the colors selected, the backgrounds on which they are printed, and the size and shape of type or image being used. The principles governing size of type and legibility are discussed on pp 48 and 84. As a guide, good color legibility is achieved when ground and the color placed on it are opposites, for example, violet (the color nearest to black) on a white ground. On the same background, as one moves the image color toward yellow, legibility will decrease. Another factor in legibility is when the ground is in a color that harmonizes with the image. Contrast is the key to legibility and this means using your knowledge of the color circle. The greatest contrast is a violet image on a yellow ground; the poorest legibility would result from a red/orange image on a red ground.

UNIT 3 | **Color Associations**

Why are certain colors preferred, or more suitable, in different situations? It is because, through history, colors have come to have particular associations that most likely derive from nature, but over the millennia have become deeply rooted in human psychology.

Red letter The copy line automatically suggests the choice of red, but the color gains added drama from the black background.

Many kinds of reference are available for the designer to consult concerning psychology of color: credit for this body of knowledge is due to people such as Wilhelm Ostwald, a Nobel Prize-winning chemist, who just prior to World War I sought to analyze why certain color combinations were perceived as pleasant or unpleasant. His search for a law based on color order led him to the conclusion that people responded to colors emotionally. Ostwald stated that the best way to understand and be able to use color productively was to study it from a subjective psychological viewpoint.

SEE ALSO: Scrapbooks and Mood boards *p52*

Color safe These two safety designs for a building company show two possible design directions. The choice of blue reflects the blue eyes of the child, which helps to individualize the feeling of danger. The yellow, by contrast, stands out from the children, creating tension, and of course it is the conventional color to express warning.

We therefore need to investigate how color works in language, signs, different cultures, and religions, and how it creates an emotional response.

Color in culture

Intelligence, memory, experience, history, and culture all play a part in the way we perceive colors. That is not to say all individuals perceive colors differently, just that those perceptions have subtly different meanings depending on psychology and cultural background. Colors have symbolic associations in all societies through their appearance in seasonal, political, environmental, and sexual contexts. Of course, different cultures will apply different meanings to color. For example, black is the color of mourning and death in the industrialized West, whereas in China and India it is white. Red does not have the instant conventional association with "stop" in those countries where automobiles are still rare. In the nineteenth century, green, through its links to arsenic,

This largely monochromatic photograph allows the red of the Underground logo—the focus of the whole poster—to be the most prominent feature.

The typography has been designed with strong colors that represent the primary palette. This use of fundamental colors, together with powerful verticals and horizontals, supports the fact that art, architecture, and engineering are all three combined in this project.

was associated with poison, whereas today it is seen as the color of spring and environmental awareness. In the U.S., if you were looking to post a letter, you would be scanning the street for a blue mailbox, but in Sweden or the U.K. your awareness of the local environment would tell you to look for the color red. These random examples show that the meanings of colors change across time and space. If you are designing in international markets you should be particularly aware of the cultural variations.

Color in emotions and language

Despite these local differences, certain colors do seem to have universal characteristics. Reds, oranges, and yellows stimulate the senses and tend to be perceived as "warm"—capable of exciting feelings of stimulation, cheeriness, good health, and aggression; opposite on the color wheel, blues and

⬆ **The color of metal** In this poster, the words "architecture" and "art" are in pink and yellow—warm colors linked to humanity—while the blue of "engineering" conjures up a sense of function and machinery.

⬇ **Playing with fire** Red's links with evil are graphically depicted here. The copy is cleverly used to evoke hellfire.

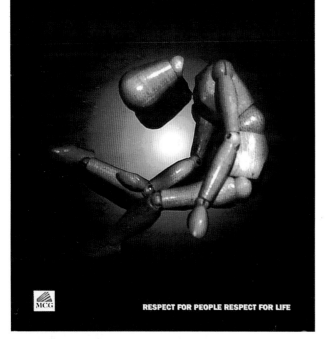

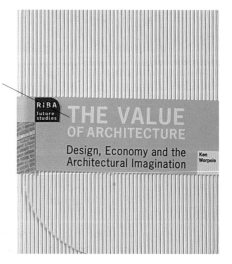

Keep type big when reversing out of yellow to avoid problems of legibility.

↑ **The color of the sun** Yellow gives a certain warmth to the design, reflecting the fact that architecture is fundamentally about shelter.

← **Danger signals** The psychological associations of red with danger and yellow with warning have here been used to good effect. In addition, the black background helps create a strong contrast.

↓ **The color of money** These experiments with bank checks create different moods. Red and brown together inspire feelings of warmth and fruitfulness, whereas purple can convey a sense of aristocracy or luxury. Which is more appropriate?

greens are seen as "cool" and have connotations of calmness, peace, safety, and depression. Warm colors can increase body heat and raise blood pressure, whereas cool colors tend to have a relaxing effect. Reds advance toward the viewer; blues recede. It's not just hue that influences how we see things; so too do the other dimensions of value and intensity. Compositions that are close together in value seem hazy, vague, or introspective, whereas dark designs are evocative of the night, fear, or mystery. High intensities of color are dynamic and create a feeling of movement.

We can tell that colors are deeply rooted in our psychology, because we use them figuratively in language to describe feelings: "He turned purple with rage," "I'm feeling blue," "She turned green with envy" are just a few examples.

These earthy and rustic colors are suggestive of harvest-time and fruitfulness.

This rich purple is associated with royalty and wealth.

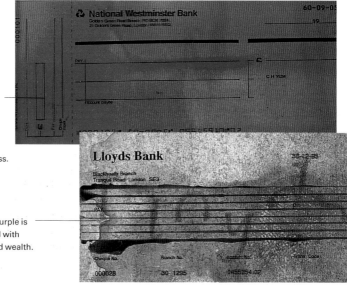

Hue Experiments
Using a format of A5 square, divide the shape into four areas of unequal size and complete the following exercises:
1 Select three hues to evoke a warm color scheme and place in three of the areas. Typeset the word "temperature" and place in the remaining area.
2 Repeating the same specification as above, this time evoke a cool or cold color scheme.
3 Again, use the same specification, but this time the theme should be "tranquillity."

The meaning of color

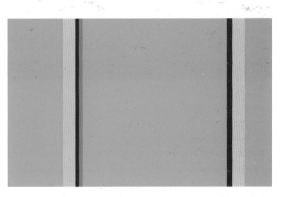

Red Associated with fire. It has an intense, vibrant, advancing, and aggressive character, increases muscular tension and stimulates higher blood pressure. Its positive associations include love (red roses), sexiness, festivity (Santa Claus), and luck, while its negative connotations include the devil, debt, revolution (red flag), bureaucracy (red tape), and danger. Indeed, our subconscious fears can be prompted by intense bright red, because our ancestors' greatest fear was fire.

Green Associated with spring, youth, and the environment, it helps people to feel calm (one reason why it is so often used as a color in hospitals). Green causes less eye strain and nerve strain than any other color, which may explain in part why looking at scenery is so relaxing. Greenish-blue is said to be the coldest of all colors. As the color of envy, nausea, poison, and decay, green does have some bad connotations too.

Yellow Associated with the sun and therefore with light, it is the center of the highest luminosity in the spectrum with the highest reflection value. For this reason it is often used as a warning color, and is the color generally seen first, particularly when placed against black. Though yellow is linked with both illness (jaundice) and cowardice, it is essentially the hue of happiness: sun, gold, and hope.

Blue Associated with the sky, water, and brightness, in many cultures blue is the color representing spirituality. Its clear, cool, transparent qualities link it to detachment, peace, and distance. The downside to blue, so to speak, is its status as the color of depression, cold, and introversion.

aggressive

When we are angry we see red. Following feelings of anger and frustration we can often feel depleted of energy. A dislike of red is fairly common, and is explained by psychologists as a characteristic of someone who has been frustrated or defeated. It stand for power, our own, others and the power struggles that can sometimes ensue between the two. Exposure to red causes measurable reactions in the body. Blood pressure goes up, breathing and pulse rates quicken, sweating begins and brain waves are stimulated. But in the case of bullfighting the red colour on the fabric is more for the audience, since the bull is acctually colourd blind It is the movement of the cape that actually atracts the bull to charge.

SECTION 1	THE LANGUAGE OF DESIGN
MODULE 2	Color
UNIT 4	**Color Contrast and Harmony**

When conceiving a graphic idea one should ask what the visual idea carrying the message is. Color should contribute by bringing an added association of meaning and feeling. Will the mood be one of quiet harmony or dynamic tension? Colors can be quiet and passive, or cold and brash, and can be used to express emotion. Analogous color schemes— those close to each other on the color wheel—create a feeling of harmony—yellow and green, for example, have softer visual associations. Complementary colors—on opposite sides of the wheel—give more movement and vibrancy: the colors red and green offer a more direct, aggressive, or dominant look.

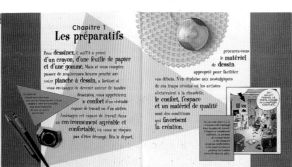

⟶ Punchy tints Strong, bright, grabbing tints are chosen for a book about how to be a cartoonist— upbeat subject, upbeat treatment.

SEE ALSO: Styles of Layout p102
Pace and Contrast p106

🄍 Red rag The choice of red for the evocative copy contrasts greatly with the matador in the dark hue. The red cloak, with its associations of provoking anger, also adds tension to the composition.

⬆ Tints as colors The interesting typographic treatment of the display copy is enhanced by the choice of color. The magenta and gray have strong contrast and the use of tints on both these colors gives the impression of another color being used.

You may want to exert humor or irony in your design. Or you may choose colors to create a quiet tranquil feel. By using the opposite (a very bright red) an idea can be reinforced in color terms. Whether you want the color combination to be aggressive or passive, quiet or loud, tense or relaxed, mysterious or obvious, learning the language of color will enable you to use it productively to make the concept work.

Correct proportions

Another factor in your decision-making should be the proportion of color to use. For example, a small amount of bright red in a complementary scheme can have a bigger impact than using equal proportions of red and green. Furthermore, if you use equal amounts of a saturated red and green together the result can be an unpleasant visual discord. Vary the saturation levels of the hues to avoid this. Contrast is often the key. By using a greater proportion of green with less saturation and a red with good saturation the red is given extra emphasis. With analogous schemes the hues tend to have less vibrancy and therefore similar proportions can be contemplated.

Selecting colors should never be an arbitrary decision. The colors you choose as a designer should

The fact that the name overlays text shows how content has been sacrificed to graphic impact.

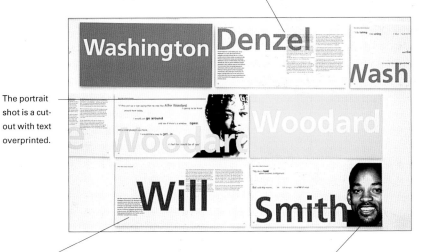

The portrait shot is a cut-out with text overprinted.

The body copy serves to make the heading more interesting, not the other way around.

Squared-up image with no type overlay: the primary colors unify the spreads so variation is possible.

⬆ **Star colors** By using primary colors the designer has created a strong contrast between the spreads but managed to unify the overall look.

⬅ **Content of color** The rich variety of color here echoes the diversity of letterforms. Color goes beyond making designs attractive and can help to communicate the point.

⬆ **Composite harmony** The harmonious color scheme here helps to bring unity to a poster created out of composite images.

⬅ **Color clash** In this other example of good contrast, the yellow against the dark blue is very powerful, and hints at the conflict inherent in the play.

enhance the layout and create a visual impact. Designers who develop an understanding of the complex and subtle ways in which colors interact will be able to explore new ways of expressing graphic ideas. Having strong predisposed opinions about color can hinder choices; one should always instead pay close attention to color relationships and their potential for creating different emotional and psychological responses in the beholder.

Today's designers are fortunate, for they are able to access software programs giving an almost infinite range of color. Printing technology has made tremendous advances, too, enabling the most complex range of colors to be reproduced. But too much choice and ease of application can create their own problems. Color should enhance designs. Using color for color's sake can be counterproductive, since sometimes using one color is more effective than using many.

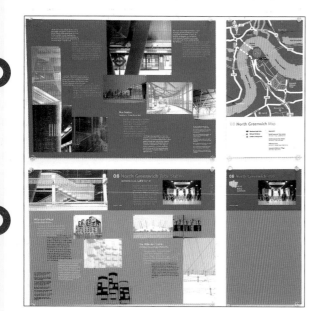

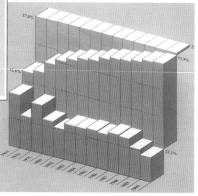

⬆ **3D** The use of three different tints of orange in this bar chart emphasizes the 3D effect.

⬆ **Color codes** Color is a real bonus for the designer when constructing maps, as can be seen from this one showing distances and traveling times between European cities.

⬆ **Coordinating hues** In this brochure, the use of orange and blue in the map is matched within the tint panels, thereby effectively linking both pieces of information.

UNIT 5 Color in Information Design

Color can be a powerful tool in the realm of information design, where it is used to help the viewer organize data into various structures. Psychologists have proved that we see the color of an object before its shapes and details. Because it works at this basic level, color is very good at keeping things delineated, and guiding the eye through systems.

SEE ALSO: Emphasis and Hierarchy *p88*

Systems can be anything that contains a flow of complex information—maps, signage, sections, structures, or web pages—and color is effective whenever that information needs to be organized into different categories. Complex buildings, such as hospitals, need a good signage system for people to negotiate through. Color is an obvious technique for helping people choose the correct path. Many shopping malls are so large that parking zones are now color-coded—a memorable way of helping you return successfully to your vehicle. One of the most famous maps in existence is the London Underground map, developed by the engineer Harry Beck. He had the idea of using color to differentiate the various lines. People using the Tube can, as a result, readily identify the appropriate route they need to take. This most original of designs is a model copied in various forms throughout the world.

Many traditional ways of using color have been in financial matters. A balance sheet showing debits would use red to denote being in arrears, hence the phrase "in the red." Balance sheets still use this custom today to separate trading figures from year to year. Catalogs and books often have different sections color-coded to aid navigation through the pages. When Penguin Books introduced the first paperbacks in

Graphic tool Color is ideal in the design of pie charts and other diagrammatic information. It quickly distinguishes the items graphically represented.

Distinct tints Color delineates the countries quickly and effectively in this piece of information design.

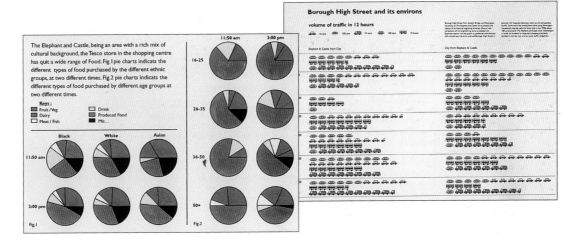

The Elephant and Castle, being an area with a rich mix of cultural background, the Tesco store in the shopping centre has quit a wide range of Food. Fig.1 pie charts indicates the different types of food purchased by the different ethnic groups, at two different times. Fig.2 pie charts indicates the different types of food purchased by different age groups at two different times.

Keys:
☐ Fruit / Veg   ☐ Drink
☐ Dairy   ☐ Produced Food
☐ Meat / Fish   ■ Mis...

Britain in the 1930s they used a bright orange background. This color quickly became fused with the books' identity. Later the same publisher introduced another imprint, called Pelican, whose books were given a blue background. Customers quickly came to recognize the differences through the use of color. The visual associations of color can also help to delineate various sections within a body of text and highlight a number of different levels of importance. The designer can set crucial parts in a bold typeface and use a different color from the rest of the text. The eye picks this up very quickly.

Web designers use color to help people navigate through the structures. Color can help identify the moves needed to execute whatever operation is intended. An economic use of color is selecting colored paper to put different items into sections. Printing a color on a colored stock gives interesting visual combinations as well as helping readers make the appropriate identification.

Colored letterforms are used cleverly here to inform about prices.

Fade to gray Diagrams do not have to be multicolored: here the gray line serves to contrast with the other information in black.

EXERCISE

Map design
Design a simple map showing your journey from home to the nearest library or railway station. Annotate the map with as many different types of labels as you wish; these could be street names, bus stops, churches, stores, etc. Use only black and white for this design. Then repeat the design, this time using color to differentiate the labels. From this small experiment you should see how important color is to the information designer.

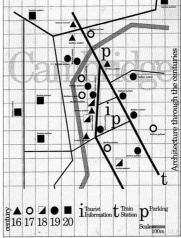

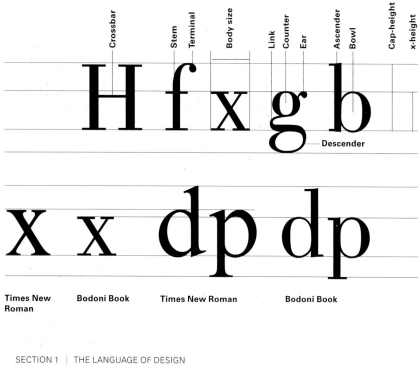

Crossbar | Stem | Terminal | Body size | Link | Counter | Ear | Ascender | Bowl | Cap-height | x-height

H f x g b

Descender

X x dp dp

Times New Roman | Bodoni Book | Times New Roman | Bodoni Book

◀ Language of letterforms
Each distinct part of a letter has its own name.

◀ Impact of x-height The x-height is the height of a lower-case x and determines the visual size of type. The x-height size varies from typeface to typeface: some, like Bodoni, have a small x-height, while Times New Roman has a large x-height. However, each type has the same body size. Type with large x-heights tend to have small ascenders and descenders, whereas type with small x-heights have large ones.

SECTION 1 | THE LANGUAGE OF DESIGN

MODULE 3 | Introduction to Typography

UNIT 1 | **The Anatomy of Type**

Type images can so easily be taken for granted, but choosing from the list of fonts to which you have access needs immense care and considerable visual understanding. Before you start designing with typography, look at a selection of various individual characters and assess the image and style each letter form represents: imagine the letters enlarged by a factor of 100 percent, which you can easily do on screen, and examine their different shapes and forms. If you think of the letterforms you choose as designs in their own right, you will be well prepared to create interesting layouts with typography.

SEE ALSO: Understanding and Selecting Typefaces *p80*

Letterforms
Knowing the structure of letterforms is essential to understanding how typefaces differ and allows the designer to make decisions about selecting and using the multitude of typefaces now available. When discussing typefaces, reference is made to terms such as the size of the x-height or counter, the type of serif, or the stress of the letter. These terms quantify the type design and indicate how the type will visually appear. Being able to compare these terms from typeface to typeface establishes a knowledge about type that is essential when making judgments as to its suitability for selection. The technological advances in

Serif letters There are general groups of serifs: bracketed, hairline slab, or slab bracket. When trying to identify a typeface, a good starting point is to identify the type of serif. A popular type with bracketed serifs is Caslon, hairline serifs are found on Bodoni, and a popular slab serif font is Glypha.

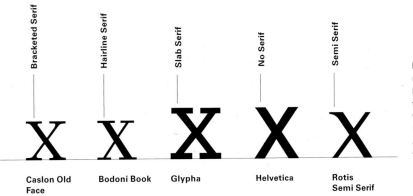

Bracketed Serif · Hairline Serif · Slab Serif · No Serif · Semi Serif

Caslon Old Face · Bodoni Book · Glypha · Helvetica · Rotis Semi Serif

Sans serif and semi serif letters Debate continues to rage as to whether sans is harder to read as text copy than serif faces. Digital typographers have begun to negate such categories altogether, introducing such forms as semi-serif and mix.

Stress The stress is in the inclination of the character between the thick and thin strokes. It can be vertical, as it is in Bodoni, or inclined, as in Caslon.

Caslon Old Face · Bodoni Book · Glypha

Counters The counter is the space enclosed within a character. It will also vary in size between typefaces. Type with small counters tends to look darker on the page.

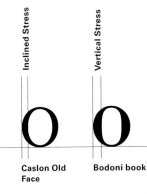

Inclined Stress · Vertical Stress

Caslon Old Face · Bodoni book

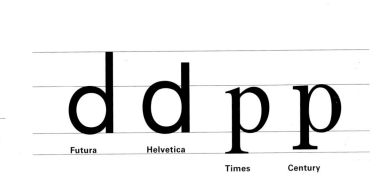

Futura · Helvetica · Times · Century

Tips

- Remember that type communicates a visual message just like a drawing does.
- Letterforms should be viewed individually as illustrations.
- Use the facility to white out of colored backgrounds and tonally adjust the visual effect.

Roman · Italic · Condensed · Expanded

The underlying structure of the font remains when it is adapted into italic, condensed, or expanded forms. Not all fonts have these variants, which can be useful for defining different pieces of information.

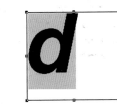

| X : 46 mm | W : 50.325 mm | △ 0° | ↦ ↕ auto | 55 Helvetica Rom. | 120 pt |
| Y : 181.297 mm | H : 44.703 mm | Cols: 1 | ↥ ◇◇ 0 | P B I U W ⊕ @ S K K | |

Impostor Never use the Quark measurement box to modify type as this creates a "bastardized" form; where possible, always use the proper italic or bold font.

ways that typefaces are designed and produced has led to difficulties in deciding which typeface to use. Because of the relatively easy method of producing type through digital means, there are now countless different fonts on the market. Some of these are best left alone, as they do not have much inherent usefulness beyond being "new." Of course, arguments can be made for using them as they may appear different or experimental: this could be a reason for their use—say, in a cutting-edge style magazine—but in general it is better to select the well-known or classical fonts. Criteria for selection should normally be made on a more rational basis rather than simply that it looks different or is unusual.

Key terms

There are over 25 terms applicable to a letterform. It's not necessary to know all of them but certain ones are essential in order to make visual judgments about type. The principal terms that determine how letterforms differ are: x-height, serif, counter, descender, ascender, and the stress of a letter. Other terms such as loop, spur, tail, and link are interesting but not as influential as the ones described.

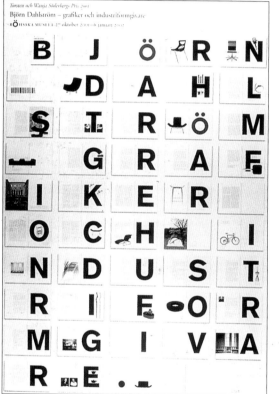

◀ ▶ ⏿ **Font furniture** The designs for this poster and pages from a catalog show that sometimes using the simple forms of letters can become the main concept of the piece. The clean sans serif face has been chosen to create an (almost) abstract graphic solution that can be playfully combined with other shapes and images.

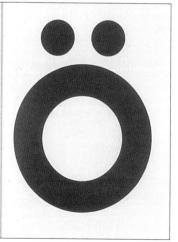

Typography leaflet

You are asked to design a series of information sheets explaining the anatomy of type to someone new to the subject. The main object of the sheets is to convey the terms as clearly as possible in a visually interesting way.

Using the typefaces given, you can enlarge or reduce, cut out sections, or change them—anything you think helps explain the terms to the viewer. Use two colors to full effect by using the second color sparingly to add emphasis. Show at least three terms on each sheet.

Select the terms from the following list: x-height, cap-height, body size, counter, serif, ascender, descender, bowl, baseline, bracketed serif, crossbar, terminal, link, ear, hairline serif, slab serif, stem.

The explanatory copy can be taken from the information in these pages. The format should be 8¼ in (210 mm) square. There are three stages to the design and a production stage, when you will produce your designs on the computer. The point of having different design stages is so that you will fully explore ideas before going to the computer to produce them. Shown on this page are examples by students who followed the brief. See how differently they interpreted it.

⬆ **Emphasis** By keeping the design simple and blocking in only the letter parts that are being discussed, this designer successfully communicates meaning in a visually arresting way.

➔ **"a"** Here a single letter has been dissected and its component parts enlarged. By keeping the complete letter as part of the design the meaning is clear and the attention is drawn to the letter's anatomy.

Stages of work

1 Analyze the information you have been given, and make sure that you fully understand all the terms. Select those terms you wish to convey in your design.

2 Fully explore your design scheme using thumbnails or half-size visuals, and develop your treatment of the material. At this stage you need to make your design as dramatic as possible, while still maintaining comprehension.

3 Work up your designs to full size, as working drawings. Use layout paper or cartridge paper.

4 Think about color. Do you want each element to be different or the same? Or perhaps you'd prefer to work with a limited palette of colors?

5 Before going to the computer you need to develop hand-rendered artwork. Work produced on the computer should reflect your hand-rendered layouts.

⬆ **Effective use** of positive and negative space gives this simple black-and-white image impact, but the diagonal slant might serve to confuse the message, misrepresenting the position of the descender.

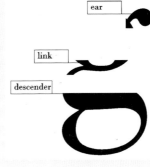

⬆ **Empty space** An interesting, though not necessarily successful interpretation. The eye is drawn more to the empty spaces, to what is missing rather than what is shown.

⬆ **Color** could have been used to better effect. The labels are not strong enough, and the eye is drawn to the expanse of white space at the bottom and right of the page rather than to the relevant points of the letter.

In many cases layouts will consist of a mixture of pictures, captions, and copy, either in the form of headings (display type) or main copy (text). In practical terms, display type ranges in size from 14 pt and upward while main copy generally falls between 5 pt and 12 pt. Space will be left in the "roughs" to accommodate display and main text, and many initial choices will need to be made regarding typefaces, sizes, and measure (width of line). You will also need to decide about spacing (letter, word, and line) and, later, adjustments will need to be made by eye.

IEFKHN
OQ
AVI|D
space needed

These upright letters appear much tighter visually than the rounded letters below.

Rounded shapes give the illusion of more space between each letterform.

The V has been moved closer to the A but there is still an unevenness of visual spacing in the word, so adjustments need to be made.

Theilowercaseiiiiisiaigoodiguide
Word spacing is traditionally based upon a space equivalent to the body width of a lower-case "i."

t o o m u c h l e t t e r s p a c e
Too much spacing between letters looks awkward and can inhibit readability.

SEE ALSO: Page-layout Programs *p62*

Letter spacing

The main objective in display and text is to try and achieve a visual evenness through the characters. This form of consistency is important for the reader because when we read we interpret shapes of words rather than individual letters. In display copy, if there is unevenness in the letter spacing the eye can easily become distracted by the space rather than seeing the shapes. As the type size increases the unevenness can get proportionally worse, requiring the designer to make adjustments. This problem is particularly prevalent when using capital letters, because the way they fit together is complicated by their inherent forms. Characters that have straight stems when placed together, such as I, J, E, and F, require more space than letters with rounded shapes, like O and Q, or those with diagonal strokes, such as A, V, Y, and W. All desktop publishing programs enable you to apply "kerning" in such circumstances, allowing for individual reductions or increments to the letter spacing. (To increase or reduce space between words, you apply "tracking.") Type designers will already have made certain adjustments to overcome the most obvious of spacing problems, for example when an A and V come together. Problems remain, however, because of the infinite combinations of letters used in the Roman alphabet. Other letters in a word may, for instance, have to have their letter spacing adjusted to compensate for the reduced space between characters such as A and V.

Although these difficulties decrease when using lower-case letters, tweaking will still be necessary, particularly in the larger sizes of type. It is difficult to lay down hard and fast rules, but certainly if characters are set too close and almost touching this will affect the ease of reading. Conversely, if lower-case characters are too generously spaced the result will be the same. Of course, extra or negative letter spacing can be inserted into lower-case type or capitals to reinforce a particular conceptual idea, but these are the exceptions that prove the rule. With regard to text sizes, in general letter spacing should not be altered from what the computer produces. Type designers for software programs are generally careful to produce settings that give a good visual spacing between letters at different sizes. However, condensed typefaces always need to be treated carefully, as do those set in justified measures:

⬆ Negative leading can produce dramatic results. Here the display type overlaps slightly, which impairs legibility but adds to the sense of foreboding suggested by the image.

② Exaggerated line spacing can add dramatic emphasis to a design and gives the copy more importance.

in these cases, small additions or subtractions can visually improve the evenness of spacing or allow a word to be taken into a line to avoid widows or orphans (single words from the end of a paragraph left at the end or beginning of a column of text).

Word spacing

In display type, a good guide for the amount of space to leave between the words is the width of a lower-case "i." Anything more than this will exacerbate the difficulties of reading, as discussed earlier. It is therefore best not to try to force display lines out to preconceived measures.

Word spacing in text type also needs careful scrutiny. The style of typesetting will here play an important part. There are two basic styles for setting type for continuous reading; justified and ranged left. With justified setting, that is, alignment on both the right and left of the measure, word spacing will vary

With justified setting, that is, alignment on both the right and left of the measure, the word spacing will vary because words are pushed out to fulfill the requirements of the measure. Herein lies the problem. The space can become excessive, particularly if the chosen measure is too small or the typeface too large. The result is often bad word spacing, which can cause "rivers" of space to run down the page

⬆ No H and J (hyphenation and justification) Justified setting with no word breaks. You can easily see the problems of excessive word spacing, which causes rivers to form.

Hyphenation can be adjusted to even out the words spacing as far as possible, and avoid ugly spacing. Hyphenation specifications are sets of automatic hyphenation rules that you can create and apply to paragraphs. You can specifiy the smallest number of characters that must precede an automatic hyphen (the default is 3), and the minimum number of characters that must follow an automatic hyphen (the default is 2). These controls do not

⬆ Hyphenation can help to reduce the problem of excessive word spacing.

With ranged-left setting you have the decided advantage of being able to space words consistently – the inherent difficulties of justified text can be avoided. For this reason, many designers prefer this style, though problems of legibility can still arise. As mentioned earlier, style of type also plays an important part in the amount of word spacing to have. Percentage adjustments can be made within the hyphenation-and-justification (H & J)

⬆ Unjustified Excessive word spacing disappears with the ranged-left style of setting. With no word breaks you can shorten lines, giving a ragged look.

because words are pushed out in order to fulfill the requirements of the measure. Herein lies the problem. The space can become excessive, particularly if the chosen measure is too small or the typeface too large. The result is sometimes bad word spacing, which can cause "rivers" of space to run down the page. Hyphenation can be adjusted to even out the word spacing as far as possible.

With ranged-left setting you have the decided advantage of being able to space words consistently — the inherent difficulties of justified text can be avoided. For this reason, many designers prefer this style, through problems of legibility can still arise. As mentioned earlier, style of type also plays an important part in the amount of word spacing to have. Percentage adjustments can be made within the hyphenation-and-justification (H & J) settings of QuarkXPress to accommodate closer or wider word spacing depending on the width of character of the typeface in question. In general, ranged-left setting is not hyphenated, although sometimes it is for shorter column widths; otherwise one can end up with lines of very uneven length.

NEW YORK PROCLAIMED

V.S. PRITCHETT

Leading

This term derives from "hot metal" typesetting (strips of lead were placed between lines of type) and refers to the amount of spacing between lines of type. In display type the designer will invariably have to adjust individual lines and not just rely on a constant setting for the line space. This is of paramount importance when you use lower-case letters that contain variable amounts of ascenders (e.g. the vertical stroke of a "k" or "d") and descenders (e.g. the vertical stroke of a "p" or "q"). When a descender and an ascender are used together in display text they can sometimes clash visually, something that doesn't happen in lines of text type. There are no clear rules regarding adjustments of line spacing for display matter; it is simply a matter of skill in developing an even look and, as they say, letting your eye be your guide. In other words, every time you use display type,

⬆ **Up and down** Too much leading (below) can hamper readability as much as too little leading (below, far right).

🔼 **No word spacing** at all in large display type can work if another tint or color is used.

Let your eye be your guide in assessing the amount of leading

Let your eye be your guide in assessing the amount of leading

Let your eye be your guide in assessing the amount of leading

Adjusting spacing

- Typeset and arrange in a US letter or A4 format the heading BOSTON'S RAILWAYS IN CRISIS in a 60 pt sans serif face. Do not adjust any letter space.
- Print out the setting and mark on the proofs any adjustment you feel is necessary to achieve visually even spacing.
- Return to the computer and apply kerning.
- Print out the new version and compare the two proofs.

Jubilee Line Extension

Architectural Features of the JLE

⬅ ⬇ Deliberate over-spacing between letters can draw the viewer through the design and reinforce the meaning of the copy at the same time.

⬆ Graphic impact Display typography may use extremes of spacing for deliberate typographic effect.

analyze each case individually. For example, designers often use negative leading (in which the leading has a lower numerical value than the type size). This can be extremely effective in giving part of the setting a dynamic visual appearance.

The consensus view is that all type settings are enhanced by the careful consideration of leading. Factors such as x-height, measure, and weight of typeface will all influence the amount of leading that you should employ. This is discussed further in the unit on legibility (see page 84).

World population with access to safe water

37%

water used in the UK by one person – litres

RuralLivelihoods : Crisis and Response

$h^2 o$

There are few absolutes in typography. In any particular case, your choice of font, weight of heading, or amount of leading all depend on the other decisions you have made. The same is true of type size: point size is an absolute measure of how big type is, but the same-sized type can look very different depending on other factors—the amount of space around it, the relative size of the text copy, the weight of font used, and so on. The central point about increasing type size is that it works as a strong form of emphasis, providing a focal point that attracts the reader's attention.

Headings and dropped capitals

Once agreement has been reached about the different levels of importance in the main text, they need to be translated into appropriate sizes. If the headings are of varying levels of importance, try to make sure they are visually segregated. For example, the top level of heading might be in 48 pt, with the next one down being 24 pt. Any closer in size, and readers might have trouble separating one from another.

There are numerous ways in which you can play with headings to improve the visual feel of a design. Breaking a line or word into different parts, or using alternating sizes with a heading, can look dynamic. For example, articles and conjunctions ("the," "a," "and," "or," etc.) could be used smaller in order to give the important words more stress. This technique might help you to achieve a more close-knit display, although it might require three or four lines to achieve the unity you are looking for.

Type performing certain functions has to be big. The names of magazines (known as the masthead), billboards intended primarily for motorists, newspaper headlines—all are attempting to catch people's attention, and they invariably have to shout loudly to be heard among the competition.

↑ **Overlapping type** in various sizes and colors creates a feeling of mental confusion, of noise and panic. It can also provide a powerful communicating tool.

↪ **Unity** The rules and combination of type sizes have together helped to give this display heading an integrated feel.

SEE ALSO: Understanding and Selecting Typefaces *p80*
Emphasis and Hierarchy *p88*

52.Summer Special Edition.

SPIRIT

The Naked Truth
A glimpse at the Erotic Minds of our Generation

The Ultimate Aphrodisiacs
Tantric Sex Tangles
Hormones, Health and Happiness
Lovely Latinos and Tempting Transexual in Rio
Sustenance to Improve your Sex Drive
Take the Silk Route for Erotic Massage
World Champion Kickboxer John Lawson
An Erotic Interlude with our Favourite Physician
All that's New in Mind, Body and Soul
Sex for the Next Millennium
Architecture with an Enviromental
In Sites to find Sex Online
The Great Art of Spoken Words

Mastheads shout for our attention, and they are often large for that reason. Particular care needs to be taken with the letter spacing, because in very large sizes any unevenness is more noticeable.

Splitting of words can be visually dynamic and, if done on the syllables, can reinforce or twist the meaning.

Another way that size is used as a display element is in the use of dropped initial letters. This technique has a long history, deriving from the earliest printed manuscripts, and is a way of enticing the reader into a piece of writing by using essentially a decorative feature. Unity is again critical: the type next to the initial should be as tight as possible to the drop letter, otherwise it looks awkward and hampers readability.

Type as image

Designers have long exploited the fact that type not only conveys meaning, but has aesthetically powerful characteristics in its own right. Indeed, if you think about how many expressive fonts are now available, and the way in which one can apply color, weight, form, and spacing to type, it is possible to see type functioning as an illustration. This is only really possible when the type is used for display, or above a certain size. Black Letter Gothic type is capable of conjuring an atmosphere of fear and mystery just as effectively as a picture of Dracula! Display type is chosen, in part, for the mood you are trying to convey, and each face has its own characteristics: Garamond Italic is elegant; Franklin Gothic is powerful; Meta is fashionable; Helvetica is bland but safe, and so on. Just

Torem ipsum dolor sit amet, consectetuer adipiscing elit, sed diam nonummy nibh euismod tincidunt ut laoreet dolore magna aliquam erat volutpat. Ut wisi enim ad minim veniam, quis nostrud exerci tation ullamcorper suscipit lobortis nisl ut aliquip ex ea commodo consequat.

Horem ipsum dolor sit amet, consectetuer adipiscing elit, sed diam nonummy nibh euismod tincidunt ut laoreet dolore magna aliquam erat volutpat. Ut wisi enim ad minim veniam, quis nostrud exerci tation

Drop caps Using an initial drop cap is a way of drawing the reader's eye to the starting point of the text. You can specify the number of letters to be larger and how many drop lines you want.

Eorem ipsum dolor sit amet, consectetuer adipiscing elit, sed diam nonummy nibh euismod tincidunt ut laoreet dolore magna aliquam erat volutpat. Ut wisi enim ad minim veniam, quis nostrud

Porem ipsum dolor sit amet, consectetuer adipiscing elit, sed diam nonummy nibh euismod tincidunt ut laoreet dolore magna aliquam erat volutpat. Ut wisi enim ad minim

Realigning words is another way of creating tension.

The large first letter in this masthead both attracts the eye and serves as a visual anchor for the rest of the copy.

In 3D work the use of large sizes of type can be extremely effective, particularly if it is shown heading in different directions, as here.

Size and variety In these mailshots promoting a furniture fair, classical soft-focus shots become a backdrop for funky type experiments.

Extremely large letters can create excellent opportunities for arranging the remaining material in a layout.

as an artist can create a mood through the style of illustration he employs, so can a typographer subtly "illustrate" the meaning of the copy by his use of font, type size, and weight. The reason this can work is that we are surrounded by letter forms throughout our lives. From an early age we become accustomed to their shapes and meanings, and they become a part of us. In addition, letter forms have inherent qualities—their forms have lovely shapes that are ripe for exploitation by the designer.

Having a good knowledge of design history enables you to pursue concepts in a more informed way. Look at the work of Josef Muller-Brockmann, Wim Crouwel, and Philippe Apeloig, and you will see how these gifted designers have exploited type as image. Often they rely solely on the use of form, weight, and color to enhance the meaning of the copy.

Working on posters gives you the most freedom, because here you have a large "canvas" on which to explore your ideas. The type can be large and fill the area, flying in different directions. Alternatively, it can be broken down into various segments. When you add color into the mix, you have a powerful armory for achieving dynamic designs.

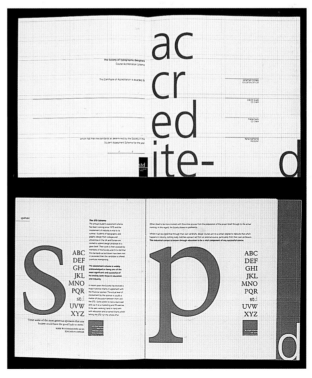

UNIT 1 Scrapbooks and Mood Boards

It's an old adage, but the first step toward becoming interesting is to be interested. Artists of all kinds—painters, designers, writers, sculptors, musicians, playwrights—make the world their inspiration. They are fundamentally interested.

➔ Keeping a scrapbook of cuttings, samples, and other ephemera can form a "catalog of inspiration" that you will always find useful.

SEE ALSO: Advertising p148

⬇ ➔ Keeping a visual diary can have a direct impact on your career. The sketches below, done for fun, eventually led to this Valentine card for a well-known restaurant.

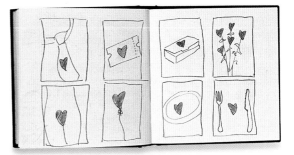

While many people's interests are often relatively narrow, as a designer you must broaden your horizons in order to be able to successfully communicate with people of all ages, professions, and lifestyles. Learning to differentiate between what you like, what exists, and what is good is an essential skill. Consequently, you should never read just one newspaper—change it every day, or read a few and compare the stories. The same goes for books. You can never read enough books, but don't limit yourself to the kind of book you usually read. Books about graphic design can be particularly dangerous! Though extremely useful for providing information and guidance, reading nothing else will have the opposite of the desired effect by turning you into an armchair expert—and you want to be an original practitioner. So add to your reading list books on sculpture, architecture, and cooking; even boxing, archeology, travel, and math—it really doesn't matter, as long as they provide you with a broad spectrum of knowledge. Equally, visit the kinds of shops, galleries, and nightclubs you'd never normally go in, listen to music you've never heard before, and eat food you've never tried before. Perhaps most importantly, talk to people. Listen to what language they use, and see how they react to life's swings and roundabouts. This is the stuff of life, the raw material common to every artist, and it's important to constantly observe and absorb it.

Recording devices

For all this, being human means that we forget things in the hustle and bustle of our own daily lives. How many times have you woken in the night with an idea, and forgotten it in the morning? Or found yourself saying, "I wish I had a camera," or "I'm sure I saw something about that recently"? Every practicing designer, without exception, carries on them at all times some form of recording device. This can be a sketchbook, a camera, a tape recorder, a video camera—whatever is most relevant to your area of interest. These are updated on a near daily basis. They also keep scrapbooks of material that interests them. Often they will not know exactly why, or how, the material will come in useful.

Mood boards

A mood board is a basic aid for visual stimulus that designers of various disciplines use in order to visually encapsulate qualities of mood, atmosphere, and voice. It serves as an aid to lateral thinking and can help to establish the character of a design and to identify the elements needed to create it.

When exploring ideas for a design project, it is important not to rely totally on your own immediate knowledge and experience. You should carry out

Inspiring images This mood board, which combines the unlikely themes of the seaside and vintage dress, was put together by a designer developing a poster for an exhibition on "Travel in the Roaring Twenties."

EXERCISE

Mood boards: likes and dislikes
Prepare two mood boards of your own. For the first, gather together material that expresses the things you like, and for the second, things you dislike.

New York story When collecting material for a mood board it is important to try to be precise. For example, if you are a tennis enthusiast, show scenes of court action rather than head-and-shoulders portraits of tennis stars, as they focus on the essence of the game, as opposed to celebrity. This designer makes graphically clear his love for urban music.

specific research related to the project in hand. Research done with an open mind will broaden your knowledge and help you mature as a designer.

The method can be used as an aid to any project: to establish an illustration style for a series of books; a scheme for an exhibition stand; typeforms for a corporate identity; a photographic style for an advertising campaign. This is visual research, so one should select items only on a visual basis. Remember, just because visual qualities cannot always be expressed satisfactorily in words that does not invalidate them. This is particularly true of color.

Start by gathering together from any source items that stimulate associations with the project at hand; they might be emotive or practical, such as colors, characteristic letter forms, textures, or format proportions—any sort of imagery from books, magazines, and newspapers. You must decide what is admissible, for there are no rules as to how a mood board is made up; the direction you take should be governed by the project in question and whatever limits you wish to apply.

The actual process of assembling a mood board may be carried out in less than an hour, or for some projects it may take weeks to slowly gather material together, while you are working on other things. A new mood board will be required for each project and sometimes helps as a springboard for discussion, particularly if a client has problems briefing the designer about a difficult or unclear project that they need resolved.

Items may be affixed to a pinboard or, perhaps more conveniently, glued to an A1 mounting board, making it easy for transportation. The advantage of mounting the collected material on boards is that they can be viewed as a whole simultaneously, making comparisons and connections easier. Scrapbooks are less effective because the turning of pages creates an isolated sequence of visual experiences.

Catalogs of inspiration

A scrapbook belonging to one of the contributors to this book contains articles on the rebirth of Rolling Stone magazine, a comparison between the philosophies of Roland Barthes and Bart Simpson, a first-hand account of life with Ernest Hemingway, Haiti's voodoo culture, the benefits of asking silly questions, Gauguin's life in Tahiti, and even an article about the nature of inspiration itself!

If something grabs your attention, draw it, note it down, photograph it, or file it away immediately. Not only will your drawing and research skills improve, but over time you will have built yourself a "catalog of inspiration" that can be drawn upon at any time in your career and especially when you are short of ideas.

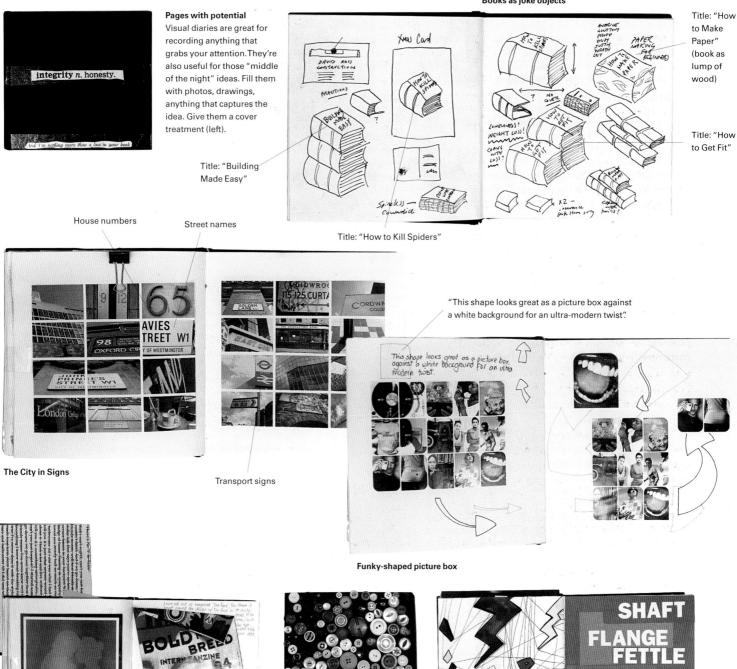

Pages with potential

Visual diaries are great for recording anything that grabs your attention. They're also useful for those "middle of the night" ideas. Fill them with photos, drawings, anything that captures the idea. Give them a cover treatment (left).

integrity *n.* honesty.

And I'm nothing more than a line in your book

Title: "Building Made Easy"

Books as joke objects

Title: "How to Make Paper" (book as lump of wood)

Title: "How to Get Fit"

Title: "How to Kill Spiders"

House numbers

Street names

The City in Signs

Transport signs

"This shape looks great as a picture box against a white background for an ultra-modern twist".

Funky-shaped picture box

SHAFT
FLANGE
FETTLE

PROBE

As a student you need to develop the skill of getting ideas down on paper. Part of this technique involves preparing rough visuals. These are given various names—thumbnails, scamps, or roughs. Quite often students tend to forget this process and set about producing ideas directly on the computer. This generally inhibits the development of ideas, because psychologically you tend to restrict yourself to what you are capable of achieving technically.

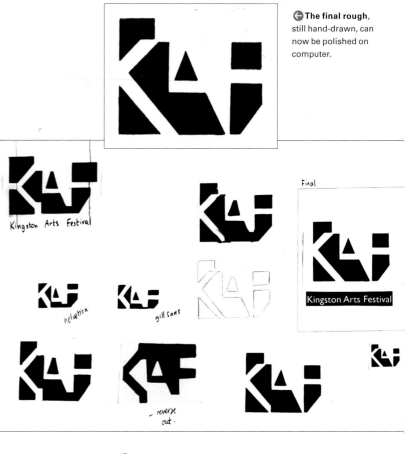

⬅ **The final rough**, still hand-drawn, can now be polished on computer.

⬆ **Less rough** The approach is narrowed down and the initial ideas developed.

⬅ **Initial thoughts**
A 20-minute brainstorming exercise resulted in these ideas for a logo comprising the initial letters for Kingston Arts Festival.

Initial ideas are more prolific if you have a brainstorming session, in which your first thoughts are scribbled down quickly on paper. The coordination between brain, eye, and hand is amazingly fast, and by working quickly you can release a good many ideas. While producing these early concepts, your mind starts integrating diverse aspects of the project and moving the thought processes forward. It is worth bearing in mind that although roughs require drawing skills, they can be learnt quite easily for this kind of unpolished work. In short, this struggle for ideas is the real essence of developing concepts.

SEE ALSO: Illustrative Typography *p92*
Corporate Design *p158*

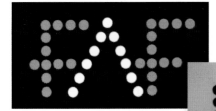

Screen idle Once a visual for this Florida Arts Festival logo has been created on screen, numerous combinations of colors for background and image can easily be produced.

Art and Technology ...
presents ...
Richard L Gregory
✗✗✗✗✗✗✗✗✗✗✗ ✗ ✗
✗✗✗ ✗ ✗✗✗✗✗
Wednesday 31 October 2004
✗✗✗ ✗✗ ✗ ✗✗✗✗ ✗✗✗✗
Saturday 13 November 2004
✗✗✗✗✗ ✗ ✗ ✗✗✗✗✗
Tuesday 16 November
✗✗✗✗ ✗ ✗ ✗ ✗✗
Carnegie Music Hall
✗✗✗ ✗ ✗✗✗✗✗
✗ ✗✗✗✗✗✗✗✗✗✗✗

First "scamps" or thumbnails can be produced quite quickly and various changes tried out.

Art and Technology ....
presents ....
Richard L. Gregory
✗✗✗✗✗ ✗✗✗✗✗
✗✗✗✗✗ ✗✗✗✗✗
Wednesday 31 October 2004
✗✗ ✗✗✗✗ ✗✗✗✗✗
Saturday 13 November 2004
✗✗✗✗ ✗✗✗✗✗✗
Thursday 16 November 2004
✗✗✗✗✗✗✗✗✗✗
Carnegie Music Hall
✗✗✗✗✗✗✗✗✗✗✗
✗✗✗✗✗ ✗✗✗✗✗✗✗✗

Once you have ideas jotted down, you can step back and make judgments regarding their value. It is at this point that computers come into their own, because they enable you to produce many alternate versions of your ideas, changing color, typeface, and images as many times as you wish. There is no definite size to which these roughs have to be worked. Thumbnails are, as the term suggests, quite small. You may feel more comfortable working to a third or a half of the actual size. One of the clear payoffs in developing the ability to do roughs is that when presenting your ideas to clients, alternate ones can be quickly sketched out, when needed, to confirm a fresh approach.

This rough visual for the Taipei Summer Arts Festival, drawn to a bigger size than the scamp (above), should have more detail and be ready to be worked up on screen.

Taipei Summer Arts Festival

Saturday 24 July to Saturday 7 August

events include:
Film shows
Live theatre
Poetry readings
Art exhibitions
Live bands

taf plus workshops in Printmaking, Sculpture, Pottery, Calligraphy
contact Festival organising team on 07919567572
email taipei@aol.com for full festival details

UNIT 1 | **Cutting and Creasing**

In addition to your drawing skills, you will need to develop a number of manual skills that, like drawing, are an aspect of your hand and eye coordination capabilities. You will need to assemble a collection of tools and equipment: a steel-edged ruler for measuring and using as a straight edge for cutting paper and cardboard; a pair of scissors; HB and 2H pencils (pencil grades are not standardized and can vary greatly from manufacturer to manufacturer); an eraser; masking tape and invisible adhesive tape; a sharp X-acto or craft knife for light fine cutting including pencil sharpening; and for heavier cutting, such as thicker cardboards, a trimming knife.

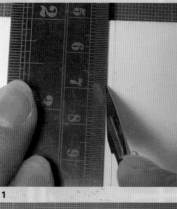

1

2

⬆ **Cutting** Always use the knife against a metal rule when cutting. Slowly make the incision, keeping the knife steady, and moving downwards.

➡ **Making a fold** You will need a thick sheet of card. Make two parallel cuts about the thickness of the steel rule apart, but do not cut right through the card (**1**). Scoop out the groove with the back of a scalpel blade. Place the card you wish to fold over it. Use the end of the blade holder and a ruler to push a groove into the card (**2**).

SEE ALSO: Packaging Design *p174*

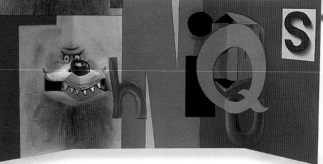

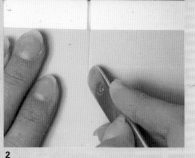

⬅ ⬇ **Constructing a pop-up** An enlarged section of Neil Young's pop-up showing the illustrative elements in great detail. Study the mechanics of the construction and produce some sample pop-ups yourself.

You should have a plastic cutting mat, which will heal up surface cuts and remain smooth. You will need adhesives, one for paper and one for heavier materials, but you should be able to reposition both after application. Because spray glue can be hazardous in enclosed spaces it is not recommended for general pasting and collage but only for mounting work.

Making a three-dimensional mock-up

Frequently it is necessary for a designer to produce a mock-up of the intended design. This is a simple process when you are designing a brochure or folded leaflet, but packaging requires more thought—a mock-up is essential in order to experience the three-dimensional qualities of the package. Test your manual skills by making a mock-up of this simple box. Use an A4 piece of 250 or 300 gsm card (paper should not be used as it is not rigid enough). At this stage it is not necessary to consider any special construction and closure details as this will come much later should the design go into production. This mock-up enables you to experience the basic form and volume and to practice planning, accurate measured drawing, and cutting skills. When planning, make a rough sketch of both the intended three-dimensional form and how the flat plan should be, so that you can see the number of panels, how they relate to each other, and where tabs should best be placed. This will help to save time and materials by spotting problems early on. Design is planning.

The flat plan

You are to make a box measuring 3⅛in (8 cm) high by 2 in (5 cm) wide and 2 in (5 cm) deep. Carefully draw a flat plan of the box so that the four panels of 2 in (5 cm) wide by 3⅛in (8 cm) in height are joined together along their 3⅛in (8 cm) edges. Start with the A4 card in front of you in a landscape format. Measure in from the left edge ⅝in (15 mm) and draw a light vertical line with your 2H pencil the full height of the card (remember, the pencil lines are just a guide for you to cut or score). Measure and draw four more vertical lines each 2 in (5 cm) apart across the card to the right. Now, measuring up ½in (14 mm) from the bottom edge of the card, draw a horizontal line the width of the card. Above that measure 2 in (5 cm) and draw another line across the card. Measure up again, this time drawing a line 3⅛in (8 cm) above the 2 in (5 cm) line. Finally draw another line 2 in (5 cm) above the 3⅛in (8 cm). This will provide you with a row of four squares at the bottom of the sheet, above a row of four vertical rectangles, and then above that another row of squares. This is the flat plan of your box. Choose one of the bottom squares to be the end of the box, and choose the top square attached to the same rectangle to become the other end of the box. The narrow edge of

card that is on the outer edge of the square should be retained to act as a tab that is tucked in (and glued if required) to hold the end panel in place.

On the left of the vertical 3⅛ x 2 in (8 x 5 cm) rectangles is ⅝in (15 mm) of card, which is required to become a gluing tab. Before continuing always check your measurements, as time and materials can be saved if there is a fault found at this stage.

Creasing and gluing the mock-up

Now the flat plan can be cut out of the card so that it can be made up into the three-dimensional form. On the right you will have a piece of card about 3⅛ x 8¼ in (80 x 210 mm), which is waste. When your flat box is cut out it should have a cruciform, created by the box ends. To increase rigidity to the box it is possible to add further tabs to each side of the box ends so that they have tabs on three sides (tabs when cut out should be tapered towards the free edge, making tucking in easier) the fourth side awaiting a crease. Now the card should be creased before folding and gluing, as explained opposite. This part of the process can be very fiddly so take your time and try to be as accurate as possible. Your mock-up is now ready for use.

⬇ **The mock-up** The three stages of making a three-dimensional mock-up.

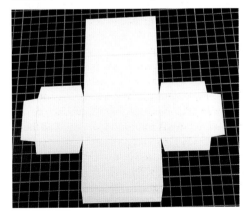

1 The flat plan with glue tabs cut out of 300 gsm card.

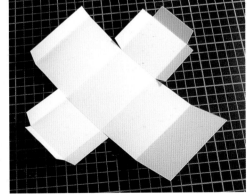

2 The flat sheet is creased before folding into the full form.

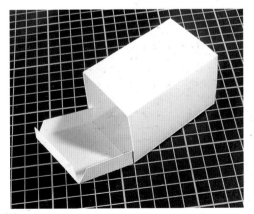

3 The completed plain box ready to be used. Computer print-outs can be pasted on in order to test the effect of different color and type forms.

UNIT 2 | **Design Publishing Software**

Today's design development software caters simultaneously for several markets: design for print; the extension of traditional printing into the modern electronic toolkit; and newly emerging technologies, including multimedia, web design, and online content.

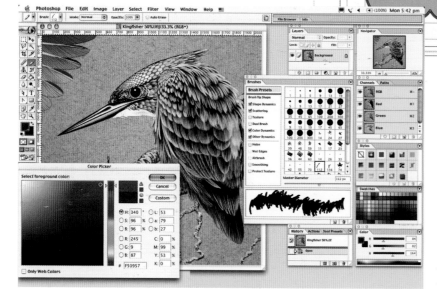

Adobe Illustrator Another very well-regarded industry leader, Illustrator works primarily with vector-based imagery and provides a wide range of tools to support designers and web developers.

For the creative professional, just a few packages are dominant. From the Adobe stable these include Photoshop, Illustrator, and InDesign; from the Macromedia stable Freehand and Dreamweaver. And very much on its own in page-makeup, but very much a market leader, stands QuarkXPress. There are alternative products with fewer features available for the non-professional.

The software market offers a wide range of applications all capable of providing you with professional-quality results. Collectively they add up to electronic publishing. You can use them to create any kind of publication, from a black-and-white stamp to a

Adobe Photoshop Pretty much the industry-accepted standard in image manipulation, Photoshop provides a huge selection of powerful image-editing tools to cover virtually all requirements. Professionals such as photographers choose it for its strengths in handling full-color high-resolution images.

multicolor, multi-illustrated magazine, and from a printed brochure to a website. Choosing how you integrate your software needs into the design and production process depends on many different factors, including the kind of publications you wish to create, how they are to be realized, whether the hardware is available/affordable, and the size of the production team.

For the budding designer this can offer too much choice, but you will generally require at least a page-makeup application and an image-manipulation application. Photographers, illustrators, digital artists, or those with a painterly approach are very likely to have a preference for Photoshop. Those at the fine-art end of the spectrum may also like to look at Painter, which offers an environment analogous to traditional brush and canvas. Typographers and graphic artists may equally prefer Illustrator or Freehand. Corporate and editorial designers will probably opt for a page-layout program.

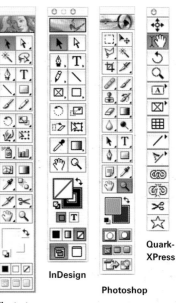

Illustrator

InDesign

Photoshop

Quark-XPress

⬆ **Toolboxes** from the four programs indicate the similarities among those from the Adobe programs and, by contrast, the rather more modest appearance of the Quark alternative.

⬆ **Adobe InDesign** InDesign is Adobe's equivalent to QuarkXPress and between the two these cover just about every conceivable need.

Programs from the various stables tend to be optimized to work together. Adobe has made an attractive selection, both in terms of cost and integrated functionality, with its Creative Suite which in its most comprehensive version includes Photoshop CS, Illustrator CS, and InDesign CS plus GoLive CS, Acrobat Professional, and Version Cue. Macromedia programs equally integrate with one another. Unfortunately, for the novice user, choosing a suite of programs is tough since personal preference tends to come from experience over a lengthy period.

➡ **QuarkXPress** In Western markets, Quark has dominated the electronic print industry for a decade. In practice the program does not have a huge number of features, offering an interface built around importing objects into boxes and manipulating them. PageMaker is the program of choice in many Far Eastern countries.

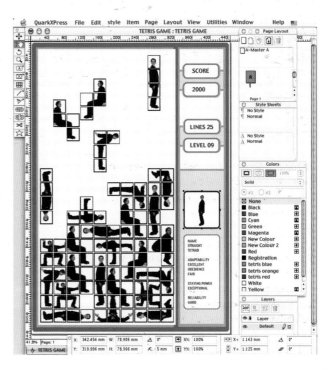

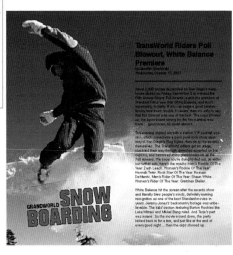

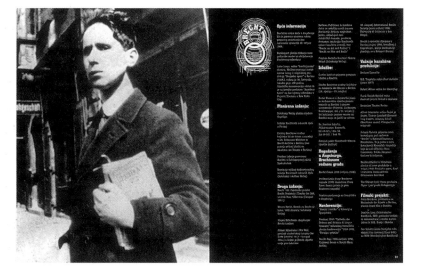

Essentially a page-layout program assembles, collates, and juxtaposes various objects in one combined document, which can then be printed. At the two extremes, documents might either be created entirely within the program or they might simply be assembled, all the elements having been created in external programs.

There are several strengths that have made page-layout programs such important tools within design for print: the ease with which components can be collated, assembled, and juxtaposed; the simplicity with which complex functions can be achieved; accuracy in visualizing and manipulating type within the design process—all are invaluable.

Basic concepts

Essentially, page-makeup programs revolve around the construction and manipulation of boxes, which contain either imported items or internally generated ones. Typically, illustrations are imported and type/text items created within the program—although raw text may well have been typed in, unformatted, using a word-processing program like Microsoft Word. Everything that appears in a Quark document, with the exception of some rule-work, is contained within boxes. The text or picture box is the basic element in all page composition. All page elements—text or pictures—are either created inside, or imported into, boxes.

⬆ ➡ Initial ideas on paper If you are working in a page-layout program, having a well-thought-out idea can save a lot of time and effort in the document's creation. Aspects such as the page size and margins can then be correctly set, right at the beginning, in the New Document dialog box.

SECTION 1	THE LANGUAGE OF DESIGN
MODULE 5	Studio Tools and Skills
UNIT 3	**Page-layout Programs**

QuarkXPress has until recently been regarded as the industry standard for professional publishing. It is used around the world to create professional-quality publications, ranging from newspapers and magazines to business cards and movie posters. It is one of a number of page-layout programs, alternatives including Adobe InDesign and Adobe PageMaker.

➡ Columns aligned Page-layout programs ensure that columns of text align perfectly, and spacing on subheads is uniform.

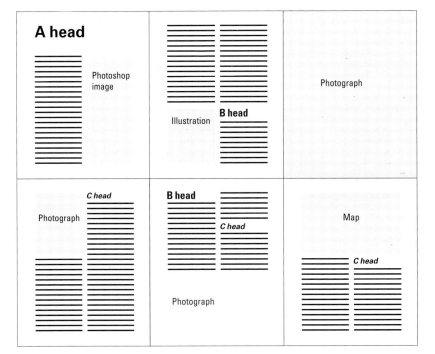

A head

Photoshop image

Illustration **B head**

Photograph

C head

Photograph

B head

C head

Photograph

Map

C head

⬆ **A multipage document**, the raison d'être of page-layout programs. Elements created in other programs—photographs, maps, text, and illustrations—are imported into picture or text boxes for a seamless appearance.

⬇ **Circular type** Text manipulation is easy, letting the designer explore extreme options in a finished form.

QuarkXPress vs InDesign

Quark has been the industry standard for a long time, and design companies and publishing houses have generally made hefty investments. But it is something of a one-horse stable, and today's market is increasingly geared up for more integrated approaches, so it now faces some stiff competition. InDesign is the new kid on the block, as it were, and offers a serious challenge to Quark's long dominance. A strong point, especially where productivity is an issue, is the fact that it shares an interface with Photoshop and Illustrator. The ease with which objects and images can be interchanged between the Adobe programs is also a major bonus.

Generally speaking, both programs are capable of doing the job, as in fact can other alternatives. But the serious typographer is most likely to go for either InDesign or Quark.

⬇ **Cropping and angles** Different typographical crops and angles can be explored.

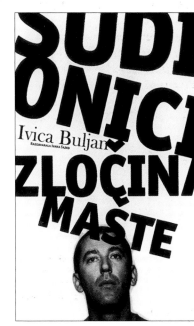

UNIT 4 | **Digital Photography**

The great change from analog to digital is now upon us. For some time, predictions of the demise of traditional means of image capture have sent ripples of anxiety through the design industry. How will technological changes affect the roles of the photographer, designer, and printer?

In fact, all the old rules of lighting and composition still apply; all that has changed is the method of capture and storage. Where film had to be purchased, stored in cool and dry surroundings, shot, developed, manipulated, printed, and stored, the digital approach allows for a single purchase of a specific amount of memory (which can be used again and again); the pictures are shot, downloaded, and stored. The process of manipulation and printing can then take place at any time by any person who has access to the files; the data can also easily be shared by e-mail.

Archiving your images
One problem yet to be satisfactorily addressed is that of archiving digital data. If a negative is scratched it can still be printed, and retouched, but the loss of a digital file can be catastrophic. For example, if your picture is stored on a computer whose hard drive is fatally damaged you will have lost the information. It is far better to back up the file on one or two of the variety of external hard drives that now exist: you will need a Zip disk, portable external hard drive, memory card, or CD burner to store the information.

Work on the assumption that if your data exists in only one form it does not really exist at all. Keep it on your hard drive, burn it on two gold archival CDs (but do not put sticky labels over the CD), keep one copy for access, and store the other copy in a different place from where you work. You should also consider rewriting the discs every few years. In short, back it up.

◄ Power supply Because digital cameras do not need to house bulky mechanical parts they can be made smaller and lighter. However, because they rely totally on electrical power to operate, they are hungrily dependent on batteries.

File format
The industry-standard software that you are likely to need if you are working in photography is Adobe Photoshop. Although it is always good to have the latest software, it is safe to say that anyone working with Photoshop 6 or higher will have no problems with 95 percent of their projects. When saving files it is crucial to choose the right format for the job in hand.

↑ Mini printers allow you to make quick prints directly from your camera.

- PSD (Photoshop Document), when you are working in layers.
- TIFF, when you have completed all the work on your piece and you have flattened the layers.
- JPEG, when you wish to compress for sending as an attachment file.

SEE ALSO: Scanning *p66*
                 Image Manipulation *p68*

There should be no loss of quality or detail when opening and closing PSD and TIF files, but with TIF you may use LZW compression as a good way of saving file space. Remember, however, that it will not open in any other software except Photoshop.

A JPEG is a format instantly recognized by any image capture software and will open on any computer. This is a very handy format for shrinking large files down to a tiny size, but there is an expensive price to be paid. Saving at too low a number will lose information from the file every time it is opened and closed. This is fine if you want to send an image as part of an e-mail, where it will only appear as a screen image, but if one were to try and print it then the image quality would be seriously compromised.

Pixels are the building blocks of any digital image. The more pixels in an image, the larger you can make a print without loss of quality.

Digital noise versus film grain

Film works by using millions of tiny light sensitive particles that react when light hits them. As you enlarge an image you will begin to see these tiny dots, which are called "film grain." By contrast, a digital camera works by using a light-sensitive chip to record the image. If we enlarge a digital image we begin to see the building blocks that go to make up an image. These are called "pixels." If you buy a camera without enough memory you will get smaller pictures that will become increasingly blurred when enlarged.

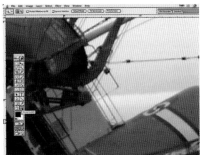
1

2

3

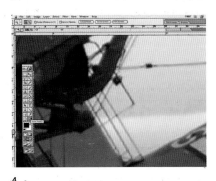
4

5

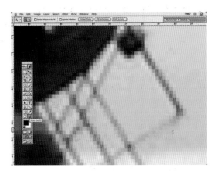
6

Why do images degrade as they are enlarged?

1	2048 x 1536 pixels	15 x 11 cm	250 dpi
2	1200 x 900 pixels	12 x 9 cm	250 dpi
3	900 x 675 pixels	9 x 7 cm	250 dpi
4	450 x 338 pixels	4.5 x 3.4 cm	250 dpi
5	200 x 150 pixels	2.03 x 1.52 cm	250 dpi
6	100 x 75 pixels	1 x 0.75 cm	250 dpi

(dpi = dots per inch)

Scanning

Although scanners from the various manufacturers may appear to be different, superficially they do have a great deal in common. This text covers mainly the mechanics of the basic scanning process, and we shall use the HP Precision Scan and Umax PlugIn Scan software interfaces by way of examples. Other machines will offer similar options, though not all scanners support all the same features.

HP Precision Scan

Umax PlugIn Scan, version 3.3

⬆ **Sample scanner interfaces**
Main scanning windows from HP Scanjet and Umax scanners.

The scanner interface window generally offers the following basics: the artwork window, artwork selection tools, menus of options, mode settings, brightness and contrast controls, gamut or color range, an indication of storage requirements (impending scan size), and preview, scan, and cancel options. If possible, it is usually easier to scan directly into Photoshop using the Photoshop Plug-in version of the software. This avoids a lot of problems associated with file formats, unnecessary saving and reloading of files, and gives immediate access to Photoshop's very extensive image manipulation, adjustment, and correction features. This is the approach adopted here.

SEE ALSO: Digital Photography *p64*
Image Manipulation *p68*

The fundamental process

In its simplest form, the process is as follows (we are working here with original reflective artwork—see below):
- Select the scanner from Photoshop, File > Import > "Name of scanner."
- The scanner window and menus will now appear.
- Reset the scanner to its default settings, if necessary.
- Set the preview scan area to maximum, if needed.
- Set the mode to the type of artwork to be scanned—line art, grayscale, color—and whether it is reflective or transmissive artwork (negative or transparency).
- Do a preview scan of the artwork.
- Select the area of artwork to be scanned.
- Set the resolution.
- Scan the image.

The scanned image should pop up within a Photoshop window.

Different artwork types

For most practical purposes artwork can be divided into two fundamental types: original artwork, either scanned directly from the "original" or from an intermediate original such as a photograph, slide, or negative; or second-generation artwork, such as images scanned directly from the printed page.

Transmissive artwork—transparencies and negatives—unless they are photographs of printed materials, normally counts as true "artwork" and needs little special treatment beyond the basics above.

Clean well-finished original "artwork" generally presents few problems in the scanning process. However, much of the time you'll be concerned not with scanning originated finished artwork, but accumulating various pieces from a variety of sources. This may necessitate the scanning of pencil drawings and sketches, various printed materials, and photocopies: plus there are many substrates, such as glossy surfaces, that often pose scanning problems. The most common difficulties come from pre-screened materials.

Sharpening scanned images

For various technical reasons images that have been scanned often need both sharpening and some degree of color correction. Scans that have included descreening as part of the process almost invariably need some degree of sharpening.

⬇ **Image resolution** Determine the image mode in which your scan will be created. RGB (Red, Green, Blue) is used for all color originals; use Grayscale for black-and-white tone (photos and pencil drawings); finally, if your image is pure black and white (line drawing, map, or diagram) use Bitmap mode.

Scanned in RGB mode   Scanned in Grayscale mode   Scanned in Bitmap mode

⬇ **Image resolution** The more pixels you create, the more detail and size you can achieve in your prints. When buying a scanner, look for a resolution capacity of at least 600 dpi.

Image scanned at 30 dpi   Image scanned at 60 dpi

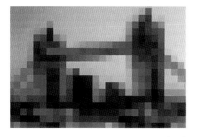 

Image scanned at 120 dpi   Image scanned at 240 dpi

EXERCISE

Sharpening "original" artwork

First-generation art, if it needs sharpening at all, can normally be satisfactorily handled using the Unsharp Mask filter in Photoshop:

- Go to Filter > Sharpen > Unsharp Mask. This will open the Unsharp Mask dialogue box. Make sure the Preview option is selected. Click on the image in the preview window to see how the image looks without the sharpening. Drag in the preview window to see different parts of the image, and click + or – to zoom in or out.

Do one of the following:

- Drag the Amount slider or enter a value to determine how much to increase the contrast of pixels. For high-resolution printed images, an amount between 150 and 200 percent is usually recommended.
- Drag the Radius slider or enter a value to determine the number of pixels surrounding the edge pixels that affect sharpening. For high-resolution images a Radius between 1 and 2 is usually recommended. A lower value sharpens only the edge pixels, whereas a higher value sharpens a wider band of pixels. This effect is much less noticeable in print than on-screen, because a 2-pixel radius represents a smaller area in a high-resolution printed image.
- Drag the Threshold slider or enter a value to determine how different the sharpened pixels must be from the surrounding area before they are considered edge pixels and sharpened by the filter.

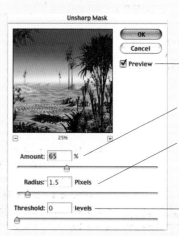

Check how the image looks in the preview box.

Use the Amount slider to increase the pixel contrast.

Use the Radius slider to change the number of pixels near to the edge pixels.

The Threshold slider determines the difference of the sharpened pixels from the surrounding area.

UNIT 6 | **Image Manipulation**

Artists and designers have been making images by a multitude of traditional techniques, founded in years or even centuries of practice— everything from pencil drawing and oil painting through to more recent techniques such as frottage and airbrushing (a skill that the program under discussion has made virtually redundant). Photoshop is the modern electronic-imaging tool par excellence, and while it may not be able to fully replace these techniques in all their guises, it goes a long way to offering a digital equivalent.

Today's Photoshop is greatly enhanced from the early versions of ten years ago. Then it was mainly used as an image-retouching tool. Since Adobe introduced its intuitive layer structure, and powerful drawing and painting tools, there is very little that cannot be achieved (or, at least, simulated) using Photoshop. The latest versions now extend these features to include web design, within both Photoshop itself and its sister program, ImageReady.

SEE ALSO: Digital Photography *p64* ● Scanning *p66*

⬇ ⬅ ⬆ **Photoshop interface** shown on an Apple Macintosh desktop, including image document, menu bar, toolbox, and layers palette, as well as potential images for inclusion in the montage, ready for dragging and dropping.

For work requiring excellent imagery, but not vast amounts of text or too many pages, Photoshop is a good choice. Programs like Photoshop have brought traditional painting techniques into a new digital arena, one adopted now by many professional artists and illustrators. The software offers a range of aesthetic techniques, and with recent improvements in printing technologies, like ink jet, computer-originated work can be effectively displayed in galleries.

EXERCISE

Adding color to a pencil drawing

1 The pencil drawing Scan the pencil drawing to an appropriate size (in megabytes). This scan is to be full size as it is this image (layer) that will define the detailed content of the image. Tidy up the image inside the silhouette. Outside the silhouette doesn't matter as it will be masked off.

2 Duplicating the drawing Move the pencil drawing from the background to a layer. A duplicate layer will suffice for this. It doesn't matter if the background also contains the same image to start off with, as the background copy will be painted out.

3 Adding the silhouette mask Add the layer mask and using pencil and brush carefully create the silhouette mask. Reset the layer application mode from "normal" to "multiply" in the pencil drawing layer.

4 Coloring the image Click on the color layer and paint into the layer to apply color. The pencil image in this layer will be destroyed by the painting process. This won't seem to happen because the drawing applied by the layer above will obscure this effect. The overall effect will be of color being applied to the drawing.

1

2

3

4

Digital techniques bring myriad new parameters to the repertoire of traditional techniques, opening up exciting avenues of exploration for the professional image maker. Just to touch on some of the possibilities: you are no longer tied to a fixed canvas; the canvas itself becomes a dynamic variable. The digital canvas has no implicit size, except when it is manifested in physical form. Freedom to endlessly juxtapose elements and images allows for experiment without commitment. The "drawing" and "paint" layers are also fluid; no longer, in general, must what lies beneath be covered by that on top.

If objects form the basic element in Illustrator, and boxes the basis of page-makeup programs, the most fundamental unit in Photoshop is the layer. Most often a layer comprises an image, the bit whose contribution you see, and a layer mask, which controls how that image combines with the images in the other layers.

At the least demanding end of the scale, a photographer may need to use only one or two layers when working on images that are already very close to the desired result. A little retouching, a little sharpening, or a little color correction may be all that is required. A computer artist, on the other hand, might require dozens of layers, some of which may include additional adjustment layers beyond the basic unit. Skillful manipulation of layers is therefore essential to mastering Photoshop.

Complex imagery

The images above and to the right show a more complex, multi-layered example than that shown in the exercise below. As the number of layers increases, the overall file size grows, the amount by which it grows depending on the size and complexity of each additional layer. To help alleviate the problem of oversized files, this design has been created in two separate files. Most of the basic images have been combined in the first image file. Here the background image of 8 megabytes has increased to 43 megabytes with all the added layers. When working toward a complex final image, building it up in several auxiliary files is often a good way of avoiding problems. One, all your eggs are not in one basket, so to speak; and two, you can work more quickly in smaller files than one huge unwieldy one.

⬆ **Montaging images together in Photoshop** The inset shows an intermediate stage in the layering process. The big picture shows the finished image.

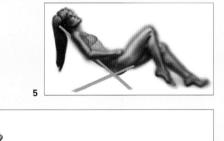

5

6

5 Painting over the edges It doesn't matter if the paint extends beyond the confines of the drawing in this bottom layer, because the effect of the mask on the layer above will be to preserve a sharp silhouette.

6 Finished image The finished image was created using the same basic working procedure, but contains other modifications to achieve independent control over additional elements.

7 Layer palette The full layer palette for this image looks like this. Note that there are layers additional to the primary layers: the color layer, the pencil drawing layer, and the silhouette masking layer. Usually some adjustments and fine-tuning are required. These are all shown here.

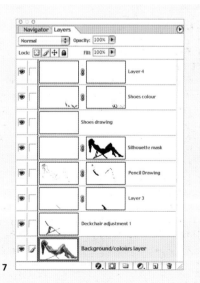

7

UNIT 7 | **Computer Illustration**

Practically the designer's one-stop answer to creating vector-based imagery, Adobe Illustrator offers a huge range of tools for object-oriented drawing and painting; for making symbols and complex shapes; for transforming and manipulating objects; and for filling, stroking, blending, and masking. You can create readymades like graphs using the graphing tools, brushes and symbols, and design and make your own objects. The toolbox alone contains over a hundred tool options. You should find no shortage of creative avenues.

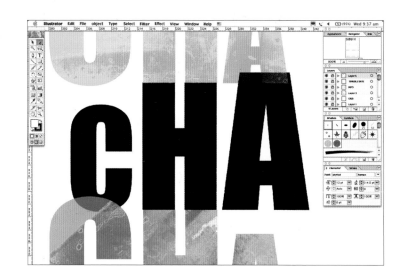

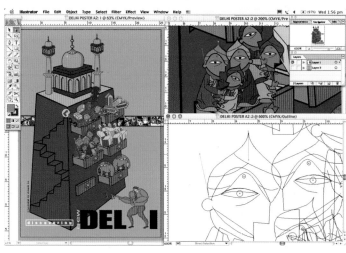

⬆ **Viewing artwork** One can zoom in within the Illustrator interface to edit iconic letter forms.

⬆ **Multiple windows** One can work with multiple windows while editing objects in the artwork. Artwork can be viewed either in color or as path outlines. In this case, editing is being performed in zoomed outline, while changes can be monitored at alternate scales in full-color views.

⬆ **Illustrator imagery** Illustrator lends itself to mixing hard-edged graphic imagery with powerful and sophisticated typographic tools. Raster (or pixel-oriented) art can be included too, as in the narrow band of photographs in this Delhi poster.

SEE ALSO: Composition *p14*

For clean crisp hard-edged graphics Illustrator offers an elegant approach, with a comfortable and easy-to-use graphics interface. Computer graphics fall into two main types, vector-based graphics (sometimes called object-oriented) and pixel-orientated graphics (also called bitmapped, or rastered). Mostly, imagery originated in Illustrator will be of the vector type. One of the big advantages of vector imagery is that it doesn't alter when magnified. An Illustrator document consisting only of vector images will rescale and print at any size with no loss of sharpness. This contrasts with Photoshop, in which if an image is blown up large enough it will start to pixelate.

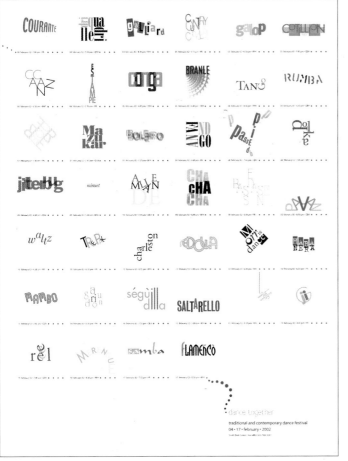

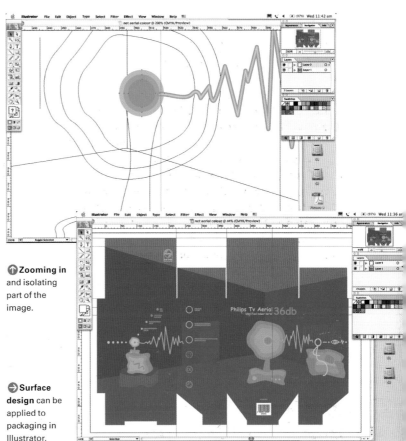

Zooming in and isolating part of the image.

Surface design can be applied to packaging in Illustrator.

Versatile This poster incorporates an amazing variety of effects and styles.

Bitmap/raster imagery versus object-oriented/vector imagery (right side); the former begins to pixelate when magnified at high percentages.

In Illustrator the main unit of design is the object. Most simply, this may be just a line. At the more complex end of the spectrum, it may be a masked outline containing a number of different sub-objects of various kinds, from simple filled objects to complex shaded objects with graduated tones. Generally it will be an outline with a simple fill. Whether complex or simple, it will be a variation on this theme. In Illustrator jargon, an object has an outline that has a "stroke" applied to it, as well as an encompassed space that contains the "fill."

As it is the edge line that defines the shape of an object, "line" drawing is an equally important feature of Illustrator. This is particularly true of Bezier lines and curves. Learning to use components like the pen tool and line-editing tools for adjusting, adding, subtracting, and converting anchor point types is key to getting the best out of Illustrator.

UNIT 8 | **Web-design Software**

Featured here are just three of the more popular pieces of software, though it should be said that many more are available, and some of them are totally free. If you have Internet access, try searching for web-design tools, software, and programs.

While there are many alternatives available to the web designer, Macromedia Dreamweaver has developed massively in its recent versions and still remains a very popular choice among professional web designers.

Dreamweaver provides a relatively intuitive user interface and offers different levels of functionality for everyone from the novice web designer to the professional web developer. The software provides various templates with which to work, code editing for

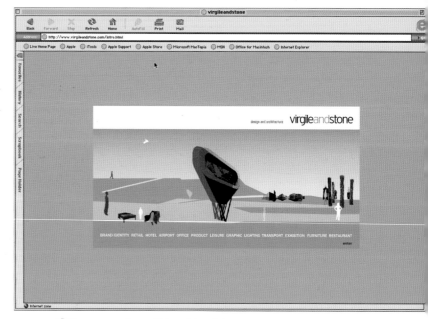

↑ Movement and sound This stylish website for interior design firm Virgile and Stone (www.virgileandstone.com) was designed in Illustrator before being translated into Flash. It features sound and animated clips.

Dreamweaver: a closer look

Although Dreamweaver comes in various versions, for the purpose of this overview we will be concentrating on MX 2004—though most of the features discussed in these pages are available in older versions. The software is available for both Mac and PC, and screen shots included here are taken from a Mac running OS 10.3.

The general principle behind Dreamweaver is that it is a WYSIWYG editor. Starting with an empty page you can insert elements such as tables, into which you can place text and images. Each page can contain links from one page to another, or to an external website. You would need to create any images and buttons used within your website in a program such as Adobe Photoshop or Macromedia Fireworks.

This is a BASIC HTML page presented in SPLIT VIEW. Under split view you can access the code and the page. Click on the other options to toggle between views.

The title of the page as it will be seen in the browser bar can be entered here.

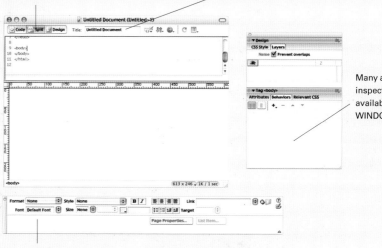

Many additional inspectors are available from the WINDOW menu.

The PROPERTIES inspector (WINDOW > PROPERTIES) is the window you will use most often. It is a "conditional" inspector—that is, its function changes depending on what you are working with. This view allows for formatting of text.

SEE ALSO: Web Design *p166*

those interested in hand coding, or a range of WYSIWYG tools ("what you see is what you get"). Developers can use Dreamweaver with server technology to build Internet applications and a range of options is available for constructing dynamic sites.

Dreamweaver's latest version has received some criticism for its instability, drain on RAM and sluggishness, although many counter these claims. Perhaps the best news is that you can try out the software before purchasing it. Investigate www.macromedia.com for a free 30-day trial and to see for yourself.

Adobe GoLive CS is battling against Dreamweaver to become the web designer's choice. It has all the features you would expect, such as visual interface and WYSIWYG tools, but it also integrates directly with Adobe Photoshop, Adobe Illustrator, and Adobe Portable Document Format (PDF), meaning that files can be worked on in GoLive without switching between applications; if you use other Adobe software, moreover, the interface is also very familiar. One major drawback for GoLive CS is its lack of support for

dynamic sites, so opt for Dreamweaver if you are interested in delving into this realm. As with Macromedia Dreamweaver, a 30-day free trial of Adobe GoLive CS is available by visiting www.adobe.com.

BBEdit is an HTML and text editor that is only available for Apple Macintosh computers. With fewer "bells and whistles" than either Dreamweaver or GoLive and requiring a sharper learning curve at first, it is pitched at those wanting to do work at a coding level. Once mastered, however, BBEdit allows for fast and easy site construction and editing.

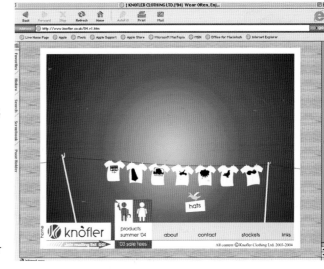

Downloading at the double
This site for a clothing company (www.knofler.co.uk) is optimized for speed, because after the main site loads, the rest of the site is made up of separate Flash movie files.

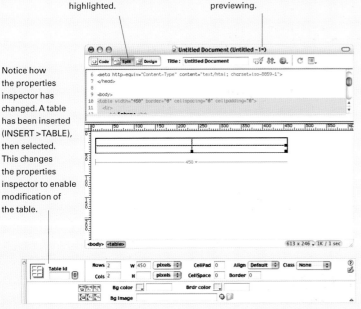

The code view now displays code relating to the table. If the table is selected the code is highlighted.

An * indicates that the document has been modified, but not yet saved. Always save your document before previewing.

Notice how the properties inspector has changed. A table has been inserted (INSERT >TABLE), then selected. This changes the properties inspector to enable modification of the table.

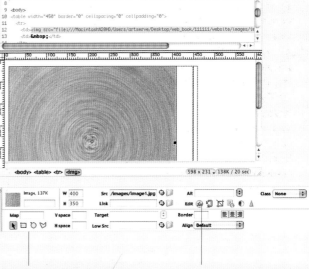

Inserting an image into the table again changes the properties inspector, and this time offers various image-related options.

If you have Macromedia Fireworks installed, you can crop, resize, and edit images from within Dreamweaver.

UNIT 9 | **Animation Software**

Despite the fact that the major animation studios are predicting the end of commercial 2D animation production, there is still plenty of room for creative 2D projects, especially web-based ones. For web animation the de facto standard is Macromedia Flash and its swf file format, which offers compact, resolution-independent files that will work with almost every installed web browser.

From its beginnings as a tool for making compact animated banners, Flash has grown into a fully fledged multimedia and web-development tool. Its diversity of application makes it one of the must-know programs for any designer, especially given the range of talents you are expected to have these days.

Flash is essentially a vector-based program, like Adobe Illustrator and Macromedia Freehand, which makes it an excellent starting-point for your animation, given its more complex drawing tools. In addition, vector drawings can be imported directly into Flash and will remain editable.

⬆ **Flash** is a great tool for producing stunning animated e-cards that will run on almost any computer. The small file size means it can be easily e-mailed at the last moment for that all-important birthday or anniversary you've "forgotten." This original Bon Voyage card was made by Cartoon Saloon in Ireland. E-cards also make excellent calling cards when looking for work.

➡ **Japanese animation** (anime) uses many tricks to achieve a sense of action without doing lots of drawing, mostly through camera movement. Simulating this in Flash is easy, using a motion path and tweening.

Timeline All the elements in your movie, on their various layers, are controlled from here.

The Motion Tweening between the two keyframes is indicated here and is controlled in the Properties palette.

Library palette Elements of your movie are stored here as Symbols. They can be dragged from the library and placed on the Stage.

Tools Palette The basic tools needed for creating and editing your movie.

Starting position of the spaceboy Symbol. This will be a keyframe in Frame 1 on the Timeline.

Motion Path This sits on its own layer and controls the direction in which the attached Symbol moves.

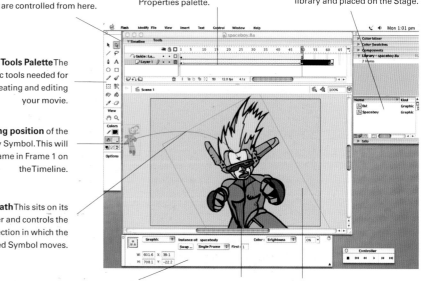

Properties Palette The attributes of the various elements on the stage are edited here.

Position of the spaceboy Symbol in the final keyframe of the sequence.

Stage The blue area is where the action takes place. The gray is a "pasteboard" area where items not in shot can be stored.

From sketch to finished frame

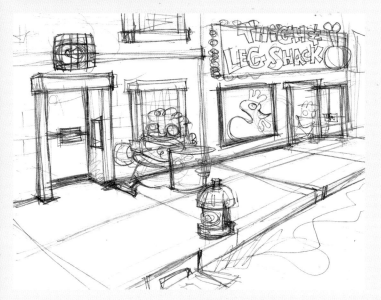

↑ The scene is sketched and storyboarded. In this instance it is a single drawing, because only one background and camera angle is used. The beginning of the scene shows Potty Mouf exiting the shop. The finishing position of the character is also shown.

↗ The original scene was redrawn and a clean, black-line version created. This was scanned and vectorized using Adobe Streamline and Illustrator. You can do the same with Macromedia Freehand.

→ Another black-line illustration was produced with the key positions of the character. The same vectorizing process used on the background was employed.

continued over the page ▶

The Stage and the Timeline

The two main components of Flash, for creating basic animations, are the Stage and the Timeline. All the visual elements are placed on the Stage and are controlled from the Timeline. The Timeline is frame-based, with each step of a movement occupying a different frame. This does mean you have to decide your frame rate before you start. Cinema films are projected at 24 frames per second (fps), but for the web you can work at around half that (12 fps).

→ **Using Flash** The original artwork for Broken Saints was created using Photoshop, a pixel-based software, which meant the finished Flash files were large. However, the universality of the swf format and the ease of integrated sound and movement made Flash the obvious choice.

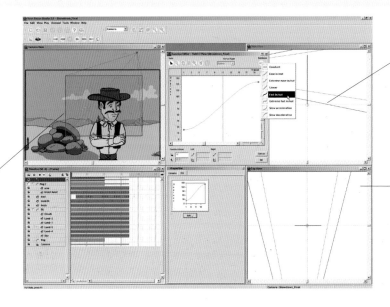

Background The newly vectorized background image was finished with some additional details and colored using Adobe Illustrator. The other advantage of working with vectors is the ease with which colors can be created and altered.

The finished background was imported into Flash and placed on its own layer, where it was locked into place to prevent accidental movement.

Character layer The vectorized and colored pictures of the character were also placed onto a separate layer in Flash. This layer also contained the open door, with its shaft of light on the footpath, which sits over the existing door on the background.

Toon Boom Studio is the tool of choice for producing a more traditional-looking animation using vectors. It has many of the features found in digital cel animation software, such as its big brother USAnimation, but at a fraction of the cost. This screenshot shows how a tracking shot is going to work.

The red box marks the area of the final frame of the tracking shot. Tracking is where the camera moves through a scene to change the viewer's perspective.

The movement of the camera is shown in graphical form. It can be altered by adjusting the curve.

A top view of the scene. The green line is the foreground character, with the other lines showing the camera's angle of view as it moves through the scene.

The final shot of the scene has the character moving out of the shadows into foreground light, before moving into a different scene. Once the animation is finished sound effects and (original) music can be added.

To simplify the animation process a walk cycle wasn't created but the three images of Potty Mouf shown on p.75 (far right) were placed at appropriate intervals in the timeline to give the impression of movement without the need for lots of drawing. Tricks such as simplifying the animation not only reduce the work involved but keep the file size down, allowing for faster playback online.

Keyframes

Like most animation software, Flash works with "keyframes." These are the extreme points in an action. In traditional cel animation the lead animator would draw the keyframes as pencil roughs, which would be cleaned up by another artist, then given to yet another animator to draw all the in-between frames. This is known as tweening. When creating simple movements, such as an object moving between two points, you set the beginning and end keyframes and Flash automatically does the tweening for you. If you move the position of a keyframe the software adjusts the tweening accordingly. This method is not recommended for complex character movement.

Where Flash really excels is in interactivity, using its own scripting language known as ActionScript. This is what is used to create content-rich websites, not to mention the myriad games available on the Internet.

Other options

Flash is by no means the only vector-based animation software. For those interested in creating a more conventional narrative animation, Toon Boom Studio is the tool of choice. This resembles a traditional approach to animation with integrated exposure sheet and multiplane cameras that can add more depth to scenes. It also has a lip-syncing tool to match up mouth shapes with recorded sounds.

As a relatively inexpensive, all-purpose animation and web design tool Flash can't be beaten, and the range and level of independent support on the Internet is unrivaled. But if your interest is pure animation then other programs, such as Toon Boom Studio, should be your choice. If animation is your thing there are still the other disciplines such as cel, CGI and stop-motion to consider, all of which have their own range of software.

Principles and Techniques

So far in this book we have looked at the fundamental building-blocks of design, such as form, color, and early concepts, as well as various media— digital and analogue—for creating images and type. This part of the book establishes the methods you will employ to generate ideas and develop them to a successful conclusion. We begin the chapter by returning to the topic of typography, but instead of examining the fundamentals—what type consists of, spacing, and size—we analyze the questions designers need to ask when actually working with type. What qualities do the different type families possess and which typefaces go well together? How do I ensure that my text is readable? When is it appropriate to use ornaments, rules, and tint panels? How do I arrange different levels of heading into a sensible hierarchy? And how can I use text as illustration effectively?

The context in which most designers specify type will either be in web design or in the printed arenas of books, promotional literature, or magazines. We will

discuss the importance of deciding the right form and shape for your work—
cost, purpose, and market are all important criteria here. Creating a workable
grid for your layout (either symmetrical or asymmetrical), with appropriate
margins, is essential to give your pictures, body copy, headings, and captions
an underlying framework. You will also learn how to build pace and contrast into
your work, to give your layouts visual rhythm and dynamism.

In such areas as corporate design, advertising, and packaging a premium is
placed on outstanding ideas expressed in original ways. But developing
concepts, though a skill in its own right, often involves more mundane
groundwork, such as finding out about your target audience and competing
brands, the ability to research and commission good-quality illustrations, and
making sure you have the production know-how to check that all your plans are
feasible and affordable. All these issues, and more, will be covered in Section 2.

UNIT 1 | Understanding and Selecting Typefaces

Since the introduction of digital forms of type, the number of faces available to designers has increased exponentially; it is virtually impossible, therefore, to know them all. However, it is advantageous to know a typeface's historical background, as it can help in harmonizing the face's characteristics with the content of the text. Very broadly, contemporary typefaces tend to work in cutting-edge contexts, whereas traditional type would be more apt for a literary classic.

Before examining the factors in selecting type, let us look at the broad categories into which they can be placed. Categorizing type is a hazardous business because of the many quirks and foibles that different fonts have. Nevertheless, a rough guide can help in recognizing typefaces and learning the different functions appropriate to the various type families. Two clear categories are text and display type, each of which has its own criteria for selection.

Text type: Old Style, Transitional, and Modern

Primarily, text types are meant to be read in a continuous form or at least with few interruptions. Certain serif typefaces, such as Bembo, Garamond, and Caslon, are ideal for the purpose of continuous reading. They have become regarded as "classic" fonts because they have stood the test of time and still warrant respect. Also known as Old Style faces, these Roman

Choose your font
Type finders group together typefaces in related families and in many different sizes and weights.

SEE ALSO: Emphasis and Hierarchy *p88*

A contemporary sans combined with geometric shapes makes for a lively design.

Dynamic poster Sans serif is an ideal choice for integrating these letters dynamically.

This slab serif has a power that effectively echoes the subject-matter.

fonts have been in use since the origins of printing in the 16th century. During the 1930s a number of new "Romans" were introduced to coincide with the new Monotype hot-metal system; many of the classics were also recut for the same purpose. Times New Roman and Imprint are good examples of this group, known as 20th-century Romans. Later the Germans Hermann Zapf and Jan Tschichold added, respectively, Palatino (1949) and Sabon (1967) to this group. Contemporary Romans, such as Minion and Swift, have now been designed using digital means.

The next group of Roman fonts is known as Transitional. Transitional faces have a vertical stress, sharp and bracketed serifs, and in most cases a medium to high contrast between the thick and thin letterstrokes. Baskerville and Century Schoolbook are prime examples. The term captures a movement away from the Old Style group, influenced by calligraphy, towards Modern faces, which are rooted in geometry rather than the pen. Modern faces also have a vertical stress, but an abrupt contrast between the thick and thin letterstrokes, fine horizontal serifs, and a narrow set width (in most cases). Bodoni is one of the earliest and best-known examples. There are many fonts in these three groups, which cover pretty much all kinds of book work. They can also be found in brochures and magazines, but other groups are more often used for this kind of publication.

Display type

Display types were introduced in the 19th century because of major changes taking place in the structure of society. In Britain, the Industrial Revolution brought the masses into the cities, and the need arose to communicate to a wider audience of people. The fonts discussed above were for books, still limited to a

⬅ **The Black Letter** form is perfect for anything with a Gothic flavor.

⬇ **Transport signage** A modern sans interacts with an Art Nouveau letter form to draw attention to this Metro station.

⬆ **Many styles** are evident in this street poster, which makes use of sans, slab serif, and outline letter forms.

Sans serif and script typefaces

The 20th century saw the extensive development of the sans serif, notably by the Bauhaus school in the 1920s and 1930s. Their philosophy was to sweep away the traditional forms characterized by excessive ornament. Simple typographic structures called for clean, functional typefaces, hence the interest in the sans serif with its monoline and functional forms. Futura was introduced in 1927, and two years later Gill Sans was unveiled. In the decades that followed, well-known fonts such as Helvetica and Optima in Europe, and Franklin Gothic and Avant Garde in the U.S., kept the sans serif among the most popular of type styles.

A significant advantage that the sans serif has over most other categories is the large number of variants that can be developed within one typeface. In 1957 Adrian Frutiger introduced a complete family of different weights and forms when he conceived the design of Univers, which comprises 21 variants ranging from light condensed to bold expanded.

Type designers have lately produced serif and sans serif versions of the same typeface, for example Officina and Stone. The advantage is that you can use a serif for the text setting and a sans for the display.

Selecting fonts

The content of the material and the purpose of the design are the main factors in deciding your choice of font. In information design clarity is essential, and it is telling that sans serif types, with their simple monoline structures, are

relatively elite sector of the population, and printers found them inadequate for the new billboards and pamphlets that were being produced. Bolder, stronger faces were needed.

This period saw the introduction of the sans serif (albeit in a minor role), slab serifs, and thickened Modern letters known as "Fat Faces." Mostly, these rather crude faces died out after 1850, but Ultra Bodoni is an example still in use today. The Victorians were extremely innovative and the invention of the pantograph machine later in the period enabled them to cut and produce all sorts of intricate fonts and ornaments, some of which are very comical. Their designs are full of vigor and still fascinate people today.

➡ **Wooden type,** originally used for producing posters by letterpress printing, is a good source of alternative letterforms.

used for road signage. Sans serif is also ideal when type has to be small size, as in some diagrams and maps.

Which font you choose can be influenced by the subject matter; in such cases a knowledge of the origins of the font can help in coming to a decision. For example, Caslon and Baskerville are classical English, Garamond is French, Goudy American, Bodoni Italian, and so on. You do not have to rely on the classical fonts; contemporary serif fonts such as Minion, Swift, and Quadraat are ideal for modern material.

Magazine designs can be more adventurous because readers tend to dip into the product rather than reading from cover to cover. Slab serifs that have been designed for text settings, such as Century, Serifa, and Glypha, are vigorous and appealing. If there are small amounts of copy, quirky fonts can bring a freshness to the overall feeling of the design.

Display types offer much more variety. Readability is less of an issue, so you can indulge in some playful experimentation. The feeling you wish to engender is naturally a major factor.

In summary, sans serif and slab serif faces are more authoritative. If you are reversing out type or printing on to tints in small sizes, these fonts are a better bet than serif types. For elegance, and a more subtle approach, serif fonts have the edge. A good technique in selecting fonts is to choose a serif for the text and a display face for the headings. This results in a harmonious feel as well as meeting both sets of criteria.

Evolving logo The middle of the word "seven" changes to reflect the different shows on this TV channel.

Effective mixture A serif italic font for "Relaxing" and a contemporary sans for the word "snazzy" nicely reflects the shift of moods.

THIS IS A PUBLIC INFORMATION ANNOUNCEMENT - GILLSANS

The Class and Sophistication of Shelly Allegro

ROLL UP! ROLL UP! - ZEBRAWOOD

THE GO-FASTER STRIPES OF SLIPSTREAM

The Swordsman like Strokes of Avalon

THE HIGH SCHOOL JOCK OF FONTS - PRINCETOWN

The Ye olde Traditions of Blackletter

The Timeless Elegance of AGaramond

Bold, brash and very curvaceous - BauerBodni Blk BT

COME AND HAVE A GO IF YOU THINK YOU'RE HARD ENOUGH! - MACHINE BT

CHUNKY AND VERY RETRO - DECORATEDO3S BT

shock of the new - BubbledotICGcoarsepositive

THE GOOD, THE BAD, AND THE UGLY - MESQUITE

CLASS IN A GLASS - CHARLEMAGNE

the informal handwritten style of - Aimee

Beware wet paint! - KidTYPEPaint

The Simplicity of Helvetica

Feeling a little uptight tonight are we dear? - Birch

Knock knock? Who's there? - Comic Sans MS

clear, gentle, and level-headed - Avant Garde

Stereotyping? Budding designers need to develop a strong sense of how the different fonts create emotional, psychological, and historical resonances within the reader.

UNIT 2 | **Readability and Legibility**

Debate continues to rage between traditionalists and modernists as to whether sans serif typefaces are more or less legible than serif faces. It must be said that serifs help letters to keep their distance, they link letters to make words and help to differentiate the letterforms—all factors that keep the eye moving along the horizontal line. However, modernists argue that sans serifs do not really decrease legibility; it is just a question of readers becoming culturally acclimatized to the sans serif face, which historically is a much more recent phenomenon.

Certain "rules" have evolved in regard to setting type and using letterforms. One principle is that long passages composed entirely of capital letters are difficult to read, since the words have similar rectangular outlines and lack ascenders and descenders.

⬆ **OK, right** The range-right setting works perfectly well here, as there is not too much text to read.

SEE ALSO: Color Differences and Legibility *p30*

learning on-line goes live

With the power of new technologies to bring lessons to your laptop at the press of a button, the old idea of institutional learning is finding a new form in *learndirect*. Out goes the idea of fixed timetables, rigid curricula and one-size-fits-all teaching. In comes learning that fits around your life, mixes and matches your personal goals and unrolls at your own pace.

This year Kaleidoscope lived up to its diamond-hard reputation for delivery when it helped make the government's vision of lifelong learning for everyone a reality. As an early development centre for the government's flagship University for Industry, our Tutors' House has ensured that even the most marginalized have been able to benefit from this ground-breaking initiative.

"It's all about building strong relationships with hard to reach groups, understanding their needs and personalising face to face support," says Alison Corbett Gibbin, UfI's Development Manager for London. "However great the technology and online support, we know people who lack confidence, basic skills and ICT know-how will fail to keep pace with the sweeping changes ICT is bringing to the way we live without

the kind of approach that *learndirect* can offer with the expert assistance of organisations such as Kaleidoscope."

In its first six months, 42 students have undertaken over 100 courses with *learndirect* at Kaleidoscope. Including ex-offenders and the homeless, mums returning to work and students in further education seeking supplementary skills, they have focussed on the potential of *learndirect* to enhance their understanding of basic ICT skills, internet and email, word processing, and databases and spreadsheets.

One student recovering from ME has just landed a part-time job as an internet services manager after training with *learndirect*. "I'm tickled pink!" she says. "I don't think it would have been feasible unless I'd had access to my own computer and someone to guide me when I got stuck."

This year our tutors will be promoting opportunities to extend online learning to a broader range of vocational skills including time management and budgeting. If you know people who would appreciate a friendly learning environment, contact our Tutors' House at scopetraing@cablelnet.co.uk.

"We know people who lack confidence, basic skills and ICT know-how will fail to keep pace with the sweeping changes ICT is bringing to the way we live without the expert assistance of organisations such as Kaleidoscope."

Alison Corbett Gibbin, Development Manager for London, University for Industry

⬅ **Ratio of type size to measure** For both column widths the optimum number of characters (60–72) has been used for the different type sizes and measures.

Type size, measure, and leading

The key factor that all agree on is that there is a readability relationship among the components of type size, measure (line length), and leading (spacing between lines). The optimum number of characters to a line is somewhere between 60 and 72. Any more than this and the eye has problems picking up the next line. Conversely, fewer characters per line can interrupt the flow of reading, since your head constantly has to move back and forth from one line to

⬆ **Mind the gap** Although the wide measure and reversed-out type could cause problems of readability, the use of generous leading and a sans serif typeface has helped to compensate for some of these inherent problems.

the next. Of course, different types of jobs will influence these decisions. In fact, context is everything. In magazine work the measures tend to be shorter because readers dip into articles rather than reading the whole periodical from cover to cover. Likewise, novels, which have to satisfy a criterion of continuous reading, look very different from advertisements, in which impact is a primary concern. Indeed it is a useful exercise to ask yourself why certain publications—telephone directories, timetables, cookbooks, and so on—differ in their standards of readability depending on the function they fulfill. Choice of type size and measure also depends on the amount of copy there is to be read. Readers can cope with small amounts of copy if the setting is smaller or on a narrower measure than the recommended optimum.

Typefaces with large x-heights have reduced ascenders and descenders, resulting in less differentiation in word shapes. Therefore, these typefaces need to have more leading. Leading is a major element in readability, for if there is insufficient space between the lines the eye will be hampered from moving to the next line. Increased leading is also required if the typeface is condensed, or if it is a serif typeface with a heavy or bold characteristic.

Justified versus ranged-left?

Another perennially hot topic is the relative virtues of justified and ranged-left setting. As the typographer Betty Binns says, "Since an uneven line ending creates a pattern of broken eye movement, you might expect that justified type would be easier to read. Again, reading experiments do not confirm this. It may be that the additional white space provided by unjustified type compensates for the less eye movement pattern." Ranged-right setting, by contrast, forces the reader to search for the beginning of each line, which over long passages of text can get very annoying and should be avoided. On a general note, if you are reversing type out of black or a color, then a sans serif typeface is a safer option than the alternative, with its finer lines and serifs. Much will depend, of course, on the size of type and quality of paper.

There are many factors to consider when thinking about readability and legibility of the text. These include the line length (measure), the size of type, the weight of type, the amount of leading, and the size of the x-height.

4 pt

There are many factors to consider when thinking about readability and legibility of the text. These include the line length (measure), the size of type, the weight of type, the amount of leading, and the size of the x-height.

8 pt

There are many factors to consider when thinking about readability and legibility of the text. These include the line length (measure), the size of type, the weight of type, the amount of leading, and the size of the x-height.

10 pt

There are many factors to consider when thinking about readability and legibility of the text. These include the line length (measure), the size of type, the weight of type, the amount of leading, and the size of the x-height.

12 pt

There are many factors to consider when thinking about readability and legibility of the text. These include the line length (measure), the size of type, the weight of type, the amount of leading, and the size of the x-height.

16 pt

⬆ **The optimum measure** of characters to a line is somewhere between 60 and 72 pt, although these parameters would be looser with smaller amounts of text. When lines are too long the eye loses its place; too short, and you become distracted by the constant returning to the start of a new line. The text throughout this panel is set in Sabon.

⬇ **Apparent size** The upper sentence is set in Bembo; the lower in Times New Roman; and both are 12 pt in size. However, because of its greater x-height, the Times text looks larger.

The apparent size of a typeface varies according to the x-height.

The apparent size of a typeface varies according to the x-height.

⊋ Film speed
Descenders and ascenders have been extended with rules, conveying the sense of motion of film frames.

SECTION 2 | PRINCIPLES AND TECHNIQUES

MODULE 6 | Typography

UNIT 3 | # Typographic Rules and Ornaments

Typographic rules (printed lines) and ornaments have been inherited from the letterpress tradition of setting and arranging type matter. The reason they are still invaluable to the designer today is because they serve both functional and aesthetic roles.

The function of rules

In their functional capacity they assist in directing the reader's eye around the page, drawing attention to specific parts of the copy and breaking copy into sections. Generally speaking, vertical rules should be used to separate blocks of text only when other means of division are not possible or sufficient. The weight, or thickness, of the rules should match the tonal value of the text to which they relate. Horizontal rules work well for organizing information and helping readability. Examples can be found in tabular matter, such as timetables and contents pages, where they can be used between each entry and to help direct the eye from item to page number.

SEE ALSO: Styles of Layout *p102*

⬆ Varying weights of rules prioritize the importance of the different sections and also help to anchor the floating copy.

⊋ Design squared
The use of rules helps construct a modular design, composed of differently sized and colored squares.

Highlighting text

Rules have gained in popularity since the introduction of computer typesetting, in which a single command can underline a word or words. Many designers regret this, arguing that there are better means available if you want to emphasize things (see pages 88–91). Nevertheless, rules can be effectively used to highlight a piece of copy by placing the rule in the margin alongside the text. The widths available range from a ½-point (hairline) rule upward. Tint panels are effectively thick rules that can be used as boxes in which nuggets of information can be printed. One can either reverse out the type, or have the rule in a tint and print the type on top. Also known as "sidebars," they are

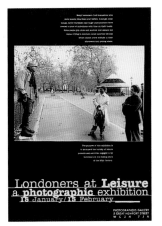

Underlining the display type unifies the different weights and emphasizes the copy.

⬇ **White stripes** The white tint panels both lead the eye to the important copy and harmonize nicely with the style of illustration.

⬆ **Sound rules** The graduating tints of the rules in this exhibition notice have a musical feel.

⬇ **Colored rules** in this timetable help to move the eye across the information.

➡ **Hairline rules** keep the items on this contents page visually differentiated.

---

particularly popular in newspapers for their ability to provide an in-depth focus on a particular editorial theme, while also relieving the eye from column after column of main text type.

Rules in display type

In display setting, rules can create drama by acting as attention seekers. The Constructivist art movement in early 20th-century Russia pioneered the use of rules in this way. They used very heavy rules running alongside, or at angles to, the copy. The popularity of the rule is still evident in today's designs in both functional and visual aspects. When a layout has too few elements and the overall look appears rather bland, rules can help in giving the layout structure, dynamism, and strength. They are a good fallback in such situations.

Ornaments

Ornaments, also known as flowers, have been in use since the origin of printing, and their primary purpose is to embellish the page. Their popularity lives on for the decorative feel they can bring to a layout. Zapf Dingbats is a well-known digital font made up of ornaments—the wide variety of different icons can be used creatively with type.

⬆ **Dual function** The hairline rules draw attention to the date and at the same time separate the books into their respective years.

UNIT 4 | **Emphasis and Hierarchy**

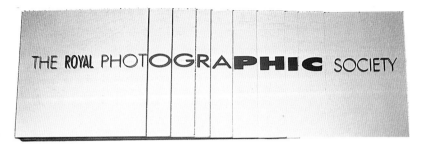

The tools of the graphic design trade need to be learned like any other in order to be able to express ideas typographically. Learning how to solve problems of emphasis using type is one such skill.

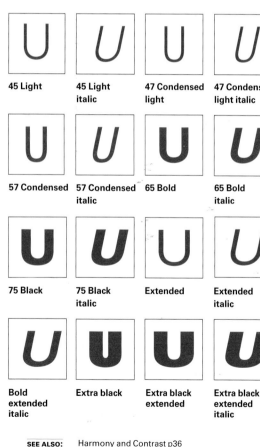

45 Light

45 Light italic

47 Condensed light

47 Condensed light italic

55 Regular

55 Regular italic

57 Condensed

57 Condensed italic

65 Bold

65 Bold italic

67 Condensed bold

67 Condensed bold italic

75 Black

75 Black italic

Extended

Extended italic

Ultra condensed

Bold extended

Bold extended italic

Extra black

Extra black extended

Extra black extended italic

SEE ALSO: Harmony and Contrast p36

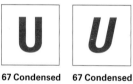

⬆ **Weight and form** are adjusted in intriguing ways in this leaflet.

🔁 **Univers** is one of the typefaces with many variants— extremely useful when many differing levels of information need to be designed.

So that form is matched by content, it is of course crucial to discuss with a client where the main points of emphasis fall in terms of headings, subheadings, intro material, captions, pull-out quotes, and so on. These different categories of importance are known as hierarchies. Once established with the client, hierarchies can be indicated in various ways. Start by having all the text copy in just one size of type, which will typically range between 9pt and 11 pt. It is from this relatively uniform typographical foundation that the display copy needs to distinguish itself.

Space, weight, and form
Emphasis can first be created by adding vertical space, in the form of a one-line space or half-line space, above or below a heading. (For a one-line space, this would mean adding an extra return or, in the other case, halving the leading. In other words, if you are using 14 pt leading, the half-line space would be an extra 7 pts making a 21 pt line feed.) It is not essential to employ extra spacing around headings if you increase the weight—that is, use bold type. The density of the black ink creates its own visual anchor. A sans serif is good for this because they typically have various weight combinations you can use: light with bold, medium with extra bold, and so on. Bear in mind that a smaller size of bold type is "heavier" than a larger size of regular-weight type. The third method is to change the form—switching from Roman to italic, for example. Italics add informality and movement to a design and are also effective for highlighting key phrases within Roman copy. Because of their more delicate form, you will probably need to increase the size proportionally in italic headings. Another shift of form is from lower-case to capitals. Although they add a degree of formality to a design, capitals need more

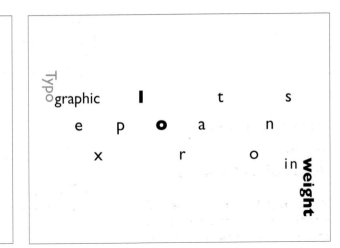

Weight and space Two variants on an exercise exploring emphasis.

Slab to sans Change of color, size, and form—from slab serif to sans—gives this design vigor and strength. Slab serif faces are heavy and mechanical-looking with unbracketed serifs; they were popular in the 19th century, the 1930s, and 1950s.

letter spacing, and thus consume more space, though you don't have the problem of ascenders clashing with descenders. Small capitals provide an even more subtle shift of emphasis.

The power of contrast: other techniques

Contrasting condensed with extended type—and thus vertical and horizontal—can work in experienced hands, but you have to be very careful not to overdo the visual shift of emphasis. Remember, too, that condensed type generally requires more leading, and expanded type pushes out the length of the copy. Contrast of direction is another method, for example having main text and the points of emphasis at varying angles.

A simple yet effective form of emphasis is to use indents, as in this book. One can indent main copy under a heading—known as a hanging indent—or indent the heading above the main text. Color is another technique you can employ. Be careful that there is sufficient contrast between the color and the stock on which you are printing. Bear in mind that there can be problems if you use fine colored type made up from the

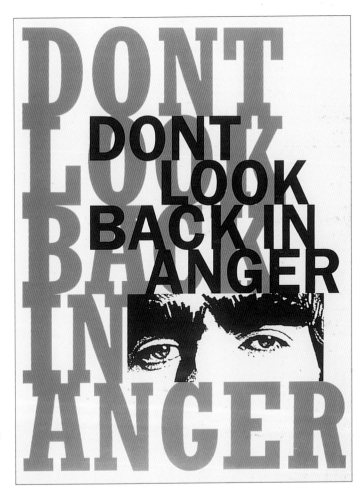

four-color set. Because the color is constructed from four separations, or layers of film, sometimes they fail to register (see pages 126–9). When adding color to type it is always worth considering using a typeface with more weight, which offers a bigger surface onto which the color can print. By making slight adjustments to the spacing you can use panels of color or black and reverse out the type, or indeed you can use rules as a way of attracting the eye.

Changing the size is perhaps the most common option. Again, be careful when using shifts of size for emphasis to ensure that there is a substantial difference between the main text and the heading. If the sizes are too close the layout can look rather awkward.

Less is more

As a precautionary note, try not to have too many means of emphasis going on at once. The old adage of "less is more" applies here. These days it is technologically easy to change things and you need to be disciplined to avoid creating a mishmash of weights, sizes, forms, and indents. Resist the temptation to set off all your fireworks at once, and remember, you do not always have to shout to be heard.

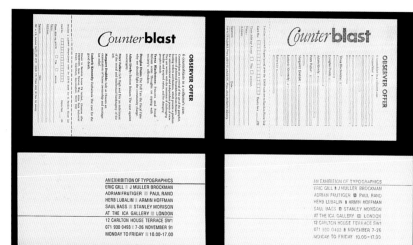

⬆ **Counterblast** Serif italic contrasted with a bold sans works typographically for such a title.

⬆ **Active but quiet** This peaceful-looking design actually incorporates changes of size, form, weight, and the use of indentation.

⬅ **The large light sans serif** in two colors creates a dynamic notice.

An **extended sans** at two different weights makes for a lively change of emphasis.

⬆ ➡ **Changes in weight** and size; weight and space; and direction show how quickly you can change the point of emphasis.

EXERCISE

Design an invitation card
Use the text below in an A5 landscape or portrait format. Choose only one size of typeface and try at least three individual techniques from above, selecting the main points of emphasis. Then repeat using only contrasts in size.

You are invited to a private view of the work of **graphic design students** *in their final year at*
[insert your own college] College of Art
on 5th October at the main college campus
St John Street, [your city or town], at 8pm
RSVP
Secretary Design School
[your own college] College of Art
[address as above]

Changing
the weight or

size of type
changes the emphasis

CHANGING THE WEIGHT OR
size of **type**
**changes
the
emphasis**

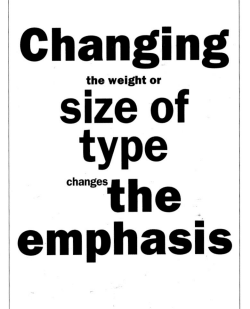

SUSHI

The glorious presentation of Japanese cuisine. Experience the taste, texture, aroma and aesthetic presentation of the impeccably freshest and best of the market place. You are cordially invited by Susan, Bruce, Bruce and Jim to an evening of adventure on Saturday, December 1, 1984, 7pm, 115 N 1st St. in Minneapolis, 3rd floor loft. Guests may bring beers and dry white wines to heighten the delightful sensations.

HONG KONG TRADE FAIR

⬅ ⬆ Illustrative text The words in these two designs were carefully considered for their illustrative opportunities. Simple graphic forms were then used, adding meaning and flair to both logos.

➡ Recognize this? Everyday objects have been manipulated here to represent the number 8.

SECTION 2	PRINCIPLES AND TECHNIQUES
MODULE 6	Typography
UNIT 5	**Illustrative Typography**

The designer has many options for communicating concepts effectively. The conventional approach is to neatly arrange type and photography on the page. This method often meets the needs of the job in hand, but sometimes a more dynamic approach is required.

SEE ALSO: Visualizing Ideas *p56*
Corporate Design *p158*

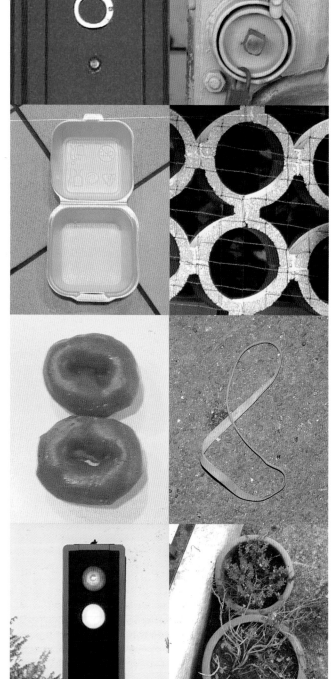

➡ **Make it plain** Many words offer obvious opportunities to illustrate their meaning.

⬆ **Fluid feel** The blurred treatment of the article's main head mimics the soft overlapping forms of the dancing figures.

blur
spin
zoom
outline

⬆ **On the baseline** Helvetica is used in this witty depiction of a sporting legend's name.

One of the fascinating elements about graphic design is that you are dealing with letter forms. The Western alphabet comprises 26 letters in both a capital and lower-case form. These letters have structures with individual shapes and forms that people grow up with and become accustomed to. Though seeing them is an everyday experience, they are so rooted in our sense of cultural, social, and historical identity that we tend to treat them with some reverence. Designers can exploit this aspect by carefully manipulating suggestive letter forms so that they become images in their own right. This means that type can actually stand in for objects: two capital "O"s can look like a pair of spectacles or the wheels of a car, a lower-case "j" resembles a hook, and an upper-case "Z" can look like a flash of lightning. Conversely, images can metamorphose into type: a pair of compasses can form a capital "A," and tumbling acrobats easily lend themselves to the letter "D."

Form matching content

The techniques for using type as illustration are numerous and go beyond trying to use type to represent simple objects and vice versa. Certain words, such as verbs indicating action, particularly lend themselves to an approach in which the typography can reflect the meaning of a word (imagine "zoom" with six "o"s instead of four; or "jump" where the "m" is lifted off the baseline). In a powerful program like Illustrator, type can be tweaked to convey myriad meanings: there can be a repetition of a word or words; overlapping of characters; distorting characters to break them up, blur, or roughen them; outlining or shadowing type; setting type along a curved path or in a circle; adjusting color, weight, or form—the possibilities are almost endless. In order to be effective, however, the positions and forms into which the type is arranged must pick up on the meaning of the copy. And do try to avoid clichés.

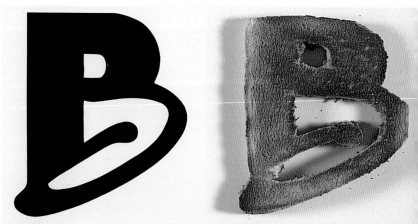

Patriotic type The typesetting is arranged to resemble the shape of the Swiss flag, an obvious yet effective idea.

Logo as toast Type becomes image in this humorous logo for a bakery.

Fun as a sales tool

People are undoubtedly attracted by playful typography, and advertisers are well aware that fun elements in a design can inspire empathy in their target audience. Of course, as has already been said, the ideas must spring from the content, otherwise the design can be criticized as being nothing more than an empty exercise in style. This practice of using type as image is not always popular with clients. They often want to use ordinary images to make the point. As a compromise, you can always consider combining image with illustrative typography in such a way that the message is doubly reinforced.

Logotypes

The design of logotypes is one area in which you can experiment with a conventional typeface. A logotype is really a signature for the organization or company, and just by altering a conventional typeface slightly you can supply that touch of individuality that makes a brand distinctive. The crucial thing is to work with your letterforms in an integrated way. You could test out your ideas within three basic shapes: a circle, square, or triangle. These

Type as network The arrangement cleverly echoes the London Underground map.

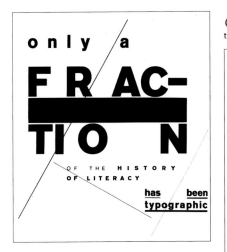

only a FRAC-TIO N

OF THE HISTORY
OF LITERACY

has been
typographic

gaudí 2002

Any Internacional Gaudí

Barcelona

Todo un año para
descubir Gaudí

A whole year
to discover Gaudí

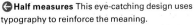
◀ **Half measures** This eye-catching design uses typography to reinforce the meaning.

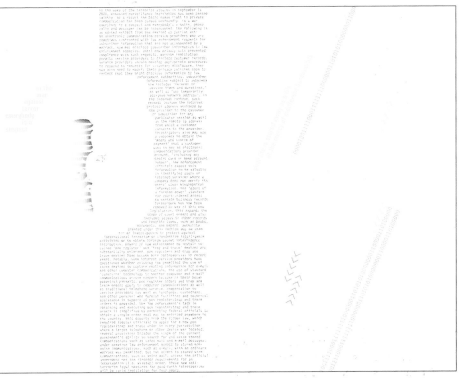

▲ **Excellent integration** of text and image creates a dynamic poster.

◀ **Angled type** The use of the letter "g" to form a double zero is an appropriately innovative touch for the iconoclastic Spanish architect, Gaudí.

days it is relatively easy to try out many ideas on the computer once you have had the initial concept—for example, you can make a positive image negative very quickly, which can add great dynamism.

TV graphics

Television is another sphere in which type is extensively modified and distorted. In that medium the possibility of movement adds a whole new dimension to graphics, and typographical effects are often blended with animation to produce exciting "living" compositions.

▲ **"Dancing" type** cleverly shadows the movement of the figures in this review of a dance festival.

UNIT 6 | **Shaped Text**

Typographic illustration or shaping text is essentially light-hearted and fun. It turns straight typography into graphic configurations with a degree of legibility, informing and entertaining the reader in an emotive way, as well as relieving the formality of conventional text.

Experiment with both symmetrical and asymmetrical text settings in order to portray a variety of different meanings. Although you will be primarily concerned with legibility, you can, through careful selection of justified, centered, ranged-left, or ranged-right setting styles, hint at the mood and echo the content of the text. You can set text into regular shapes such as squares, triangles, diamonds, and circles, or format more irregular shapes. The text need not cover the entire surface, for words, letters, or numerals can be used in a linear fashion—bending and curving to describe the contours of a particular form. Text can be shaped or wrapped around images; it can define spaces or provide silhouettes; and form an image itself. Controlled changes of typeface weight within the main text area will create subtle secondary typographic shapes or images. For a more daring approach, shape the text into representational objects associated with the meaning of the words—thereby pulling together text, design, and image into a direct and decorative expression of content. This eye-catching technique requires an inventive touch, and a sense of humor.

To be used effectively, our Latin alphabet, composed basically of straight lines, circles, and part circles, has to be resourcefully manipulated. Calligraphic scripts such as Arabic, which are flowing and organic, lend themselves much more readily to such graphic decorative techniques.

SEE ALSO: Computer Illustration *p70*
Illustrative Typography *p92*

⬆ **Christmas tree** Three typographic interpretations of Christmas tree shapes, ranging from the random to the carefully controlled. Each shaped text captures the festive spirit in its individual way.

⬆ **"T"** In this design by Total Design, the architectural character and size of the "T" is underlined in the configuration of the main body of text. A dynamic contrast in the curving line of text adds movement and depth.

⬆ **Hand-drawn letters** This charming anonymous design demonstrates the flexibility of hand-drawn letters when used for shaped text.

⊙ Convincing typographic portraits can be generated by digitized phototypesetting systems. Facial features can be effectively described by making subtle changes in weight, style, and size.

⊙ Seasonal moods Diana Wilson captures the moods of spring, summer, fall, and winter in window-like areas of drawn text through color, rhythm, and texture.

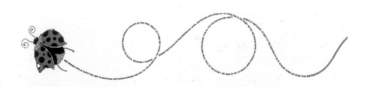

⊙ A single line of text traces the flight path of a ladybug in a decoratively informative way. Single lines can be designed into shapes equally as well as areas of text, depending on the degree of legibility required.

⊙ This shaped text printed on tracing paper forms part of a design by Total Design and typographically mirrors the photographic image to which it relates.

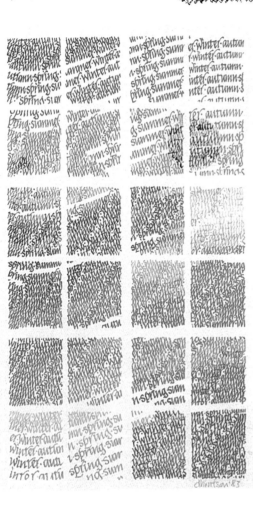

The decorative nature of shaped text transforms reading into a visual experience. Advertising uses this technique to give slogans or short pieces of text an embellished form with the visual impact to convey a message. Logotype designs also make use of this device. Text might be composed into the shapes of shoes, wine glasses, bottles, heads, complete bodies, animals, birds, fish, trees, or whole townscapes. Usually, the particular form in which text is shaped stems from the content.

Written portraits created through the texture and tone of words—where virtual photographic likenesses of the subject, human, or animal, can be achieved through an inordinate amount of dexterity and skill— are feats of decorative typography. Digitized portraits or pictures, however, can be far less arduously originated on a computer that allows you to experiment freely with typographic shading by changing the weight of the relevant parts of the text. Typographic illustrations generated on a computer tend to have a curious, tapestry-like decorative quality to them, whereas handwritten ones retain the individuality of the designer's lettering with its more subtle texture.

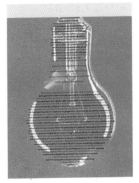

⊙ The dense texture of printed letters in this typographic illustration by Armando Testa visually parallels the feather pattern of the chicken.

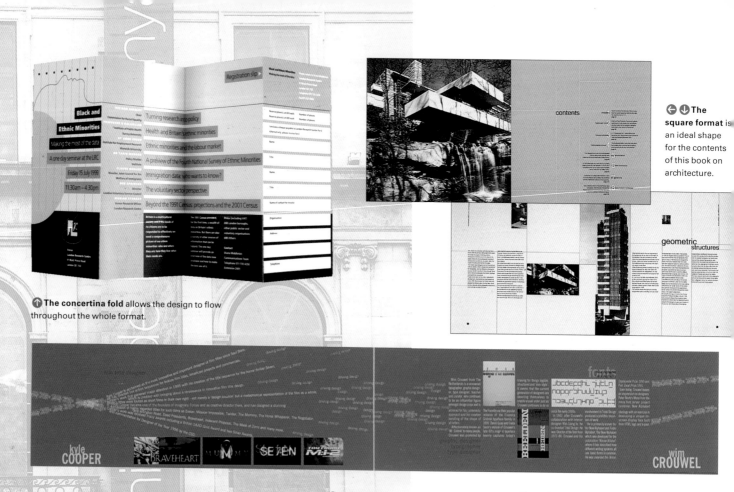

The concertina fold allows the design to flow throughout the whole format.

⬆ The square format is an ideal shape for the contents of this book on architecture.

geometric structures

kyle COOPER

wim CROUWEL

⬆ The long landscape format gives the right shape to show off the flow of this virtuoso typography.

SECTION 2 | PRINCIPLES AND TECHNIQUES

MODULE 7 | Layout

UNIT 1 | **Size and Format**

Earlier in the book it was stated that good design is a result of collaboration between all the interested parties in the project, from editorial, sales, and marketing through to production and design. One of the big decisions that those involved in preparing the project's specifications need to make relates to format and size.

SEE ALSO: Basic Principles of Layout p16
Styles of Layout p102

Cost issues

Part of the appeal of a design consists in how the product actually feels in the hand. Often the designer is limited to what the format can be by external factors. Certain items such as reports, stationery, and official forms are typically required to be in a standard size. Sometimes, however, other factors have to be considered. Cost issues normally loom large: Will the size you select be cut economically from a bigger sheet? Will the finished work have to be mailed out? If so, a larger format will prove more expensive to send out by post. Can you fold your job economically with the grain of paper?

Content determines format

In book publishing, the format should be determined by the book's purpose or nature. Text-only books pose fewer fundamental problems than illustrated books. For continuous reading, a good type

⬆ **Rollover** This square-format brochure reveals the whole title when folded out. This is a cost-effective shape, as the standard-size sheet is exactly three times the size of the finished version.

measure with adequate margins will normally determine the (portrait, or upright) format, and in the case of paperbacks, which need to be both cheap and portable, the size is typically small. In illustrated books, the images need to be of a reasonable size, and so a larger format is required. The danger may be that the book becomes unwieldy. Illustrations do not necessarily lose their information value if they are smaller than first anticipated, and there are benefits in making a product easier for the reader to handle. The biggest sizes are generally reserved for fine art books and museum catalogues, in which good-quality illustrations are central to the book's success.

Where possible, content should determine the format. Illustrated books about trains, rivers, and panoramic views would, because of the shape of their subjects, lend themselves to a landscape (or sideways) format; whereas those about skyscrapers, totem poles, and giraffes would be better suited to a portrait shape. Multilingual publications pose their own set of problems. It is probably best to try and accommodate two or three languages side by side to achieve a consistent flow of text and, if illustrated, to ensure that text references are on the same page as pictures. A landscape format will probably be the best answer.

Although the fact that paper sizes are standardized internationally helps to keep prices down, the same old formats can become a little boring. There are several ways to overcome this problem. By folding the sheet differently, you can effect a simple format change. For example, fold the sheet on the short side and you have an elegant long format. Another idea is to trim off areas from the standard size giving you an unfamiliar shape with no extra cost.

⬆ **Sideways** This clever format idea ensures that the text doesn't predominate over the mountain images behind the building windows.

Folds and binding

With leaflets and brochures folds can play a big part in enticing the reader into the subject matter. The aesthetically pleasing square format is simply achieved by folding the sheet in a different way. Organizing your copy to follow the folds—be it a roll fold, where the folds go into each other, or a concertina fold, where the folds go in alternate directions—creates a sense of fun and is an excellent way of enticing the reader into the publication.

Simple binding ideas also enhance the appeal, such as trimming each spread a little shorter than the preceding one, giving an area at the end of the page to use as an information tag. Leaving the fore edge untrimmed makes for an attractively hand-crafted feel, as does using colored thread for the stitching. These are some ideas that you can easily implement in your designs. They don't necessarily have to cost a lot but can make your designs visually different and memorable.

⬆ **Gatefold** This brochure has been cleverly planned so that a double-page opener invites the reader into the leaflet where the whole of the copy can be viewed in four columns.

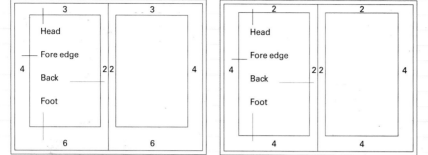

Diagrams showing simple proportions of type area to format. Far left, the head and back margins are half the amount; left, a deeper text area results in a smaller foot but it is still proportionately bigger than the head.

The three grids below range in complexity: one single horizontal measure (left); three equal columns for more complex text (center); and a vertical and horizontal grid broken into 16 units (right).

SECTION 2	PRINCIPLES AND TECHNIQUES
MODULE 7	Layout
UNIT 2	**Grids and Margins**

Once the format has been agreed the next step is to work out the type area and margins. Margins are the space surrounding the type area on the page. Guidelines have been established over time and these are discussed well in Jost Hochuli and Robin Kinross's book, *Designing Books, Practice and Theory*.

Margin proportions

If you are working on a book or other publication, you should first construct a double-page spread. This is important, for you need to see how the verso (left-hand page) relates to the recto (right-hand page) and judge how well they balance. Established practice suggests that the back (inner margin) should be roughly half the fore edge (outside margin), and the foot (bottom margin) greater than the head (top margin). These rules should ensure a balanced look to the spread with the type area sitting comfortably in the format. Remember that the eye will need to move from one page to the other, and so the gap, or gutter (the two back edges combined), should not be too large.

When establishing the margins, bear in mind the type of material with which you are dealing. For example, paperback books tend to have tight margins to keep the number of pages (and therefore costs) down, whereas illustrated books have more generous margins. Economic considerations play a part: sales brochures and promotional items tend to have bigger budgets, so more white space is possible.

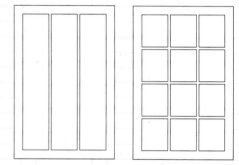

The grid: underlying order

The layout of columns, margins, and area for text and images is usually marked out as a grid—the means by which structure and order can be introduced to a design solution.

The grid divides up the available type area into a number of proportioned subdivisions (units), providing a visual structure on which the design can be based. The grid helps to unite all elements of design. The most basic grid structure—used primarily for text-based material, such as reports or novels—is that of a single measure. The actual measure chosen should be related to overall legibility (see page 84). With complex material, in which text, images, diagrams, and captions have to be integrated, a more sophisticated horizontal grid will be needed. Grids comprising three, four, five, and six columns will allow you to use all kinds of material. The more units in your grid the more flexibility you will have to accommodate both smaller pieces of copy, such as captions; longer measures, such as section openers; and boxed material. Do not simply follow your computer's default settings for columns, but decide your own, which ought to be in whole numbers for every unit.

Drop at the top Here the horizontal grid incorporates a large drop at the top, allowing plenty of space for the heading.

Up and down A good example of a horizontal and vertical grid at work: the top third is reserved solely for imagery, leaving the bottom two thirds open for a mixture of text and pictures.

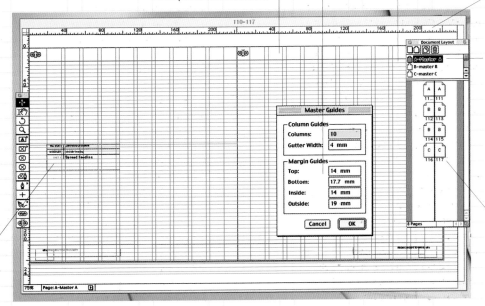

Picture variables The greater number of horizontal units there are in a grid, the more flexibly sized the pictures can be.

Proportion Although the text is set to only one measure, the grid shows how images can be varied in their size and shape yet remain in proportion with one another.

Ideally, a grid should have vertical controls, allowing for structure down the page and giving order to the material. Give headings, subheadings, captions, and page numbers set positions that give the overall job continuity. Finally, you need to be flexible. After you have designed two or three spreads the grid may seem too rigid for the compositions you desire, so simply adjust the grid to suit your requirements. Grids are not restrictive. Just look at all the possible shapes and sizes and the variety of measures you can adopt. The grid is less likely to be at fault than the way you are using it.

This is one of the master page grids used for this book. It has been divided into 10 columns, with 4 mm column spaces. The main text here will be set across 4 columns, although you could be working with just 2 or 3 columns. The captions are set across 2.

You can set up the margins around the text areas.

The baseline grid and leading for the main text. By using "lock to baseline" in the view menu you guarantee the text is in the correct position.

Further positional guides can be pulled down from the measurement bar.

You can set up more than one master page if you have different grids. Double-click on Master A; go to Page on the menu headings; then scroll down to Master Guides.

Working to a grid is essential if you are working on repetitive pages of pamphlets, brochures catalogues, magazines, and books. It is far easier to organize the layout, leaving you to focus on the more creative aspects. You can break the grid if you wish, but working to the same measures and positions will give your work an overall unity and style. Practice will make them easy to set up and you can make alterations throughout the design process.

You can place text that repeats throughout the document onto the masterpage. The designer added this, even though the words in the heading block change and it appears in different positions.

The program's page numbering system automatically changes if the pages move around.

THE NEW
DESIGNER'S
HAND**BOOK**

Alistair
Campbell

SIGNS
AND
SYMBOLS

Their Design and Meaning

ADRIAN FRUTIGER

Arts Council

ART IN
REVO
LUTION

Soviet Art and Design since 1917

◀◀◀**Bold book**
This simple asymmetric composition works very well, with its clear alignment of copy emphasizing the word "book."

◀◀**On balance** A centered arrangement, using capitals for the main title.

◀**Constructivist feel** Interesting word breaks give this asymmetric layout a good dynamic.

UNIT 3 **Styles of Layout**

Layouts can be divided into two basic styles, namely symmetrical and asymmetrical. In broad terms, the symmetrical style is associated with a traditional approach in which the design is structured around a central axis. This type of layout has its origins in early printed books, which, in turn, borrowed their style from the hand-written manuscripts of the medieval era. Designers today use this look to engender a feeling of tradition, elegance, or dignity.

The symmetrical tradition
Such work is most commonly seen on the title pages of books, each line of type being centered on the others. Part of the same tradition, so to speak, is the use of serif typefaces, often set in letter-spaced capitals, with, perhaps, the addition of an ornament or printer's flower. The reason this is considered traditional is because, until the 1920s, most publications were

➡**Follow the layout**
These enterprising exhibition panels use ranged-left setting for entry on the left and vice versa.

SEE ALSO: Basical Principles of Layout *p16*
Grids and Margins *p100*

symmetry

Lorem ipsum dolor sit amet, consectetuer adipiscing elit, sed diam nonummy nibh euismod tincidunt ut laoreet dolore magna aliquam erat volutpat. Ut wisi enim ad minim veniam, quis nostrud exerci tation ullamcorper suscipit lobortis nisl ut aliquip ex ea commodo consequat.

Duis autem vel eum iriure dolor in hendrerit in vulputate velit esse molestie consequat, vel illum dolore eu feugiat nulla facilisis at vero eros et accumsan et iusto odio dignissim qui blandit praesent luptatum zzril delenit augue duis dolore te feugait nulla facilisi. Lorem ipsum dolor sit amet, consectetuer adipiscing elit, sed diam nonummy nibh euismod tincidunt ut laoreet dolore magna aliquam erat volutpat.

symmetry

Lorem ipsum dolor sit amet, consectetuer adipiscing elit, sed diam nonummy nibh euismod tincidunt ut laoreet dolore magna aliquam erat volutpat. Ut wisi enim ad minim veniam, quis nostrud exerci tation ullamcorper suscipit lobortis nisl ut aliquip ex ea commodo consequat.

Duis autem vel eum iriure dolor in hendrerit in vulputate velit esse molestie consequat, vel illum dolore eu feugiat nulla facilisis at vero eros et accumsan et iusto odio dignissim qui blandit praesent luptatum zzril delenit augue duis dolore te feugait nulla facilisi. Lorem ipsum dolor sit amet, consectetuer adipiscing elit, sed diam nonummy nibh euismod tincidunt ut laoreet dolore magna aliquam erat volutpat.

Lorem ipsum dolor sit amet, consectetuer adipiscing elit, sed diam nonummy nibh euismod tincidunt ut laoreet dolore magna aliquam erat volutpat. Ut wisi enim ad minim veniam, quis nostrud exerci tation ullamcorper suscipit lobortis nisl ut aliquip ex ea commodo consequat.

Duis autem vel eum iriure dolor in hendrerit in vulputate velit esse molestie consequat, vel illum dolore eu feugiat nulla facilisis at vero eros et accumsan et iusto odio dignissim qui blandit praesent luptatum zzril delenit augue duis dolore te feugait nulla facilisi. Lorem ipsum dolor sit amet, consectetuer adipiscing elit, sed diam nonummy nibh euismod tincidunt ut laoreet dolore magna aliquam erat volutpat.

symmetry

Lorem ipsum dolor sit amet, consectetuer adipiscing elit, sed diam nonummy nibh euismod tincidunt ut laoreet dolore magna aliquam erat volutpat. Ut wisi enim ad minim veniam, quis nostrud exercition ullam corper suscipit lobortis nisl ut aliquip ex ea commodo consequat.

Duis aute vel eum iriure dolor in hendre rit in vulputate velit esse molestie consequat, vel illum dolore eu feugiat nulla facilisis at vero eros et accumsan et iusto odio dignissim qui blandit praesent luptatum zzril delenit.

asymmetry

Lorem ipsum dolor sit amet, consectetuer ad ipiscing elit, sed diam nonummy nibh euism tincidunt ut laoreet dolore magna aliquam erat volutpat. Ut wisi enim a minim veniam, quis nostrud exercition ullam corper suscipit lobortis nisl ut aliquip exea com consequat. Duis autem vel eum iriure dolor in hendre rit in vulputate velit es molestie consequat, vel illum dolore eu feugiat nulla facilisis at vero eros et accumsan et iusto odio dignissim qui blandit praesent luptatum zzril delenit

asymmetry

Lorem ipsum dolor sit amet, consectetuer adipiscing elit, sed diam nonummy nibh euismod tincidunt ut laoreet dolore magna aliquam erat volutpat. Ut wisi enim ad minim veniam, quis nostrud exerci tation ullamcorper suscipit lobortis nisl ut aliquip exea commodo consequat. Duis autem vel eum iriure dolor in hendrerit in vulputate velit esse molestie consequat, vel illum dolore eu feugiat nulla facilisis at vero eros et accumsan et iusto odio dignissim qui blandit praesent luptatum zzril delenit augue du dolore feugait nulla facilisi. Lorem ipsum dolor amet, consec

asymmetry

Lorem ipsum dolor sit amet, consectetuer adipiscing elit, sed diam nonummy nibh euismod tincidunt ut laoreet dolore magna aliquam erat volutpat. Ut wisi enim ad minim veniam, quis nostrud exerci tation ullamcorper suscipit lobortis nisl ut aliquip ex ea commodo consequat. Duis autem vel eum iriure dolor in hendrerit in vulputate velit esse molestie consequat, vel illum dolore eu feugiat nulla facilisis at vero eros et accumsan et iusto odio dignissim qui blandit

both styles

◀ **Symmetrical layouts** carry associations of tradition, order, and rationality.

◀ **Asymmetrical layouts** were pioneered in the 1930s by designers of the Bauhaus School and developed in conjunction with sans serif type. These days both styles— symmetry and asymmetry— are often integrated within one layout.

designed this way. Actually achieving a genuinely balanced-looking composition is no mean feat. Lines need to be of varying length so that they look balanced with each other and information has to be grouped so that most of the width of the measure is used.

The asymmetrical revolution

Asymmetrical layouts emanated from the modern movement in the 1920s and 1930s, and in particular from the German Bauhaus school. Artists such as Kurt Schwitters and Theo van Doesburg rejected the symmetrical style and experimented with layouts based on an off-centered axis, which they saw as creating more tension and dynamism. In this style the typesetting is primarily ranged left, although one sometimes sees ranged-right setting: this is best kept to a few lines, because reading from left to right is so ingrained in us Westerners. The modern movement also rejected ornament and serif typefaces, in particular. The work of the Bauhaus and their stylistic descendants,

such as the Swiss typographers of the 1960s, is always in sans serif faces, and often completely lower case. Rules in a number of weights were another distinctive feature, often in two colors, such as red and black. This gives the designs a very strong—some would say harsh or authoritarian—look. Apart from those already mentioned, designers whose work is predominantly in the asymmetric style and who are worth investigating are Armin Hofmann, Wim Crouwel, and Josef Muller-Brockmann. Another interesting case, whose work over a long career shows both styles really well, is Jan Tschichold. Early in his career he was much influenced by the modernist philosophy propounded by the Bauhaus. Later in his career he changed direction, rejecting the hard-line approach he advocated in his book *Asymmetric Typography*. He likened his youthful standpoint to the rigidity and authoritarianism of Hitler's Nazi Party and came to accept that the symmetrical approach has its place, too.

Integrating both styles

Today designers often integrate both styles in their layouts. The division between them is somewhat arbitrary, and contemporary typographers such as April Greiman and Philippe Apeloig use both in their search for visual solutions. As a student, it is necessary to understand both styles and their historical contexts so that your judgments are based on sound knowledge rather than guesswork. I think the best advice is to follow the philosophy of Jan Tschichold and use both styles in your work. Apart from anything else, keeping your options open will give you much more flexibility in reaching solutions to your graphic design problems.

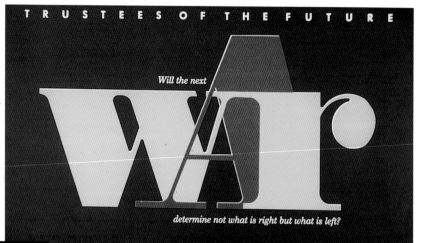

⬆ **Hybrid** This poster shows a mix of styles, a centered arrangement for the main copy with the subsidiary copy laid out off-center.

⬅ **The asymmetrical letterhead** is balanced by the letter itself, which is naturally ranged left.

⬆ **Mirror image** The typesetting is centered, reflecting the symmetrical image on the facing page.

The cafe theatre
company presents
intimacy
adapted form
a story by
jean paul sartre
directed by
michael almaz
together with
lulu-maslen george
riette-vicky carpenter
the cafe theatre
ecology centre
shelton street
london wc2
telephone
0171 240 5982
tuesday to
saturday
8:30 pm
matinee sunday
5:30 pm tuesday £3
then £5 and £4

⬆**Leaning line** The four letters sit comfortably in this central position, but the dynamic diagonal white stripe—itself a witty reference to Pisa's Leaning Tower—relieves the tedium.

➡**Signature style** In this very dynamic off-centered layout the information is aligned at the extreme top edge.

SECTION 2 | PRINCIPLES AND TECHNIQUES

MODULE 7 | Layout

UNIT 4 | **Pace and Contrast**

Pace and contrast are essential qualities for maintaining the reader's interest. This is true of many categories of design, but particularly in magazines and illustrated books when it is essential to be able to direct the eye to different elements of information. In a middle-distance athletics race runners often alternate between fast and slow, and end with a sprint finish. This is a useful metaphor for pace in design.

⬅ **Angle of attack**
A combination of unusually cropped images and angled type creates a quick pace in this spread.

⬆ **A quiet feeling** is engendered on this spread by use of white space and an uncomplicated serif type.

In continuous text, the reader takes more time to cover information, whereas in a highly integrated design— with panels, pictures, captions, quotes, and so on— there is much more variety: an article may be skim-read; some pages will be scanned for exciting pictures; in another section, the reader might be seeking a specific piece of information. The pace will be dictated by the content and space available. Contrast is closely linked: when you want to inject pace into a design you can create drama in the form of large type and imagery, or interesting cropping. Alternatively, you can create a lull by having text-only spreads or employing white space liberally.

➡ **A functional, restrained spread** with the chapter title given a whole page. The subtle use of rules, however, avoids blandness.

SEE ALSO: Basic Principles of Layout *p16*
Color Contrast and Harmony *p36*

◀ **The element of surprise** is often used to good effect in magazine design; having type running at an unexpected angle can achieve this.

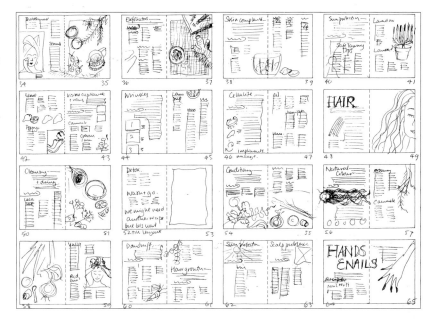

▲ **Thumbnails** fulfill two key functions: first they show how text and images work in combination, and that the designer's math works; and second, they show where the visual "splashes"—main headings, full-page images, and so on—occur.

Thumbnails

In order to achieve a good pace, with contrast built in, an overall plan is needed. Too many visual fireworks are counterproductive, but a succession of similar-looking pages stifle interest. An invaluable technique is to construct a flatplan, which shows the total number of pages in the publication. The flatplan can be drawn quite small (thumbnail size is adequate) in double-page spreads. It should contain the page numbers, titles, and the content to be included. A quick survey of this plan will give you a broad overview of how your material is set to unfold.

A prior meeting with the editor/client should be the first step. The content is all-important. You should draw up a list of questions before the meeting to find out how much contrast and pace is needed. The editor/client should know what information they are trying to impart, and how dynamically it needs to be done. Text with a complicated argument may need a gentler pace with clean, clear typography, whereas strategic messages may require a bold, lively image for the point to get across effectively.

Creating momentum and rhythm

The start of an article or section can offer a powerful statement in the form of large headings, or the introductory paragraph can be set differently from the main text. You could, for example, use a large italic type set to a wide measure. Dropped initials are another attractive way of starting an article. Alternatively, well-written copy can provide humor or an enticement into the subsequent pages. All these elements build momentum and visual excitement, pulling the reader in. Another way of interpreting pace is to view the spreads as a unit comprising 100 percent. You can vary the percentages according to the pace you wish to engender. An even pace may have 50 percent text and 50 percent image, whereas a faster pace will have maybe 80 percent image, 20 percent text. These proportions can be adjusted according to the desired pace, the available space, and the content.

When laying out images and text, many variations are possible. You could use the pictures as a frieze—a narrow sequence of images running along the top of the spreads. You could have one very large picture and five subsidiaries, or you could cut the picture into nine pieces and reassemble the fragments. Another method would be to integrate same-sized pictures within the text. Depending on the picture's content, you can create vertical movement in the layout by having narrow vertical images. Conversely, with landscape pictures, you can create horizontal movement. Contrast can be achieved by having vertical and horizontal movement on the same spread, or on consecutive spreads.

En realidad, siempre he pensado que no
hay memoria colectiva, lo que quizá sea
una forma de defensa de la especie
humana. La frase todo tiempo pasado fue
mejor no indica que antes sucedieran

5

The HOUR RECORD

Aunque ni el diablo sabe que es lo que ha de recordarla
gente, ni por qué. En realidad, siempre he pensado que
no hay memoria colectiva, lo que quizá sea una forma de
defensa de la especie humana. La frase todo tiempo
pasado fue mejor no indica que antes sucedieran menos
cosas malas, sino que felizmente la gente las echa en el
olvido. Desde luego, semejante frase no tiene validez
universal, ya, por ejemplo, me caracterizo por recordar
preferentemente los hechos malos y, así, casi podría decir
que todo tiempo pasado fue peor, si no fuera porque el
presente me parece tan horrible como el pasado;
recuerdo tantas calamidades, tantos rostros cívicos y
crueles, tantas malas acciones, que la memoria es para
mí como la temerosa luz que alumbra un sórdido museo
de la vergüenza. ¿Cuántas veces he quedado aplastado
durante horas, en un rincón oscuro del taller, después de
leer una noticia en la sección policial? Pero la verdad es
que no siempre las más vergonzosa de la raza humana
aparece allí, hasta cierto punto, los criminales son gente
más limpia, más inofensiva; esta afirmación no la hago
porque yo mismo haya matado a un ser humano; es una
honesta y la sección policial! Pero la

Desde luego, semejante frase
no tiene validez universal, ya.

Large images crossing the gutter bring drama and often signal the start of a section.

Wheel good This clever crop, nicely balanced by the text, suggests the movement of the bicycle.

You can create pace by juxtaposing black-and-white images with color, or black and white with duotones. With text, varying type measures between narrow and wide will certainly add pace to your pages. Furthermore, you can surprise your reader by either throwing in a spread with a colored tint background, text reversed out, or tilting the grid, which will result in all the material being at a different angle. Indeed, any kind of formal variation will result in a change of pace.

Magazines versus books

Magazine design is one area where pace and contrast is fundamental. There is probably more variety in magazines than in any other category of design. Magazines range from high-brow political, economic, or philosophical journals to pornographic, teenage, sporting, arts, satirical, and leisure titles. They will all require different kinds of pace depending on their content and readership.

Magazine readers differ from book readers inasmuch as the way they view the product is unpredictable. Some will be led by the cover straplines to the contents page, where they will select their articles in an ordered way; others will dip in and out of any part of the magazine; while others will always read certain sections in a peculiarly personal order. This is why some kind of buzz has to be created on almost every page; one can't rely on a gradual build-up of rhythm, as though the title were being read cover to cover.

Illustrated books also require changes of pace, although normally less pizzazz is required. Generally, readers behave in a more logical way, moving through the publication from start to finish. Of course, they too will dive in but not to the extent of magazine readers. Economic factors will also play a part in this category. If plenty of pages are available then you can introduce section openers, and use plenty of white space to create drama with headings and so on. As a general guide, try to create a style that has a strong visual identity. If the spreads are too diverse this can have a hazardous effect on the book, sowing confusion and visual disunity. Try not to place all the text in one place together. Readers often find this off-putting after viewing lots of images. If the text has to be positioned in one area, then at least introduce subheads and, perhaps, quotations to give the reader visual relief.

The digital revolution

Magazines for the electronic age will be different. Type and images interact much more readily on the screen. Imagery is much easier to manipulate and adapt to a variety of purposes. Some of the principles discussed in relation to print-based work may not apply directly to screen-based designs. One obvious difference, for example, is that viewers, instead of turning pages, scroll up and down a screen, which poses a separate set of challenges. Again, instead of using weight, form, or rules to emphasize type, type can actually move or a headline can be flashed up. Sound and graphics will increasingly integrate more effectively. In short, a whole new aesthetic is developing hand in hand with digital technology. Ultimately, though, the main points that have been covered for print still apply in part to screen. How do you as a designer navigate the viewer through the maze of available information? Learning the basics of print design can be the stepping-stone for you to form ways of working in this new age of design.

● **Type as image** Type used to reinforce an image's meaning is a much-used technique to liven up the pace.

The black verso page makes the recto image leap out all the more powerfully

Continuation arrows serve as headings and running headlines

A witty approach that ensures that image and text reinforce the other's impact

The type actually appears to be TV graphics, an idea reinforced by the remote control in the foreground

Good graphic design is not simply a result of brilliant execution of technique. It is the strong expression of clever ideas. Research is often the key to successful projects.

Research

We live in a media-saturated world. We are constantly bombarded with images. As a designer you need to have a heightened awareness of what is going on around you. Looking at the work of other designers and artists will influence you. Make notes, keep sketchbooks. You never know when something you have seen will help you solve a design problem.

Customers and audiences

It is vital to remember that everything you design is going to be seen by other people. You are not working in a vacuum. It is part of your job to discover what your audience wants.

Think about the people who will be looking at your designs. What is your target market? Try and get inside their heads. Your designs need to communicate with real people—not just look good. The more you can find out about your audience and their habits, the better informed your work will be, enhancing the chances of its favorable reception.

Large companies have whole departments devoted to what is formally called market research. These people spend their entire time conducting surveys into their customers' needs and preferences. They do this by a variety of means, including questionnaires, telephone surveys, and focus groups (where people carefully selected as representative of the target audience are brought together to discuss a product or campaign before it is launched into the public domain).

If you don't have time for this, then you should at least ask yourself the following questions every time you start a project: Who is the design aimed at? What messages are they supposed to get from looking at it? How will you grab and retain their attention?

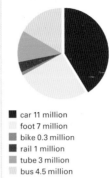

Number of journeys made into the city every day

- car 11 million
- foot 7 million
- bike 0.3 million
- rail 1 million
- tube 3 million
- bus 4.5 million

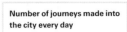 **Going underground** These pie charts summarize the findings of a survey of transport into a European metropolis. Without building up a picture of your target audience, and the factors that underlie their decisions, it is impossible to develop successful advertising solutions.

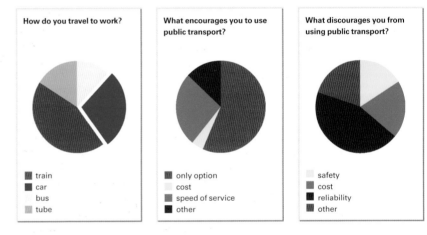

How do you travel to work?

- train
- car
- bus
- tube

What encourages you to use public transport?

- only option
- cost
- speed of service
- other

What discourages you from using public transport?

- safety
- cost
- reliability
- other

EXERCISE

Market research

Conduct your own market research into driving schools, imagining that you are going to design a promotional campaign for your local one.

Write up your findings into a report, as if you were presenting it to your local driving school as evidence to back up your ideas.

- Go to the library to look at market analysis reports/statistics
- Read newspaper/magazine articles
- Look at company websites
- Compile your own survey
- Speak to customers/users
- Try using the product/service yourself
- Speak to people who work for the companies

EXERCISE

Customer profiles

Think about customers for a new range of denim. Draw up three different customer profiles. Think about the personalities and lifestyles of the three individuals. Give them names. Where do they live? Occupation? Salary? How much do they spend on clothes? Likes/dislikes? Shopping habits?

Developing concepts

Market research leads directly into early conceptual thinking, because knowing who your audience is, their likes and dislikes, immediately narrows down the approaches that are appropriate. Previously we have equipped you with basic design rules and techniques that will allow you to express your ideas visually. But where do the ideas themselves come from? Coming up with clever new design solutions that no one has seen before is a bit of a daunting prospect. And yet it is something that most designers aspire to. How do you actually dream up innovative concepts in the first place? Don't panic! The first thing to bear in mind is that creativity is not magic. It is not an intangible quality but a skill that can be improved over time with practice. The starting point is often a piece of a paper, a pencil, and an open mind.

Brainstorming meets research

Many designers start by writing and drawing initial ideas about a project onto a single sheet of paper (use the biggest you can find).

Let's take an example project: branding for a new dance music TV channel. What words and images immediately spring into your mind from this single concept? Noise, sound and rhythm: how can you convey these visually? What kind of type could express the broken, disconnected beats? Think about the people who listen to dance music. What do they look like? What about the musicians? What is the role of the DJ? What other things do fans of dance music like? What clothes do they wear? How about graffiti? Where do you normally hear this type of music (clubs, festivals, radio)? Explore other formats through which you can listen to dance music (i.e. record, mini-disc, CD, MP3 etc). In what way are these formats differently presented in graphic terms?

This is just the beginning. It is important to note down your ideas, rather than relying on your memory, because one idea will often obscure a previous thought. Each single idea can spark off others. These can be connected together or followed up separately. At this stage it is important to have as many ideas as possible down on paper, so you can move onto the next stage.

don't be behind it, **be in it.**

from A to B **with ease.**

our doors are **always open**

The elimination process

Your next task is to explore your ideas visually to see which have the most potential. At this stage, do not be too precious about detail. Concentrate on expressing your ideas. Quick sketches are the best way of doing this. Use color if it helps, but do not get bogged down in shades and tones.

These rough drawings should be enough to show you which ideas work well and have immediate impact. Discard any that are too complex, or rely on visual clichés. Getting rid of the bad ideas will keep you focused on the good ones.

Talking about things often sparks off other trains of thought. Explaining your ideas to others can help you really understand what you are trying to achieve. Be prepared to listen to the opinions offered (remember: you do not have to act on them if you think they aren't relevant or helpful). Try not to take any criticism personally. Use it constructively to uncover which aspects of your ideas aren't working and what you can do to improve them. As a designer you will often have to listen to comments about your work, and they will not always be positive.

Select the strongest idea. Now put together a presentation visual that demonstrates why your idea is so brilliant. This is the point where you can start working on the detail. Be aware that the best ideas are often the simplest. You need to show that careful thought and preparation have gone into your work. Consider how you will explain your idea to your client. You might need to "sell" it to them, so think about what you would say to support your images.

⬆ Research factors This suite of ads for London Underground uses an eye-catching two-color format. The copy lines focus on reliability and speed of service, the two most important factors identified in market research (see pie charts opposite).

EXERCISE

Brainstorming
Think of a major hypermarket chain and brainstorm ideas for rebranding it. Come up with three adjectives to describe it. If it was an animal what animal would it be? What color is it? What mood is it? If it had a favorite drink what would it be? What place would it be?

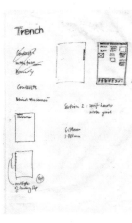

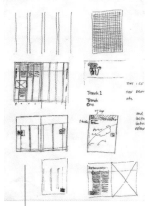

⬅ ⬆ ⬈ **Preliminary work**
Initial lists and thumbnail
sketches give visible form to
ideas: shown here are just a few
rough sketches and workings.

Doodles sketch the look of
the contents page

Early experiments using a
two- and a four-column grid

SECTION 2	PRINCIPLES AND TECHNIQUES
MODULE 8	From Concept to Visual
UNIT 2	**Organizing Thoughts**

The organization of your thoughts
into a coherent form is the end product of the
design process, although the process of
organization starts right at the beginning. You
should start with a broad approach (Exploring Ideas
is covered on pages 52–7) and gradually narrow
your ideas down until you are ready to finalize
decisions and resolve the minutiae.

Often you will have to give the information an order and
structure as well as a form. Design briefs sometimes
have to be interpreted, and sometimes clients have
very little idea what they need: they look to the designer
for a clear analysis of, and a solution to, the problem.

You should remember that there are as many
different ways of solving the same problem as there are
designers. Your job is to choose the solution that you
think is the most appropriate. This decision-making isn't
subjective; it comes from informed judgment.

SEE ALSO: Basic Principles of Layout p16
Visualizing Ideas p56

Research

Research can be very time-consuming so
bear in mind that there has to be a cut-off point at which
you have to start generating a visual concept. If you
need further information you can do this alongside the
visualizing. Remember that "design" is a verb as much
as it is a noun: it's about doing things. When you are at
the point of comprehending the problem you have to
apply that knowledge to get to the next stage.

⬆ ⮕ **Record keeping
and list making**
Recording and ordering
tasks can be done roughly
and quickly in sketchbooks
or as handwritten lists.

Visualizing initial ideas

Remember that hand-drawn ideas can be vague and can leave a lot to the imagination: this is a good thing. You don't read any detail into the sketch and are forced to leave your options open. Designers use "thumbnails" to work out ideas. Usually these are generated on a sketchpad—thumbnails made on a computer tend to look too fixed and polished: you are disinclined to change them or to be so critical. One way to capture the spirit of a thumbnail at full size is to enlarge the thumbnail on the photocopier to the desired size. Typefaces and exact grid measurements can be fluid decisions. It's easy to change these on computers and some decisions can be prioritized.

Criticism and evaluation

Look for constructive criticism but it is important to be careful who you ask. Though it can be frustrating to hear your work being shot down in flames, criticism is a vital contribution to the process. You can also work with an imaginary critic overseeing you and questioning your solutions.

Don't work with blinders on. Often we get too close to our potential solution and need to step back from it to reassess what we are actually trying to achieve. A common fault with work is to try and put too many ideas into one project—select the most appropriate for

Schedules If it is a simple production task, a schedule may be a handwritten list with dates. However, if you are working with a client, it's always a good idea to send a typewritten schedule, so there can be no confusion later on. More complex projects, with many disparate elements to pull together, may require a more formal schedule; a spread sheet is ideal for this.

Electronic "Post-it" notes Designer software programs come with electronic notes, which act as a useful aide-mémoire. You can attach them to pages on which you are working with reminders of what needs to be addressed or other members of the team can write their thoughts or critical evaluations.

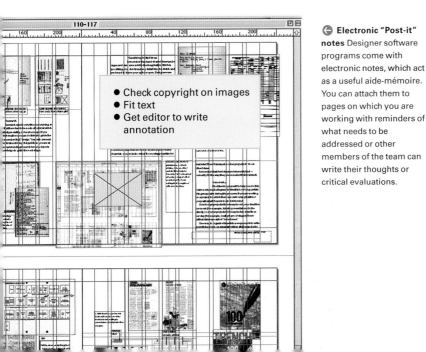

- Check copyright on images
- Fit text
- Get editor to write annotation

that brief. There will always be other projects for those other ideas. Remember that few ideas are inherently bad—it's the way they are executed that is at fault.

Scheduling

Fix dates for yourself: to help you do this, make a schematic diagram to identify how long certain things may take during the process. If you are working on a project for which there are various applications you particularly have to bear this in mind.

Over longer projects there may be only one deadline per week (for example, interim presentations to the client); on shorter projects this may be two deadlines per day (for example, multiple proof stages). One way to organize ideas into a sequence is to write everything down on self-adhesive reminder notes and only then put things in a logical order: you may surprise yourself with the final order.

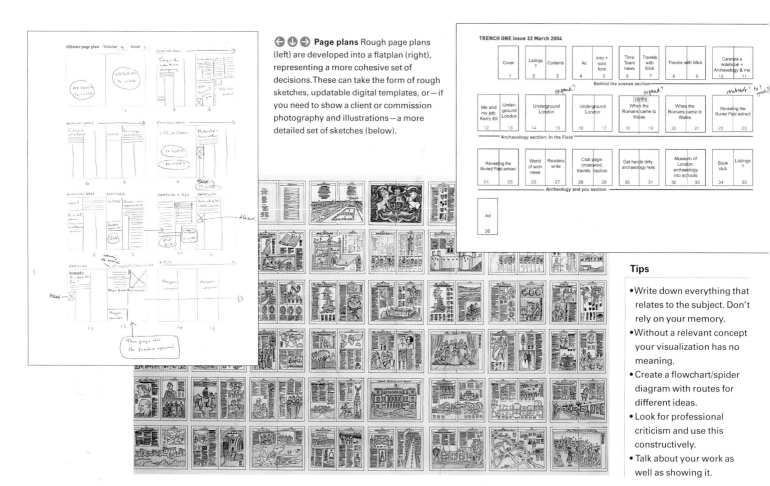

Page plans Rough page plans (left) are developed into a flatplan (right), representing a more cohesive set of decisions. These can take the form of rough sketches, updatable digital templates, or—if you need to show a client or commission photography and illustrations—a more detailed set of sketches (below).

TRENCH ONE Issue 22 March 2004

Cover	Listings ?	Contents	Ad	Intro + subs form	Time Team news	Travels with Mick	Travels with Mick		Carenza s notebook + Archaeology & me
1	2	3	4	5	6	7	8	9	10 11

Behind the scenes section

Me and my job: Kerry Eli	Under-ground London	Underground London		Underground London		When the Romans came to Wales		When the Romans came to Wales		Revealing the Buried Past extract
12	13	14	15	16	17	18	19	20	21	22 23

Archaeology section: In the Field

Revealing the Buried Past extract		World of arch news	Readers write	Club page: crossword, travels, caption		Get hands dirty: archaeology hols		Museum of London: archaeology into schools		Book club	Listings ?
24	25	26	27	28	29	30	31	32	33	34	35

Archeology and you section

Ad
36

Tips

- Write down everything that relates to the subject. Don't rely on your memory.
- Without a relevant concept your visualization has no meaning.
- Create a flowchart/spider diagram with routes for different ideas.
- Look for professional criticism and use this constructively.
- Talk about your work as well as showing it.

Ways to organize thoughts

Something as simple as making lists of tasks, of approaches, or of time can clarify exactly what a particular problem is. Try organizing your ideas by the following criteria:
- Alphabet—from A to Z
- Category—by type
- Chronological—by time
- Continuum—for example, from "good" to "bad"
- Magnitude—by size
- Location—by place

Storyboards

The idea is to give the client or production person enough information so that each member can take the storyboards and begin to design their assigned spreads or pages of the final product.

Website plans show how pages link up with other pages in a logical order. The organization of a website reflects the actual body for which the site is being designed. It is important to get the structure right before designing the look of the pages.

Storyboards are used to design individual pages or sequences before engaging a web designer. As well as in multimedia design, storyboards are commonly employed in films, comic strip, animation, and TV commercials. The storyboard contains a sketch of the visual aspect of the screen, information which will be present, descriptions of animations, interactions (for

example, dialog boxes), sounds, and any other media. Although storyboards were originally linear (for film), non-linear elements are incorporated.

Page plans

There has to be a logical visual (and intellectual) sequence in any design project. A magazine or a book illustrates this point quite well. Magazines and books are normally laid out in miniature on a "page plan" several times before full-size layouts are started. The page plan may consist of no more than the article title but can be much more specific including a list of all the page elements or a thumbnail drawing of the layout with text blocks and artwork sketched in. The page plan is intended to clarify logical sequence, distribution of color, change of pace, and so on.

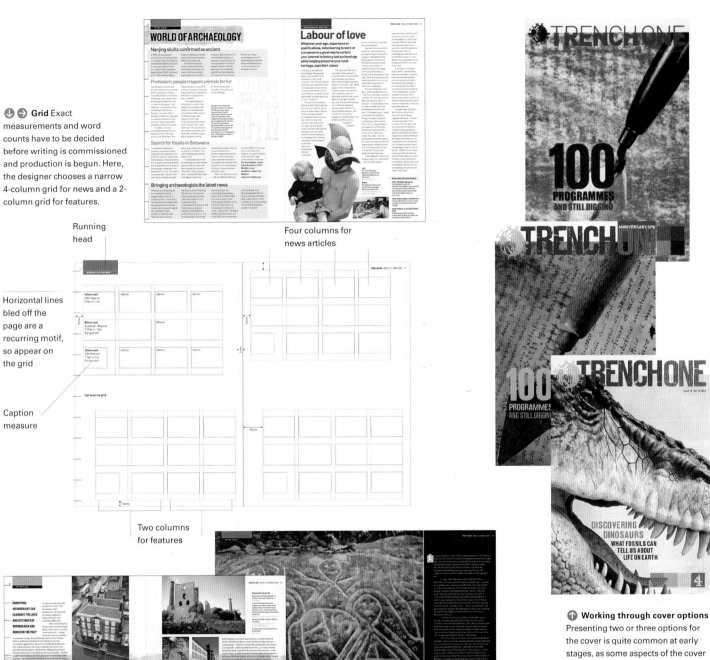

Grid Exact measurements and word counts have to be decided before writing is commissioned and production is begun. Here, the designer chooses a narrow 4-column grid for news and a 2-column grid for features.

Running head

Four columns for news articles

Horizontal lines bled off the page are a recurring motif, so appear on the grid

Caption measure

Two columns for features

Working through cover options
Presenting two or three options for the cover is quite common at early stages, as some aspects of the cover will determine the look and organization of the inside pages of brochures, catalogs, books, and magazines. Usually one will be chosen to take further.

Most design work, whatever the brief, will usually feature some kind of image, be it a photograph or an illustration. Whereas generating type on a printed page has become relatively straightforward since the advent of desktop publishing, representing images successfully can be a bit more difficult.

↑ **Image libraries** operate websites from which a vast range of images can be acquired. They also regularly publish books of image collections according to subject, provided to designers free of charge. Whatever image you are looking for you will come across a huge number of similar images, so it's best to know exactly what you are looking for in advance.

SEE ALSO: Scrapbooks and Mood Boards *p52*

How you represent an image when you show your work to a client will have a massive impact on the success of that presentation. Strong, convincing visuals capture the imagination of the client, and make them eager to see the work taken forward. You have a number of options when visualizing, and which option you choose will usually be dictated by your budget.

By far the best option when presenting working ideas is the well-executed marker visual. Not only are they cheap to acquire (as they are generated by you or your team) but they allow a lot of flexibility of interpretation by the client. Marker visuals imply what you want to do rather than explain exactly, firing your client's imagination and keeping them feeling involved. It will also allow you the freedom to locate the perfect image later on, one that's in line with the thinking behind the visual.

However, there are times when a presentation will require a more finished visual, and for this you will need to take another approach.

How to start looking

When sourcing photographs or illustrations for a project, it's important that you first know what you're looking for. For example, if you're looking for images of a baby, what kind of baby are you looking for? Is it a boy or a girl? Are they happy or grumpy? Are they indoors or out? Do you want a color photo or black and white? Good conceptual thinking early on will help you establish this, narrowing the field of research and making your life a lot easier.

Many young or inexperienced designers begin looking for images on the Internet, using a standard search engine like Google. You should avoid this for three reasons—first because, if you find an image that the client loves in the presentation, you simply won't be able to acquire a high-resolution version for final artwork; second, because you don't have the right to use any images you find, and you could be subject to prosecution if you do; and third, because such searches usually prove to be a frustrating and distracting waste of time anyway.

Image libraries

Instead, your first stop should be a bona fide image library. There are a number of image libraries in existence, and all of them can be found online. Once you've registered with one, sophisticated search engines designed for professionals will help you find what you are looking for. From here you can download low-resolution images that you can use for rough "comping." However, these images often have a watermarked name of the image library across them, which can distract from the impact of your design. Therefore, they should be avoided except for all but the roughest of roughs.

Your next option is to pay the library a small fee for a genuine comping image, which is of a higher resolution and not watermarked. This is done on the assumption that, if your presentation is successful, you will return to the library to purchase the full-resolution, full-price image.

Image libraries come in particularly useful when you need an image you can't feasibly acquire at presentation stage. Let's say that baby you're looking for needs to be wearing a big pair of spectacles. Whereas paying a photographer and model for this would be a prohibitive waste of time and money, image libraries have lots of pictures just like this in their files that you can acquire for a reasonable sum.

Remember, though, that many of the images available from image libraries are royalty free. This is good news for your budget as they are inexpensive, but it may not always be the right thing for your client. Let's say you've been to the image library and found the perfect photo of your bespectacled baby. It may be that, at the same time, another design team has found it perfect for *their* client. Your client may not be happy about the possibility of seeing "his" photograph used in someone else's campaign, however unlikely an event that may be. One way to get round this is to use an image which is not royalty free. Fewer people do this as they are, obviously, more expensive, so the chances are much greater that you won't see that image again for a considerable period of time.

Marker roughs

At the end of the day, there are no hard and fast rules for visualizing, as the chief aim is simply to be utterly convincing. You can use a digital camera to shoot quick, rough images yourself, but once again this can confuse a client when you try to explain that this wouldn't be the "actual image" you want to use. The best solution by far is to present great marker visuals and persuade your client to pay for a photographic shoot to make them reality. You then have a unique photograph that belongs to the client forever. But when this just isn't possible, image libraries provide a good opportunity for a fair compromise.

🔄 ⬆ **Marker roughs** are still regarded as the best way to present ideas. While photographic visuals do look more "finished," they may inhibit your flexibility later on.

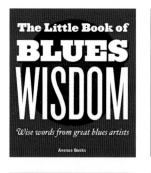

Keeping a sense of unity *The Herald Tribune* newspaper demonstrates how coordinated design helps to forge a unique identity. A good exercise for any designer is to recreate exactly, using QuarkXpress, any page from a newspaper.

So how is this sense of identity achieved? The answer is good coordinated design and an effective design strategy that will allow for changes of text and image, that is applied throughout. With newspapers, this is achieved by creating a number of strict rules and principles that never change. For example, major headlines will be set in one font and ranged left; secondary headlines in another font and centered; body text in yet another font with fixed point size, leading, and justification rules; feature articles perhaps in a bolder font with looser leading and alternate justification; and so on. These rules are never broken, but they are comprehensive enough to allow for any eventuality while maintaining the established "look" of the newspaper.

Few designers get the opportunity to design newspapers, and such a task requires monumental quantities of time, skill, and application. But coordinated design is still a common requirement of almost all graphic designers. For example, seeing as most authors write more than one book, publishers almost always use coordinated designs to produce their book covers. If a publisher is repackaging the back catalog of one of their bestselling authors, they will require a coordinated design strategy for the covers

In the commercial arena, very few things are designed to work as stand-alone pieces. Look at a successful piece of direct mail, for example, and you will notice that the sales letter, application form, leaflet, and envelope all have a commonality of design binding them together and identifying them as a set. Equally, look at any newspaper. The information a newspaper contains changes every day—different headlines, articles, photographs, etc.—yet somehow the paper also looks the same every day, and when a number of them are on a shelf we can easily and immediately identify which paper is which with just a quick glance.

Bold as brass These simple, cheerful little books make bold use of color and type. Only the color and the differing elements of the title change between books, leaving the remaining elements intact to unify the set.

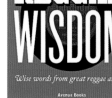

SEE ALSO: Packaging Design *p174*

Because the copy is short
and punchy it can relax in the
open space of the layout.

Full-bleed images have a powerful
impact because they contrast with
the airy page opposite.

50-54
Clerkenwell Road

You are invited to
attend the BIG studio
opening night party

BIG studio

1st floor, 50-54
Clerkenwell
Road EC1

on Thursday
29th April
2004 at 7pm

think **BIG**

It's time
for a BIG
night out.

RSVP
chris.harding@bigpictures.co.uk

BIG studio

The strip of colored tabs features on all
items in the set and adds a flash of fun
and folly—exactly what the studio
wanted to project.

The boxes of flat color, punctuated with tightly cropped images
of patterns and textures, bounce around the page giving the
impression of an abundance of space.

The logo, set in two
contrasting but
complementary typefaces,
maintains its proportions
throughout the set.

Size matters Coordinated
design can mean working
across a range of items of
wildly differing dimensions.
This set for a photographic
studio consists of a letterhead,
a compliments slip, a series of
business cards, an invitation to
view the studio, and a
brochure. Each item works
individually, but takes on
additional impact when viewed
as part of a set, giving the
studio a strong sense of
identity.

Franklin
Gothic, a
sober but
characterful
typeface that
is eminently
readable, is
selected for
the body text.

BIG studio

BIG studio

Chris Harding Photographer

First Floor,
50-54 Clerkenwell Road
London EC1M 5PS

t: +44 (0) 207 250 3500
+44 (0) 7813 308 284
e: chris.harding@bigpictures.co.uk

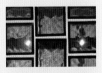

BIG studio

The backs of the
business cards.

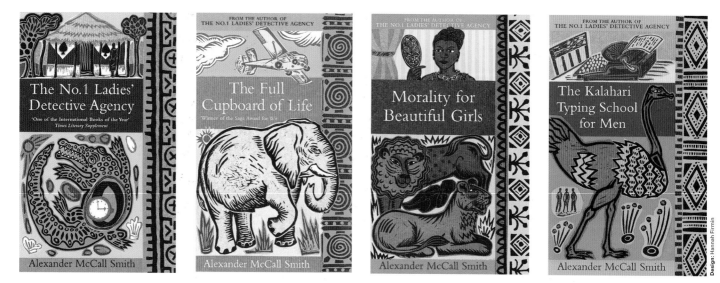

FROM THE AUTHOR OF
THE NO.1 LADIES' DETECTIVE AGENCY

The No.1 Ladies'
Detective Agency
'One of the International Books of the Year'
Times Literary Supplement

Alexander McCall Smith

FROM THE AUTHOR OF
THE NO.1 LADIES' DETECTIVE AGENCY

The Full
Cupboard of Life
Winner of the Saga Award for Wit

Alexander McCall Smith

FROM THE AUTHOR OF
THE NO.1 LADIES' DETECTIVE AGENCY

Morality for
Beautiful Girls

Alexander McCall Smith

FROM THE AUTHOR OF
THE NO.1 LADIES' DETECTIVE AGENCY

The Kalahari
Typing School
for Men

Alexander McCall Smith

Design: Hannah Firmin

that will allow for changes of color, image, and title, but at the same time allow book buyers to identify the titles as being part of a set. It could be that the element that stays the same throughout the series of covers is the type, set in the same face, at the same size, and in the same position on the page throughout. Equally it could be that the common element is the style of the photographs used (black and white, full color, over-saturated, vignetted) or of the illustration (pen and ink, scraperboard, collage).

A good designer will tie up all the elements, creating a template that not only makes each individual jacket striking in its own right, but also ensures that it is easily identifiable with its counterparts.

A book jacket is, in effect, a piece of packaging that advertises both the product and the publisher. Therefore it should be approached in the same way that you would approach an advertising campaign. Each jacket must compete with all the other jackets on display, leaping out from the shelf before going on to inform potential buyers as to what the book might be about, and why they should buy it. However, in many bookstores limited space dictates that only the spines will be visible, so how these appear as a "patch" will be crucial. For example, a series of covers that have spines designed with bold black text on acid colors will create a very impressive patch when a dozen or so of those books are stacked along a shelf.

The creation of these patches is what motivates all manufacturers competing in a fickle market, whether the product is books, chocolate, soup, or soda. Next time you go out shopping, open your eyes to this principle and you will notice that all the products that have the most eyecatching patches are always those of the most successful and best-known manufacturers in the world. It's no coincidence, and the designer that can successfully coordinate a brand will always find her services are in demand.

Know the content!

A concept for a book jacket design will be influenced by a number of things: whether the book is fiction or non-fiction; whether it is the author's first book, or whether they already have a band of loyal followers; what genre the book belongs to; whether the subject matter is fun, grave, romantic, or scary; and, most importantly, who the book is being aimed at. When designing book jackets, good designers make it their business to ask the publisher lots of questions—and to read the book! After all, your jacket must inspire people to buy the book, so what does it contain that makes it a "must read"? The covers shown here are all great examples of powerful, thoughtful, and (most importantly) very successful work.

Out of Africa These covers for Alexander McCall Smith are powerful. The bold colors and African-inspired illustrations are warm, welcoming, unique, and lively, but also intriguing—exactly the nature of the books themselves.

Gridlocked This catalog of photographs by Fin Costello makes use of a complex piece of coordinated design. While each page looks different, strict design principles and commonalities maintain the continuity of the pages.

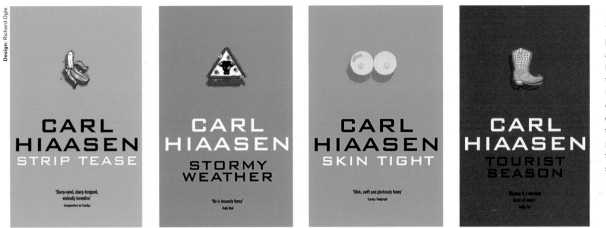

Design: Richard Ogle

CARL HIAASEN
STRIP TEASE

'Sharp-eyed, sharp-tongued, wickedly inventive'
Independent on Sunday

CARL HIAASEN
STORMY WEATHER

'He is insanely funny'
Daily Mail

CARL HIAASEN
SKIN TIGHT

'Slick, swift and gloriously funny'
Sunday Telegraph

CARL HIAASEN
TOURIST SEASON

'Hiaasen is a one-man force of nature'
Vanity Fair

← Drop shadow
The covers of these books by bestselling author Carl Hiaasen leap from the shelf with their striking designs. Both vibrant and elegant, the bold use of color and type ensures they will be equally powerful when only the spines are showing.

Consistent use of Clarendon Light as a text face gives the book authority.

The oversize drop caps inject some fun and maximize the impact, and because they are such a light tint they don't overwhelm.

The caption headers are 100% black throughout, while the captions themselves are a 30% tint of black.

Fine red keylines round the smaller images help to lift them from the page.

Photography or Illustration?

A designer will often have to enliven spreads with pictures and know how to get hold of something appropriate. Deciding whether to use photographs, illustrations, or even type as image (or all three together) can seem daunting, but a well-coordinated look that avoids a mishmash of styles is one of the hallmarks of a good design. Beware of including too many forms and styles of visual material—you need to edit your options logically and with panache. Try to banish preconceived ideas: if you know exactly what you're going to do before you start, you will be less creative. Sometimes even a mistake can turn into a new approach.

The medium and the message

The boundaries between photography and illustration are becoming blurred by digital art techniques, so although a straightforward choice between a realistic photograph and an illustrator's stylistic interpretation is still possible, computer-montage techniques allow for a merging of the two. Within the three categories relatively direct or obscure approaches are possible, so you need to think how you want your message to be understood and interpreted. Much will depend on the industry in which you are working. In advertising, for example, it is often crucial to show the brand your client is endeavoring to sell. Food packaging or car advertisements tend to feature beautifully photographed and highly realistic pictures showing the product in as flattering a light as possible. Conversely, a new brand of coffee (not intrinsically distinctive) could have a contemporary illustration that conveys the message of a trendy lifestyle. At the other

⬆ ↗ **A range of options** can be seen in these images commissioned over several years for an art-materials company: a highly detailed watercolor painting, an almost abstract shot of colored inks, a decorative stylized illustration, an atmospheric photograph, and a richly colored piece of abstract art.

⬆ ➡ **Mixing photographs and illustration**
Photography and illustration merge in these two images. The illustrator collected, colored, and photographed the objects above for a lifestyle magazine article. In the right-hand image leaves were either scanned in or photographed, then digitally colored using Photoshop's brush, blending, and gradation features.

SEE ALSO: Exploratory Drawing *p20*
Photography Basics *p22*
Digital Photography *p64*

end of the realism scale, imagery for a sneakers advertisement might be completely obscure, but the target audience would still be fully aware of the unspoken message. If you are working in corporate design, the company's ethos, enshrined in its "mission statement," is as important as its products or services. Here a more abstract or analogous set of images could also work. In magazines and books, the look of the images will have been considered at the initial styling stage, when all the questions about the target audience will have been discussed. Here a mix of diverse styles—illustrations and photographs—is possible to differentiate the editorial sections.

Creative constraints

Clients might send you the pictures they want you to use along with the initial brief. So sometimes the decision has already been made for you. Photography might not always be possible for logistical reasons—because of distance, budget, or difficulty of gaining permission—and then commissioning an illustration is the best and only route.

Technical manuals, company reports, educational books, or anything that aims to explain how things work all benefit from visualization. This tends to be a specialized area of illustration, in which the designer, illustrator, and author/originator of the material have to work together closely.

Budget and schedule

Commissioning a very intricate illustration of, say, a busy street scene for a large design might not be appropriate unless you have a large budget. Better to get a photograph. Conversely, asking a photographer to set up a shoot involving several models, a make-up artist, and a hair stylist, as well as complicated sets and props, would also be expensive. Here, it would be cost-effective to commission an illustration.

Occasionally you may have to produce something for which there is no budget. Don't be despondent—there are always possibilities. Sometimes, for instance, evocative type can function as an illustration, and copyright-free pictures can always be found if you know where to look.

Where to start

You may be working on a self-initiated project or you may be working to a brief; either way, the illustrative angle may magically spring into your mind or you may have to work harder at deciding on the right style of image. First, you should ask yourself what would be suitable for the market and the message you are trying to put across; then you must research a source that does the job within the constraints of budget and schedule.

Take a look at the checklist on page 125. Armed with these options, you can now apply some of your own creative spark. Start to research sources for the images. You might have to create them yourself or you may be commissioning a freelance illustrator or photographer. There are many ways of looking at people's work beyond flipping through someone's portfolio—on the Internet, at exhibitions and agencies, and in other graphic works such as magazines. There are picture libraries that represent photographers and illustrators,

Take a look at the checklist on page 125.

EXERCISES

Making choices

An investment company wants a brochure that will convey an image of risk-taking combined with sound financial practice. Create a set of three photomontage images.

An architect's practice is selling space in a building before it is built (you can choose either an office or living accommodation). Photograph a series of images that capture the excitement, lifestyle, and positive aspects of the area.

A local history club wants to encourage new members. Research old local engravings and create a design that is contemporary in feel.

or that buy in their work and then sell it on to the media. If you tap "picture library" or "illustration agency" into a search engine you will get many names. Generally, such companies allow you to use a low-resolution version for rough concepts, either for free or for a small fee. Then when you have finalized your idea you can buy the rights to use that picture from them. You should always check what the final fee will be before committing yourself. These sources now produce CDs of royalty free images, which means that you can use the images in your layouts without paying further fees. If you intend to cover a certain subject or style repeatedly it might make sense to buy one of these. Another source is (copyright-free) clip art, which can be useful as backgrounds to text. Although mainly old black-and-white engravings, they can be used in both modern and traditional ways.

← ↑ ↓ **Food for thought**
Food can be rendered either as mouthwateringly realistic photography, or more decoratively, as is shown by the fresh stylized illustrations in graphic monochrome and the watercolors, with or without a black outline.

← ↑ **Shopping shoot?** The decision whether to photograph or to illustrate might be influenced by cost. For professional work you can't just go out and photograph your friends. This would require a good deal of organization: hiring models (with release forms to be signed for permission) and professionals to do make-up and hair; choosing a location; talking to the shop owner; getting the car; choosing and borrowing clothes; and, not least, commissioning a photographer. By contrast, the illustration just requires a careful brief to your chosen artist.

Finally, keep a resource bank. Most designers keep notebooks or files of photographers' and illustrators' work, mainly torn from magazines. Sometimes you'll receive promotional work that has been sent in speculatively. If you like it, or think it might prove useful in the future, file it away carefully in your image bank.

Checklist

- Age/gender/social class of the target audience? The visuals for the horoscope page of a teenage magazine, for example, could be more fun, up-to-the-minute, and abstract than the imagery for a company report and accounts.

- How long is the shelf life of the work? The images in a weekly magazine can be transient, while those in an expensive book with a selling potential of 10 years or more need to have more lasting resonance.

- How clear does the information have to be? The images for a CD cover could be obscure, while those for a technical manual have to be clear and didactic.

- The perceived value. This is tricky to pinpoint, as quite often something that is cheap is being marketed as more expensive through its image, and something that is expensive can seek to appeal to a mass market.

- Design criteria. Do you want a dynamic cut-out shape or a square image bled off the page? Do you want it in black and white or color? Should it be soft- or hard-edged? Can it be stylized? Do you want it to have a retro feel? Or should it look aggressively modern? Should there be one strong focal point or a collage of ideas?

- Theme. Often it is important to create a set of images that all work around the same theme or style.

- Be contrary. Just for a moment or two, consider the opposite of what is expected: this will either give you a new angle or help to consolidate your original thoughts.

- Budget and schedule. Check that your solution is affordable and feasible in the time available.

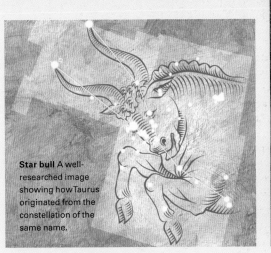

Star bull A well-researched image showing how Taurus originated from the constellation of the same name.

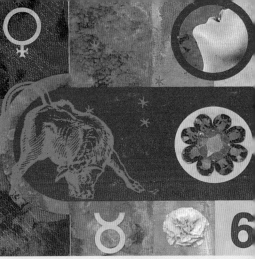

⬆ **A mixed-media collage:** paper was painted and textured, then scanned in with other elements.

⬆ **Bull icon** Here the symbol for Taurus was used to create a mosaic, which was then photographed.

EXERCISE

Zodiac symbols

You are briefed to create the first of a series of 12 images for the horoscope page of a magazine. The illustration can be created in any medium, and it should not just be the astrological symbol; you should research the sign and incorporate some of its associated characteristics. The image should be able to be reproduced in four color and will be used at 2.6 in (65mm) width.

⬅ **Free style** A decorative but realistic approach to Taurus the bull (and its attributes) in a lively pen-and-ink-wash style.

Stages of work

- Research the astrological symbols, finding out how they evolved and the characteristics associated with each sign. Keep photocopies and tearsheets for reference.

- Start doodling. Should it be a square, round, or free shape? Is it to be one image or multi-image? Do you want to apply a grid or structure to the image? Think about your design being implemented across all 12 signs, and gradually resolve these questions.

- Your sketches will help you decide which medium to use.

- Think about color. Do you want each sign to be different or the same? Or perhaps you would prefer to work with a limited palette of colors?

- Work up the image in your chosen medium; then either design or scan a horoscope page from a magazine and incorporate your illustration.

UNIT 1 | **Print Media**

The print-production procedure is often seen as merely the last stage in the design process. This isn't really true at all. A more holistic approach and knowledge of print-production issues are absolutely vital to the designer for several reasons:

- There is an inherent intention in the design process: the final printed job looks and feels the way it does because it was intended so. This "intention" can only be monitored by a designer with an excellent grasp of technical issues.
- A printed object has a tactile quality: use of a special-effect ink, stock, or ancillary process will only be available to you if you have an understanding of the print-production process.
- Late (and costly) changes caused by technical respecifications can be avoided.

SEE ALSO: Color Definitions *p26*
Correcting Color Proofs *p130*

Printing

In all printing methods your digital artwork needs to be separated into the constituent colors in which it will be printed in order to make plates. The important thing to remember is that each plate is used for one color only.

Most work that you produce for print is likely to be printed using offset lithography but other methods of printing include the following:

- Screen-printing (uses stencils) is used for T-shirts, hoardings, some special effects.
- Flexography (uses rubber relief plates) is used for certain types of packaging and plastic bags.
- Gravure (uses plates with recessed cells of varying depths) is generally used for long-run magazines or catalogs.
- Digital printing (uses a plateless computer-controlled press) is used for short-run full-color work.

Most presses feed one sheet of paper through at a time but larger web presses, which are used for long runs, draw paper in from a roll.

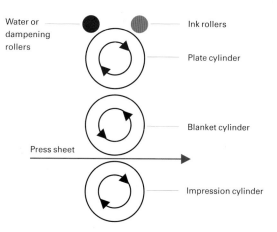

Water or dampening rollers

Ink rollers

Plate cylinder

Blanket cylinder

Press sheet

Impression cylinder

⬆ **The offset lithography principle** This printing process is based on the principle that water and oil do not mix. The digitally produced printing plate is treated chemically so that the image will accept ink and reject water. This simplified diagram of a press shows an exposed plate wrapped around the rotating plate cylinder, where the image is dampened and inked. The inked image on the plate is then transferred onto the blanket cylinder. The rubber blanket transfers the image onto the stock, which has been carried around the impression cylinder (adjusted depending on the stock used). This process is rapid, and the plate is inked on each rotation. There is no raised surface in this process, which is termed "planographic".

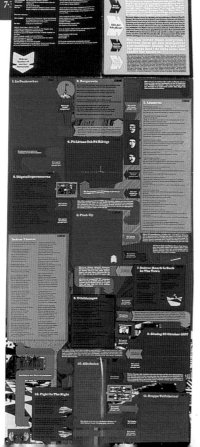

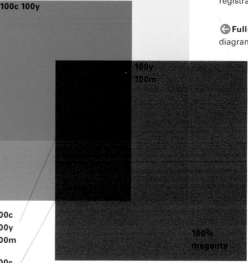

POULENC
Trio
Quintet in E flat K407
MOZART
Introduction & Allegro
RAVEL
THE
FIBONACCI
SEQUENCE
MARTINU
Trio
An Evening
IPPOLITOV-IVAN
in Georgia
DOHNÁNYI
Sextet Op. 37

Jonathan Rees	*violin*
Catherine Manson	*violin*
Yuko Inoue	*viola*
Michael Stirling	*cello*
Anna Noakes	*flute*
Christopher O'Neal	*oboe*
Julian Farrell	*clarinet*
Richard Skinner	*bassoon*
Stephen Stirling	*horn*
Gillian Tingay	*harp*
Kathron Sturrock	*piano*

Monday 8th December 1997 7:

Quality-control strip
Printed sheets usually incorporate a control strip outside the grid to monitor the quality of plate making, inking, registration, dot gain, and so on.

Full-color printing This diagram shows the principle behind full-color printing. The cyan, yellow, and magenta squares are seen overprinting each other and making secondary and tertiary colors. With the use of tints, it is possible to make thousands of subtle variations.

100% yellow

100% cyan

100c 100y

100y 100m

100c 100y 100m

100c 100y

100c 100m

100% magenta

Use of two Pantones
These flyers were both printed in two colors. Above, yellow and blue are overprinted to create a third color (dark green) in the background script font.

Flat tints This fold-out poster shows strong use of flat tints obtained from the full-color-set (CMYK). The photographs have been reproduced in full-color black to contrast with the bright tints.

Color

Various factors determine how many colors we choose to produce the job.

Single- (mono-) color printing can be used when there are budget constraints or when there is a particular color to be adhered to – for instance, most companies specify a particular Pantone ink for consistency across all their printed work.

Two- or three-color printing allows for interesting mixtures of Pantones: overprinting two inks can generate a third color, and printing black-and-white images in two colors (duotone) or three colors (tritone) can enhance their effect.

Full-color printing uses cyan (c), magenta (m), yellow (y), and black (k = "key") inks specified in percentage tints in order to create a huge variety of other colors. This method is used for reproducing full-color photographs or flat colors.

A relatively recent development is that of Hexachrome printing, which uses the full-color set as well as orange and green inks to give an even more comprehensive color range.

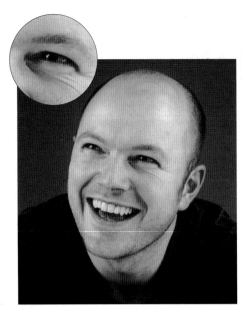

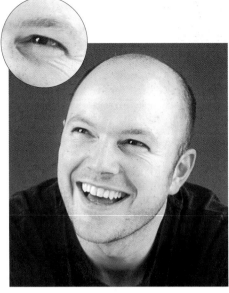

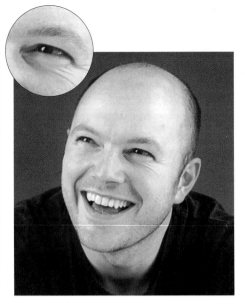

⬆ **CMYK** When you wish to reproduce a full-color image you must generate a CMYK file.

⬆ **Grayscale/mono** is used when you wish to reproduce an image with a range of tones and in a single color.

⬆ **Duotones**—in this instance cyan and black—can enhance mono images or equalize images of varying qualities.

Printing images

Photographic prints or transparencies are known as "continuous tone originals"—meaning that there's a smooth gradation from tone to tone. When we look at a printed image, it is actually made from "halftone dots"—many small evenly spaced dots of varying sizes, usually between 100 and 200 per inch (lpi—lines per inch). The lpi can be much coarser for carrier bags or much finer for art books.

In order to reproduce continuous tone through a printing process we must first generate a digital version (usually through scanning) and then convert the digital version to the halftone dots that create the illusion of continuous tone. What's important about this stage is the resolution of the digitized image: see illustrations.

Images for print should be be saved as either eps or tif files.

Stock

Do not underestimate the potential of printing stocks: there are a huge variety of colors, finishes, and weights available. When choosing a stock think about the effect you want (luxurious or rough-and-ready); the suitability to the type of job; the budget; and the printing method.

Stock is generally categorized into two types:
- coated stock is smoother and reproduces color better.
- uncoated stock has a softer feel and is slightly bulkier at an

equivalent weight: because it is more absorbent, colors flatten out and tints print heavier than intended (dot gain).

Paper weight is measured in grammes per square metre (gsm) and board thickness in microns. An A5 leaflet is generally printed on 115–150 gsm; a business card may be printed on something like 300 gsm.

Proofing

This is your (and the client's) last chance to check the quality and content of the work:
- Digital color proof: cheap and easy to produce but not entirely accurate for color.
- Wet proof: expensive but accurate: uses the final plates and ink on the proper stock.
- Soft proofing: a printer's pdf: useful when time is an issue.

Finishing processes

Any processes carried out to the printed sheet are known as finishing. Some are ancillary to printing while others are related to folding and binding. Use these processes as a creative element: wire stitches and foil blocking are available in many colors; to enhance a color image use spot varnish; etc. Other terms to familiarize yourself with include: folding, trimming, embossing, die-cutting, thermography, stitching, sewing, laminating, binding, and tipping in.

⬆ **Resolution** For full color, duotone, and grayscale images, at the size the image is to be reproduced, the resolution of the digital file should be two times the lpi.

⬆ **Ways of reproducing images** There are various ways to scan and reproduce images. The enlarged part of the image shows how the halftone dot structure differs for each method.

⬆ **Line art** is used when you wish to reproduce an image in purely black and white with no intermediate tones. At the size the image is to be reproduced, the resolution of the digital file should be eight times the lpi.

Tips

Preparing a document for print

- After a final designer's proof is signed off by the client there often remain many issues to be tackled before the work can be printed. Remind yourself that because every piece of design work is unique, it creates a unique set of problems: this stage is your last chance to check your work before handing it over to a printer.
- Be meticulous: check everything from tint specifications, document size, and image quality as well as tidying up documents of unused colors, stylesheets, and double word spaces. All these things are your responsibility; fortunately, programs such as Flightcheck can help.
- When you send a job to a printer include: your final approved document; all images used; all fonts used; a print-out of separations or a color composite of the work; and, finally, a clear covering letter with detailed instructions. Do not assume they are mind-readers.
- It is also quite common to send the printer a postscript or pdf file—a locked document including all fonts and images thereby reducing the potential for errors at the printers.

⬅ **Three-color brochure** The brochure required great attention from the printers, in respect to both the die cut and gluing as well as the spot varnish on the cover and the interior.

The arrival of color proofs is second only to the arrival of a finished printed piece of work you have created. However, at color proof stage, it is still possible to correct any flaws in photography, whether it is digital or conventional.

Transparency Viewer (lightbox)

These are available in various sizes, but what is more important is that the lighting conforms to the international standard ISO 3664:2000. This standard defines the color and intensity of the light source and is the one to which most transparency viewers used at color separation houses and printers conform.

Screen-angle Tester

The different process colors have different screen angles, and the tester consists of a piece of film. Your color separation house will probably be able to let you have one free of charge.

Screen Tester

This tests the screen ruling. Like the screen-angle tester, it consists of a piece of film and should be obtainable from your color house.

Linen Tester

This is the type of magnifying glass used by color-separation houses and printers to view 35mm color transparencies. The folding stand means that the lens is the correct distance from the subject and the hands are left free. The linen tester is used to view both transparencies and color proofs.

SEE ALSO: Color Differences and Legibility p30

Color control patch
This tells the designer whether the proof is faithful to the film being proofed. For example, if the proofer has used too much yellow ink, so that the proof looks too yellow when the film is correct, the color bar will help to show this.

Register Check registration marks to see if the job has been proofed in register. If it is correct, all you will see is black. If it is out of register, one or more colors will show next to the black.

Trim and bleed Check trim marks for position and that the bleed allowance is correct.

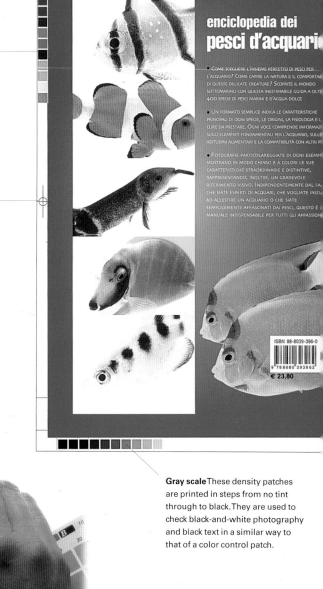

Gray scale These density patches are printed in steps from no tint through to black. They are used to check black-and-white photography and black text in a similar way to that of a color control patch.

Fit If the register marks fit, but you can see colors sticking out from the edge of the picture, the job has been planned out of fit.

Mechanical tints When first specifying the tint, always give percentages of the process colors, which can be obtained from a tint chart, rather than giving a Pantone color swatch of reference number to match, as many special colors cannot be obtained from the four-color process. The tint on the proof can then be checked against the tint chart. Watch out for mottled tints, which can be caused by the film or plate being exposed out of contact. Look also for moiré.

"Flopping" When a picture appears reversed left to right in a color proof, if should be marked "flop". This correction is not simply a matter of the color house turning the film over, as the emulsion would be on the wrong side and therefore out of contact with the plate. Instead, a new contact film has to be made so that the emulsion is on the right side.

Always check the following:

- Register
- Trim and bleed
- Sizes—if a grid is used, check proof against it
- Type—broken, missing, illegible, too fine
- Color—check the color bar
- Flopped subjects
- Artwork overlays
- Tints
- Special colors
- Returns—check that the color house has sent back all artwork and color transparencies originally supplied
- Gutter

Backgrounds of tints or special colors If a common special color or tint background is required for several pages in a publication, the designer should be aware of problems the printer might have in maintaining consistency between pages. For example, if a buff background is used, consisting of a percentage tint of process yellow, and there are some pages that require a heavy weight of yellow to be run for the pictures, the tints on those pages wil be heavier than on the other pages. The use of a special fifth color (a Pantone color, for example) for the backgrounds only should prevent this problem. But remember that it is more expensive to run five colors than four.

As a companion to the print-media unit on pages 126–9 this unit discusses issues relating to electronic production. This is a vast subject, and, depending upon your particular area, could bring you into contact with issues relating to film, video, sound, animation, print, and web design—to name just a few. So this is inevitably a rudimentary look at some of the key areas.

File naming

We have all had to deal with files that when clicked on either do not open or launch the wrong program in an attempt to open. This usually happens because files have been incorrectly named: a few very basic steps will save lots of time later.

The important thing is to name files using the correct extension. This is the suffix, usually written at the end of the file name in the form of ".xxx," replacing "xxx" with the actual extension. Generally speaking, a three-character suffix is the most common, for example ".jpg." The purpose of the extension is to describe what the file type is, as well as helping the application program recognize it, if it is a relevant file format for that particular application.

File-name length can also cause trouble. Although some operating systems and programs can read long file names, such as, "thisismyverylongfilename.txt," others may not. Try to keep the file name to within eight characters, and remember to add the file extension.

File naming Go to "SAVE AS" and type your file name, selecting and replacing an existing name if necessary. Then, select the appropriate file format from the drop down menu and press "Save".

A few other suggestions:

- Do not put any spaces in the name or the extension; if you need to separate words, use an underscore "my_file.jpg."
- Use lower-case and NOT UPPER-CASE characters.
- Only use alpha (abc) or numeric characters (123). Other characters such as @%^&*() should be avoided, and only use a full point (.) to separate the name and the extension.

File formats

Different applications store and compress data in various ways. Misunderstand or misuse these formats and you are heading for trouble. For example, you might spend hours scanning in files and creating artwork for a magazine only to save your hard work in the wrong format. The best-case scenario will be that you can resave, but this may have cost you time and suggest to others you don't really know what you are doing. The worst-case scenario will be that everything has to be re-created, costing you hours of time and possibly losing the job.

Opposite is a list, by no means exhaustive, but one that covers some of the most frequently used formats.

File type unknown In this situation, select the application you feel is most relevant and try to open the file (e.g. Photoshop for an image file). If this still doesn't work, open the application and go to "FILE > OPEN."

Font sizes

Macintosh and Windows operating systems display information differently; not only is there a brightness difference (gamma), but the same font on different platforms will look dissimilar. On the whole, type on a Windows platform will look slightly larger than the equivalent font on a Macintosh.

Gamma

Gamma is a measure of contrast in an image, usually based around the midtones. The higher the gamma value, the darker the tone. Unfortunately for the designer, gamma varies across platforms, so that the same file viewed on a Macintosh will appear different than on a PC.

Macs have a default gamma value of 1.8, but PC users have a value generally higher than this (the actual value depends on the actual card installation in the particular PC). The effect of this is files produced on a Mac will appear darker when seen on a PC, and conversely the file produced on a PC will appear lighter when seen on a Mac.

Graphic file formats

In general, the default settings should be correct, so unless instructed, do not change these. Also, bear in mind that the screen grabs on the right will appear different depending on which software package you are using.

JPG is a format which uses "lossy" compression—meaning that a certain amount of the image quality is lost during the saving process. With a complex photographic image, this would usually remain unnoticed (unless the image is over-compressed). However, if you save an image with large areas of solid color you will get blurred and distorted areas.

EPS is probably the most widely used file format in artwork preparation for print. It can contain either vector or bitmap information and contains two components, a preview and high resolution data from which to print.

TIFF creates one of the largest files because it saves an alpha channel in the file. It enables compression that is non-"lossy," in the form of "lzw" compression. It also allows for cross-platform saving (images for MAC and PC).

GIF was created by Compuserve as a "machine-independent file format." Shown here in the Indexed Color screen grab, GIF files differ from TIFF, JPG, and EPS, in that they can only hold up to a fixed 256 colors. For this reason they are good for flat graphic images using blocks of color, but not good at saving photographic images. GIF files are most widely used within the web-design field.

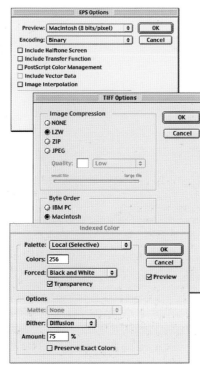

Audiovisual file formats

Similar to the graphics world, those involved with audiovisual work employ a range of file formats. The following list covers some of the most widely used.

AIFF was developed by Apple and is used for storing uncompressed sound files on the Macintosh platform.

WAV is the Windows equivalent to AIFF, used for storing high-quality, uncompressed sound.

QuickTime is a file format for storing movie and audio files. You need to run **Quicktime Player** in order to view the files. The format works across platforms.

MPEG is the name of a group of compression formats for movie and audio files. Compared to other formats, MPEG files are smaller but at the same quality.

Commercial Practice

By now you should have learned how to interpret a client's brief, generate from it some worthwhile design concepts, and see one or more of those through to a successful conclusion. You should also have realized the potential of the various media and digital tools at your disposal and come to understand how practical issues—budget, target audience, production matters, and so on—set constraints on the art of the possible. Working with type and color should, moreover, be increasingly second nature. But it is one thing to absorb the theory, quite another to put it into practice.

This section brings you face to face with the working reality of the graphic-design industry. Each sector will have slightly different demands. What a design consultancy seeks in a would-be employee will not be the same as an advertising agency; and magazines and books, while superficially similar, call for highly specific sets of skills. To some extent, your own temperament, likes, and dislikes will govern your choice of direction.

You may be better at creating images for their own sake, or you may be more suited to generating promotional ideas. A specific area, such as typography or web design, could be your passion, and you may be looking simply for practical guidance on how to launch a career that you've long mapped out in your head. Equally, you may still be casting round for that spark of inspiration. This section, covering everything from corporate design to packaging, should help. Each module is written by a design-industry practitioner and contains a seminar of careers advice, an overview of that industry sector, and in-depth commercial assignments that you can use to test what you have learned up to now.

Finally, remember that there is more than one right path. The creative professionals who have contributed to this section offer a variety of approaches, and the industry is itself broad, employing everyone from efficient proofreaders through to the most colorful thinkers. If you are dedicated and strive to be original, this section should help you find an outlet for your creativity.

UNIT 1 | **Seminar: Professional Pointers**

Books and magazines, whether weeklies or quarterlies, adhere to tight schedules within an established structure of format and grid. But despite their strict calendar of deadlines—with heavy financial implications if missed—they rely on you, the designer, to manipulate type and image creatively.

My introduction to editorial design came with my first job after college, on a weekly magazine. I liked it from the start: for its pace and teamwork, its topical nature, and for the second chances that I was given to improve my design skills. With every week came new layouts, and every issue meant an opportunity to improve on the previous ones.

With greater experience, I went on to design books. Designing books felt like a more serious matter, for they have staying power. Long after your magazine vanishes, the book you have designed may be reprinted using your original design. It is a slower, more considered process, in which your creativity is spread evenly between format, stock, binding, and content. Whether designing a series style, a one-off book, or an art catalog, your responsibility as a designer is to produce an appropriate visual vehicle for the content of the publication.

Since starting EDT, a small design consultancy consisting of three designers and the occasional freelancer, I have made sure that magazines and books are our mainstay. Our studio handles multilingual publications, promotional brochures, exhibition catalogs, and limited editions of artists' books. These design projects are all multipage documents that require more than an engaging layout. We take great pleasure in devising design systems, such as grids, page navigation, hierarchy of headings, a limited color palette, and any number of graphic devices that will create a strong visual identity for the publication. It is generally referred to as "branding" but I prefer to call it "bespoke."

I like the sense of value in working on projects where designers, writers, editors, illustrators, and picture researchers share the same platform and collaborate closely to produce a desirable end-product. We extend this collaborative style of work to our printers, binders, illustrators, and photographers. Engaging these professionals in the design process can turn a competent project into an excellent one. As a small studio with limited human resources we have to remind ourselves constantly that for every magazine we need to produce to an impossible deadline, there will be a long-term book project, for which completing the job on time and budget is less of an issue.

Our relationship with our clients is personal and informal. This is particularly important in our kind of work—responsibilities are less defined and there is a constant dialogue about the product among all the participants. Through meetings and discussions we try

to understand the product and the clients' vision of it before embarking on the design. I believe that most clients are far better judges of how their publications should appear than designers. The client may not know how to achieve the required effect, or articulate their vision, but when presented with the right solution, they will generally warm to it. The designer must develop a well-informed graphic vocabulary in order to achieve a good balance between the visual and the practical.

Problem-solving

Although technology has not helped us to develop concepts or solve creative problems, the digital environment has given us a range of tools for realizing visual possibilities in a flexible and cost-effective way. More printed matter is being produced, not to mention on-line editorial, than ever before. Endless publications on every imaginable subject compete for our attention. Their general design standard ranges from adequate to excellent.

Where does this leave the design student or young professional? My advice is to be aware of what other designers are creating in all visual disciplines. The cross-fertilization of all forms of creativity encourages us to fashion new forms of expression. To design a music magazine or a photography book innovatively you should be aware of the current state of those disciplines and how other designers have dealt with them. With the means to produce a publication available to anyone with a computer and DTP program, the designer must be a problem-solver and a thinker.

Eugenie Dodd

⬆ Voluntary-sector international funding magazine *Alliance* is a two-color quarterly magazine with a modest photography budget. The concept and template of the covers had to reflect the magazine's humanitarian social concerns and create a clear visual continuity of style.

The cover concept combines three elements: a consistent typographic style and arrangement for the masthead and contents display; a prescribed palette for the second color, which changes annually, namely every four editions; a large black-and-white portrait which identifies a topic in each edition, and which reflects the magazine's broad appeal. The visual effect is of a gallery of faces in the global community.

⬆ Art book The aim was to design an artist's book that reflects her journey through the process of assembling a collection of rocks that she has hand-wrapped with string and other materials. The structure and layout had to express the pace and nature of discovery and include the artist's narrative.

The choice of uncoated off-white stock and the grainy color linen embodies tactile and natural aspects of the art. The pages are folded at angles that hint at the text and images held within the book. Only by unfolding the pages will the reader discover the objects, their description, and narrative. Thus, the reading process mimics the collecting act. The images of the rocks are brilliantly colorful in contrast to the gray text.

Periodicals, be they newsletters or magazines, are issued at regular intervals, usually quarterly, monthly, or weekly. They range from intellectual journals through satirical broadsheets to consumer and lifestyle titles. Their visual impact depends to a great extent on the initial planning and brainstorming sessions, in which clients, editors, and designers form the character of the publication.

Preliminary discussions usually focus on the aims of the publication and its target audience, as these are the two decisive factors that influence the design style. Developing or changing a publication requires a heavy financial investment. Therefore it is the responsibility of the designer to fully understand the visual tone that will attract the projected readership.

The structure of a magazine can be broken down into two elements: the front cover and the internal pages. The front cover's function is to attract and sell the magazine and to reflect the intellectual level of its editorial content. The internal pages form the contextual framework for the subject and their visual rhythm defines its nature.

Style guidelines

If you were to design a publication for an established publishing house, you may be handed a document entitled "style guidelines." This will include an editorial and typographic set of rules covering spelling, abbreviations, punctuation, the use of italics, capitalization, and so on. You may also receive separate design guidelines, covering color palette, type style, image preference, and so forth. These guidelines describe the basic elements of the organization's branding and how to implement them. As they may conflict with your design decisions, it's best to study them before beginning work.

Editorial Assignment

Promotional booklet: The International Society of Typographic Designers set this brief for their student assessment project—the example project shown here was designed by Fabio Cibi.

Brief: Design a full-color 16-page booklet and a title identity for a new television channel, Channel 7. The typographic content should include the use of display type and text matters. You will decide the format, binding, and imagery.

Concept: Develop a scheme where the number 7 is associated with the programs that the channel will broadcast. A fable from ancient history should be the basis of the design and its concept. The days of the week were named after seven Roman Gods, whose virtues and colors represent the channel's various programs; for example, Saturn (Saturday), the god of festivals—color indigo—represents variety programs, and so on.

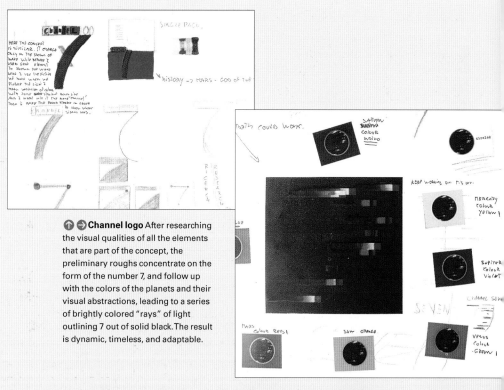

⬆ ➡ **Channel logo** After researching the visual qualities of all the elements that are part of the concept, the preliminary roughs concentrate on the form of the number 7, and follow up with the colors of the planets and their visual abstractions, leading to a series of brightly colored "rays" of light outlining 7 out of solid black. The result is dynamic, timeless, and adaptable.

Identity and styling

Once you are satisfied that you understand the subject-matter sufficiently to start the actual design process, it's best to list all the elements you need to consider. The first ones to work on are the format, masthead, and grid as they create the shell for a consistent structure of every future edition. Together with the ratio of images to text, they define the distinctive look of the magazine.

Formats

It's best to start developing ideas away from the computer. If the format of the magazine has been left to you, spread out a selection of existing periodicals in front of you and choose a few options. Try to stay within the standard formats for periodicals as non-standard paper sizes are more costly. Make up full-size blank dummies to your title's specifications, using an approximate weight of paper and roughly the right number of pages to check out the feel and weight of the final item in each case.

Typography

Looking through a type reference book will help you select possible typefaces for the masthead, and body and display text. Even if you end up customizing type for your masthead design, it's advisable to start with an existing one. Deciding on one typeface over another is a matter of visual judgment, fitness for purpose, and style. An academic periodical will be text-heavy and contain long words, so a narrower font will be more suitable as more words will fit into an acceptable column width. A traditional consumer title might be better expressed through an elegant classic serif typeface; a modern title through a recent digitally-developed one.

As a general rule choose typefaces that contain a fair number of weights and variations—a family—for example, Univers, Frutiger, Officina, Garamond, and Minion. This way you can vary the tonal quality of different layers of information using one typeface. Try to limit yourself to two typeface families, making sure that one is primarily a good display face and the other a

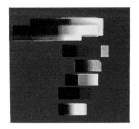

⬆ **Selecting backgrounds**
The designer tries the number 7 against a range of different backgrounds.

⬇ **Against white** The brightly colored rays punch out well against white.

continued on next page ▶

body text face. Their function may be interchangeable for certain sections of the publication. It is important to remember that the magazine is written to be read, and it's the quality of your typesetting, the choice of size, weight, and measure that will determine its readability.

Grid

What's important in multipage documents, and the foundation of most editorial projects, is clarity, efficiency, economy, and continuity. The grid is an ideal starting-point for these aims. Constructing a relevant grid for your content is the most important phase of your design. You must account for multiple kinds of information: the nature of the images and how you intend to use them, the likely variation in the length of headlines, standfirsts, pull-out quotes, and captions. The grid can be obvious—as in a column, hierarchical, or modular grid—or it can be hidden, as in an interlocking or floating grid. It is designed as a canvas offering several possible solutions.

Page navigation

Developing a visual hierarchy throughout a publication will order information and identify locations. By creating a system of signposting based on graphic or typographic elements, color-coding or a change of stock, you can navigate the reader through the different sections with relative ease. Color-coded blocks, a typographic reference, or a series of icons are examples of common practice. These functional schemes often become decorative elements and become part of the branding.

Photographs, illustrations, and color

Photographs and illustrations "tell a story" and form the backbone of a pictorial magazine. Assuming you are given the responsibility, it is your choice of image that contributes to the message and mood of a feature or cover. Your first decision is whether to use an illustration or a photograph, whether to use black and white or color, line or half-tone. On

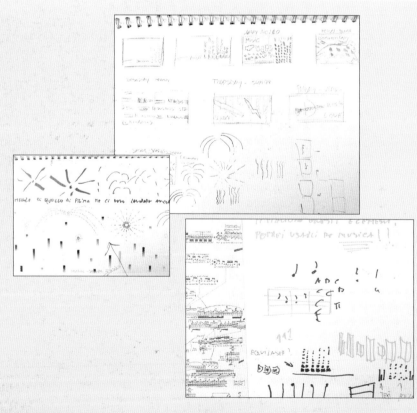

← ↑ A series of roughs showing stages of the design process of graphic representation for double-page spreads. For the spread representing the company's musical programming, musical notation is abstracted and re-created on the computer. A style for headings uses type and a graphic mark for page identification.

most occasions your decision will be dictated by the material that you've been given or by what you can source within the magazine's budget and schedule. This should not be a problem, as any image has got the potential of a range of images. When selecting or commissioning photographs or illustrations, prepare a detailed written brief, starting with concept, style, format, and all technical information needed for a satisfactory delivery. Choose photographs that are "long shots" and ensure that illustrations have large margins around them, thereby allowing for cropping and different layout options. Remember that magazine imagery is primarily journalistic: you will achieve the kind of visual impact that transforms an article only through skillful cropping, scaling, and placement of the images within the text.

Color is an integral element of your layout. It will help you to change pace and mood in your publication. With digital technology designers have a virtually limitless color palette with which to highlight, soften, identify, and modify. Color is symbolic and emotive, and when applied to type, image, or space will influence the readers' perception and their sense of the hierarchy of these elements within the layout. You need to be aware of all these factors in order to avoid sending mixed messages in your design.

Layout

The layout of a magazine is determined by the factors we have covered, and is a summary of your decisions to date. Digital technology has made it possible to experiment and explore different arrangements of type and image at the push of a key, which is great fun, as long as you remember that the final design has to subscribe to the magazine's aims and target audience. Your decisions to use horizontal or vertical axes in your layout, or how you "cluster" your elements, should be the basis for a coherent look. The pages should be visually linked but your scheme should allow for changes of pace and proportion.

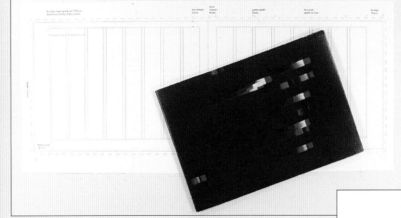

The final music spread A series of photographs of music personalities at the foot of the spread creates a strong dynamic element that underpins the easy rhythm of the rest of the spread. Typography merges smoothly with graphic forms. This framework of elements is repeated throughout the publication, but using different photographs and graphic themes, and thereby changing the mood for each spread.

Grid Although you may not be aware of a grid in this type of publication, its existence is crucial. Only by having a rigid structure to support such loose elements can the designer control the overall feel of the spreads.

continued on next page

Tips

To navigate the reader through a publication use:
- Headings—to label chapters, sections, major topics, subheads.
- Captions—to explain illustrations, photographs, charts, tables.
- Numbers—to identify pages (folios), paragraphs, footnotes, cross-references.
- Quotations—to highlight speeches and extracts.

Readers tend to dip into magazines, so you should create various levels of entry in your layouts: headlines and engaging images for the viewer, clearly set captions and pull quotes for the casual browser, and well-structured main text with engaging visual material for more committed readers.

Materials and finishing

Although the choice of papers and finishes for periodicals is limited by printing methods and budgetary constraints, there will still be many options to explore. As with other elements that we have discussed, it is important to choose the appropriate paper and binding for your publication. Art or matt-coated papers give a sleek appearance to text and photographs. Printing on uncoated paper results in a softer, more graphic print quality and a more tactile feel. Some publishers change stock for certain sections, printing all photographic matter on coated paper and information sections on uncoated, and sometimes even tinted, paper. Ask printers to supply you with samples of available papers, and discuss your ideas with them, as binding technicalities will affect your decisions. Whether you decide your publication is "self cover" or uses heavier card to protect its pages will depend on the number of pages within it and the budget. The only way to make an informed decision is to get the printer to make up different blank dummies of all your preferred options—the weight and texture of the item will be the best guide.

Design in action The vertical grid enables the designer to hang columns of type on a fixed axis while letting it travel vertically with no restraint. The landscape format of the publication unfolds a wide canvas of events that supports our idea of watching television.

One-off publications

Promotional literature such as exhibition catalogs, sales brochures, and information-intensive documents fits somewhere between periodicals and books in style, and between editorial and advertising as products. If you are designing an exhibition catalog or a sales brochure, the emphasis will be on the pictorial information, with the grid and text playing a subsidiary role. The format of the publication will be informed by the images—whether landscape or portrait—and the grid may consist of small modular units to accommodate short paragraphs of varying length and width. Layouts for these publications can ignore structure to create specific emotional responses in the readership. On these occasions you can use your digital skills to enhance type and image creatively, by altering size, density of tone, and how elements are juxtaposed. If you're designing an exhibition catalog, the starting-point should be the gallery's layout, and your design solution should be restrained and sympathetic to the display. The text accompanying these publications may consist of different sorts of information that will need careful analysis. You will need to apply a great deal of attention to typographic detail and choice of font. This is particularly true when designing primarily informative material, such as price lists, directories, and timetables.

As budgets for one-off publications are usually more generous than those for magazines, your choice of materials, special finishes, and binding is broader. Don't let the brief or the clients intimidate you. Surprise them with an interesting fold, embossed title, unusual format or layout. The key to a solution acceptable to the client is your ability to produce a visually exciting product with a clear message.

⬇ ➡ **Room for improvement**
Spreads from the finished booklet. The end result is a very successful publication that would have benefited from more imaginative binding and a slipcase to enhance the "keepsake" aspect.

⬇ **The title page** The adaptability of the solution is tested on the title page, where the 7 becomes a multicolored narrative without losing its form. The verso page, whose color palette is identical to the cover, creates a point of reference for the transformed 7.

◀ **The format** of this book hints at an authoritative reference, while being small enough to enable extended reading.

SECTION 3 | COMMERCIAL PRACTICE

MODULE 10 | Editorial Design

UNIT 3 | **Books**

More books are printed today than ever before. There are paperbacks—fiction and non-fiction—with linear reading and a simple typographic structure; large-format "coffee table" books with images and text set to various measures with a complex internal typographic hierarchy; artists' monographs that consist mainly of images with restrained informative typography; and limited-edition books that defy all laws of structure, production, and budget. Although each book is a single product retaining its own individuality, the emphasis throughout is on conceptual integrity and legibility.

Books have a prescribed general structure of covers, title pages, prelim pages, main text, and back matter. Computer software has meant that flat-planning a book and formatting continuous text can be done in a matter of minutes rather than hours, leaving the designer time to design and layout. You should relate the format and structure of a book closely to its subject and function. Books for serious reading should fit into our hands, so margins should be sufficiently wide to allow room for fingers to hold the book. Type and leading should be geared toward extended reading in standard lighting conditions.

Larger-format books will probably be set down on a table and browsed through rather than read. They typically contain more than one level of information, expressed through different type sizes, and possibly more than one type style and type color. The layout should reflect the pace of the browsing activity.

No rules apply to the limited-edition book. The design should not only express the book's subject but become an embodiment of it. Design and production considerations are mainly conceptual in such cases, and you will probably be working closely with the author or artist, the final book being the fruit of your collaboration.

In the current competitive climate publishers are eager to present their products in new ways. Although this allows designers greater scope for innovation and experimentation, it makes the design of books even more challenging.

Editorial Assignment

Project: Film book

This brief was set for students on a typography course. The example was designed by Clarice Trevisan.

Brief: Design one of a series of books on "Icons." These books are intended as serious biographies, so the emphasis is on text rather than pictures. The books should be 240 pages in length and of a similar visual style. For the presentation of your solution produce a series of rough designs showing your working process, a few final spreads, covers, and a full-size blank dummy.

Concept: Create a template for a double-page spread flexible enough to accommodate the different "icons" without losing the identity of each one of the individual subjects. Now design, as the first in the series, a book about Pedro Almodóvar, the acclaimed Spanish filmmaker, that parallels through format, space, and typography the director's points of view as represented in his films.

⬇➡ The planning stage

By working over numerous points of reference, like preliminary layout ideas, page structure, and typographic considerations, your visual ideas are being formed. Remember that continuous text needs special attention to readability. Experiment by typesetting paragraphs in different fonts and styles to achieve both the look you want and the readability you need.

century gothic
Pedro Almodovar
The most internationally acclaimed Spanish film-maker since Luis Buñuel was born in a small town (Calzada de Calatrava) in the impoverished Spanish region of La Mancha. He arrived in Madrid in 1968, and survived by selling used items in the flea-market called El Rastro. Almodóvar couldn't study filmmaking because he didn't have the money to afford it. Besides, the filmmaking schools were closed in early 70s by Franco's government. Instead, he found a job in the Spanish phone company and saved his salary to buy a Super 8 camera. From 1972 to 1978, he devoted himself to

letter gothic
Pedro Almodovar
The most internationally acclaimed Spanish filmmaker since Luis Buñuel was born in a small town (Calzada de Calatrava) in the impoverished Spanish region of La Mancha. He arrived in Madrid in 1968, and survived by selling used items in the flea-market called El Rastro. Almodóvar couldn't study filmmaking because he didn't have the money to afford it. Besides, the filmmaking schools were closed in early 70s by Franco's government. Instead, he found a

Futura regular
Pedro Almodovar
The most internationally acclaimed Spanish filmmaker since Luis Buñuel was born in a small town (Calzada de Calatrava) in the impoverished Spanish region of La Mancha. He arrived in Madrid in 1968, and survived by selling used items in the flea-market called El Rastro. Almodóvar couldn't have the money to afford it. Besides, the filmmaking schools were closed in early 70s by Franco's government. Instead, he found a job in the Spanish phone company and saved his salary to buy a Super 8 camera. From 1972 to 1978, he devoted himself to make short films with the help of his friends. The "premieres" of those early

Futura light
Pedro Almodovar
The most internationally acclaimed Spanish filmmaker since Luis Buñuel was born in a small town (Calzada de Calatrava) in the impoverished Spanish region of La Mancha. He arrived in Madrid in 1968, and survived by selling used items in the flea-market called El Rastro. Almodóvar couldn't study filmmaking because he didn't have the money to afford it. Besides, the filmmaking schools were closed in early 70s by Franco's government. Instead, he found a job in the Spanish phone company and saved his salary to buy a Super 8 camera. From 1972 to 1978, he devoted himself to make short films with the help of his friends. The "premieres" of those early

Frutiger light
Pedro Almodovar
The most internationally acclaimed Spanish filmmaker since Luis Buñuel was born in a small town (Calzada de Calatrava) in the impoverished Spanish region of La Mancha. He arrived in Madrid in 1968, and survived by selling used items in the flea-market called El Rastro. Almodóvar couldn't have the money to afford it. Besides, the filmmaking

⬆ Investigating the typographic identity

from the start helps in finding a cohesive look for display type, page navigation, and the cover. You need only develop and apply one strong visual element in different ways throughout your book to give a unique look to your design.

⬇ Picture research

Early on, this is also the stage where you should start considering color and images.

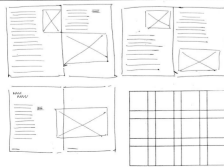

continued on next page ▶

pedro _almodovar_

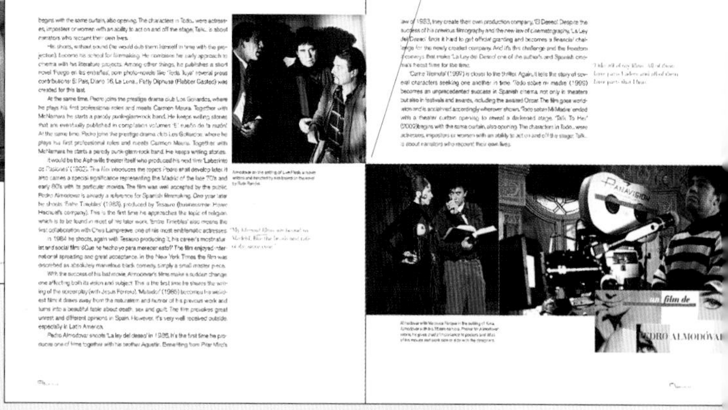

[Body text illegible at this resolution]

The way in which the pictures meet in the corner echoes the typographic treatment of headings.

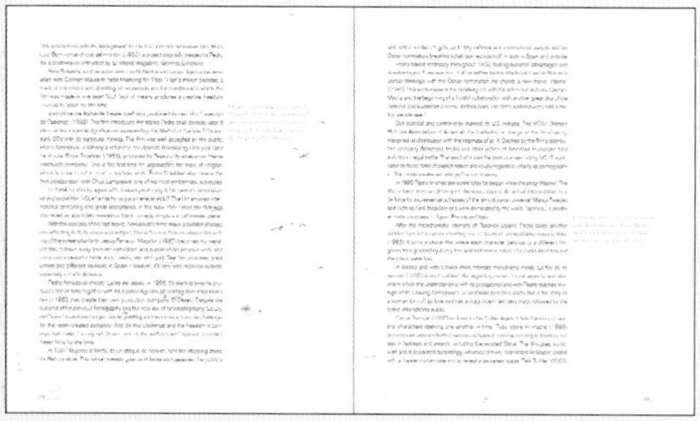

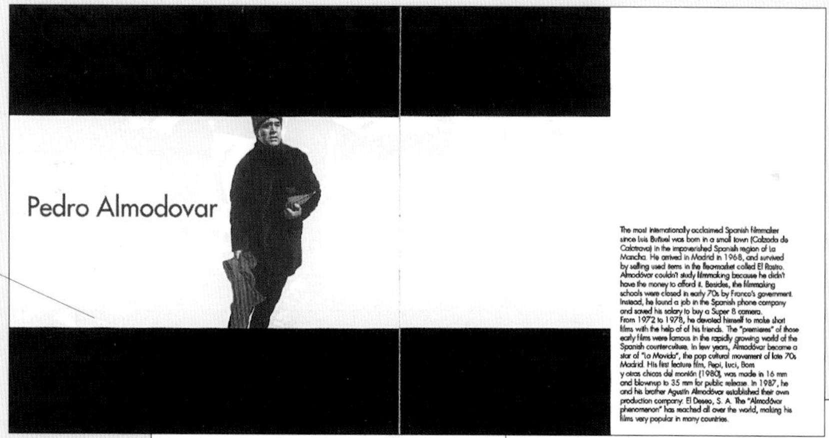

un film de
PEDRO ALMODOVAR

⬆️ ➡️ **Page layout** The size and format of a book, together with juxtaposition of type and image, are the decisive elements in determining the appearance of a page. The double-page spread in this book has generous margins and interesting spatial proportions. The vertical justified columns of type create a strong visual contrast to the images that butt up to each other horizontally across the spread.

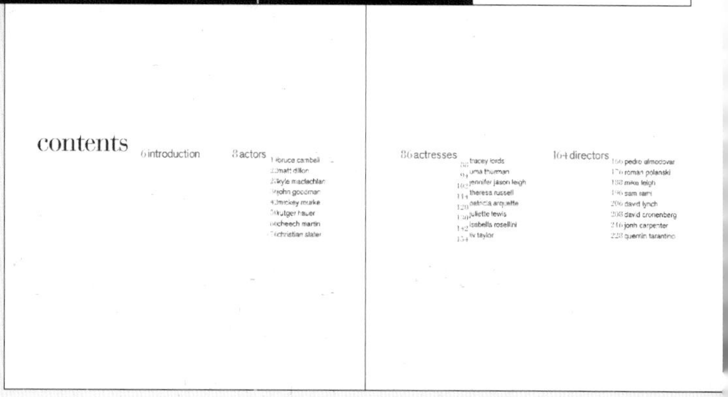

Dark panels, above and below, create a spread evocative of wide-screen cinema.

Pedro Almodovar

The most internationally acclaimed Spanish filmmaker since Luis Buñuel was born in a small town (Calzada de Calatrava) in the impoverished Spanish region of La Mancha. He arrived in Madrid in 1968, and survived by selling used term in the flea market called El Rastro. Almodovar couldn't study filmmaking because he didn't have the money to afford it. Besides, the filmmaking schools were closed in early 70s by Franco's government. Instead, he found a job in the Spanish phone company and saved his salary to buy a Super 8 camera. From 1972 to 1978, he devoted himself to make short films with the help of his friends. The "premieres" of those early films were famous in the rapidly growing world of the Spanish counterculture. In few years, Almodovar became a star of "Lo Movida", the pop cultural movement of late 70s Madrid. His first feature film, Pepi, Luci, Bom y otras chicas del montón (1980), was made in 16 mm and blowen up to 35 mm for public release in 1987. he and his brother Agustín Almodovar established their own production company El Deseo, S. A. The "Almodovar phenomenon" has reached all over the world, making his films very popular in many countries.

➡️ **Contents page** The collage device used on the spreads is echoed in the typography of headings, contents page, and page navigation. In contrast to the angular type and photographs the page space is punctuated by looser typographic elements of lighter color and texture that create an additional level of information for the browser.

contents

6 introduction

8 actors
10 bruce campbell
12 matt dillon
14 kyle maclachlan
16 john goodman
18 mickey rourke
20 rutger hauer
22 cheech marin
24 christian slater

26 actresses
28 tracey lords
30 uma thurman
32 jennifer jason leigh
34 theresa russell
36 patricia arquette
38 juliette lewis
40 isabella rossellini
42 liz taylor

164 directors
166 pedro almodovar
170 roman polanski
172 mike leigh
174 sam raimi
176 david lynch
178 david cronenberg
180 john carpenter
182 quentin tarantino

Section openers By using a familiar image on this section opener, the designer made sure that we are visually informed about the content of this book. Although this spread is alien in style to the rest of the book, it has a light touch that fits with the nature of the movie industry.

film directors

pedro almodovar
roman polanski
mike leigh
sam rami
david lynch
david cronenberg
jonh carpenter
quentin tarantino

film icons

clarice trevisan

Studio Vista

The "stepped" section opener mirrors the treatment of type on the front cover, title page, and chapter opener.

Title page The type treatment echoes the jacket but with the title in a smaller point size.

The book cover is discreet and evocative of the moviehouse experience. The abstraction of the cinema space works well with the typographic arrangement of the title and other texts, but the subject of icons, who are people larger than life, deserves a stronger and more memorable design.

Film icons is one of the three first titles in the icons series. Music and sport icons are also available.

Film icons is a unique venture which aims to unravel the multi-layered language of film, by exploring each of the crafts which combine to make a film, through the biographies of some of the notable characters who make our cinema. The icons in this book are culturally, as well as artistically, diverse.

film icons

clarice trevisan

film

icons

clarice trevisan

Studio Vista

Studio Vista

ISBN 1-85669-160-8

UNIT 1 | **Seminar: Professional Pointers**

Malcolm Jobling has spent over 20 years in advertising, and now teaches Design for Advertising at the School of Art & Design at Dunstable College. Nick Jeeves has been a graphic designer for ten years and also lectures at the Cambridge School of Art. Here they talk about their experiences in the advertising industry.

"You dine off the advertiser's 'sizzling,' not the meat of the steak." J.B. Priestley

" Advertising has become one of the most powerful agents of change in the modern world. It can sell us a toothbrush, a car, a home; even a town, a government, or a country. It surrounds us virtually from the moment we wake up to the moment we go to sleep, and persuades us to accept what's "in," what's "out," and what's "the next big thing."

Over time, creatives have found increasingly brilliant ways in which to do this, although its basic principle is unchanged: To attract people's attention for long enough to make them interested in a product.

For the most part good advertising today depends on three things: simplicity, originality, and skill of execution. As our primary task is to arrest people's interest quickly, simplicity is at the top of the list. The oldest and best analogy goes thus: Throw a dozen tennis balls at someone, and they'll catch none of them. Throw just one, and they'll catch it.

Throughout our careers, both of us have seen dozens of portfolios from young creatives that are full of excellently rendered but ultimately uninformed ads. What's often forgotten is that before you can consider a career as a designer, copywriter, or art director you first need to demonstrate that you are passionate, dedicated, and obsessively curious. This is really what counts in advertising, and what we don't see enough of. Strive to understand what makes people of all backgrounds tick—what motivates them, what language they use, what aspirations they have, and

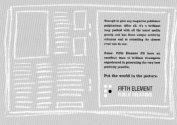

"He's the cute one that used to be in that band with the other one."

"It's one of those glossy celebrity mags with a one-word title."

⊝ ⊙ **A teaser ad** doesn't reveal what it's selling straight away. A snatch of conversational chat is enough to draw you in to this blurb for a PR company.

you'll be far more likely to impress cynical art directors. The section on scrapbooks and mood boards earlier in the book (see pages 52–5) applies to all designers, but for those with ambitions in advertising it is absolutely crucial. Also, all aspiring designers and writers should consume old awards annuals and absorb their basic principles. That said, we would also recommend that once you've done this, you should feel free to ignore it all, as by their very nature these books are full of old ideas, and advertising is about nothing if not new ideas.

Finally, and perhaps most importantly, you must set out to be good. As in all walks of life, the only thing worth investing in is your reputation, so you should always be prepared to go the extra mile on every occasion—and then go another two. Good advertising is not just the result of a passion for the profession itself, but for the world and all its mysteries. If this is you, welcome to Adland. "

Malcolm Jobling and Nick Jeeves

UNIT 2 | **The Business of Advertising**

Some people want to be novelists. Others want to be photographers. These are skills, and careers, in themselves. But because advertising employs writing, photography, illustration, animation, music, and theater in its remit, you'll need to be well versed in all these skills. You won't need to be an expert, but you will need to be able to spot the good stuff when you see it and be able to use it as both a means and an end. Happily you will rarely, if ever, be working alone, as teamwork is fundamental to the advertising business.

An agency team usually consists of a number of highly skilled people working together. At the front end of the business, account executives first find clients for the agency. The art director and copywriter then develop concepts for the client using visuals and words respectively, although there is rarely an absolute line of distinction between these two roles, and their relationship is essentially symbiotic.

At the top of the creative totem pole is the creative director, who is in control of all the artistic output, and whose responsibility it is to hire and fire. It is perhaps the most prestigious job in advertising. Naturally, the creative director is more than capable of carrying out every aspect of the creative process, but it is the support of an excellent team that enables him or her to concentrate on developing the best concepts and strategies for the client.

Developing a concept

Advertising is highly competitive. Only the best ads succeed and therefore agencies only employ the people best at creating them. Your ads must stop people in their tracks in a world crammed with ads designed to do just this. This is where the subject of USPs comes into play. A USP—a unique selling proposition—is the thing that makes the product you are advertising different from the rest, and therefore desirable. It doesn't always matter what this difference

Two hours to deadline, and all's well.

HYPHEN
PREPRESS MANAGEMENT SOLUTIONS

is, as long as there is one: bigger, softer, cheaper, tastier than the competition. It is the USP that forms the core of a campaign's concept: Compare the USP of a Volkswagen with that of a Cadillac, and you will begin to understand their ads' strategies.

While the effectiveness of selling a product by focusing on the USP is almost beyond dispute, there are no hard and fast rules when it comes to creating ads. Except one: Don't be boring. You must use your creative resources to come up with an idea that is memorable and therefore effective. Adland supremo David Ogilvy once said, "I do not regard advertising as entertainment or an art form, but as a *medium of information*. When I write an advertisement, I don't want you to tell me that you find it 'creative.' I want you to find it so interesting that you *buy the product*."

You may have noticed that you'll have done no graphic design yet. That's because conceptual development—the bulk of the work in advertising—has nothing to do with design and everything to do with ideas. The advertisement at the top of this page is not good because of how it looks, it's good because it's a great *idea*. Design is simply the mechanism used to convey information effectively—pointless if you have no information to convey. Also, until you know where your concepts are going to be placed, there is nothing to design. An agency's media planners will work out the most effective and budget-conscious way to expose the target audience to the product, using either billboards, press ads, direct mail, or a combination of these.

A memorable visual is always a useful sales tool. The potentially "boring" business of production management systems is brought to life by a shot of staff walking through treacle.

Tips

- Consume books, magazines, and newspapers; visit stores, galleries, cinemas; get to know the country you live in. Talk to people. Aspire to be the best-informed person you know.
- Keep a visual diary and make a note of anything that inspires you or grabs your attention, every day.
- Simplicity, originality, and skill of execution are the principal ingredients of a good advertisement.
- Learn from old awards books but don't treat them as gospel. Be original.
- Set out to be good, and invest everything in your reputation.

The assignments on the next few pages are designed to give you an idea of the kinds of project you might be expected to work upon in the advertising industry. Normally your team would generate perhaps a dozen initial ideas and work and refine from there. Due to the constraints of space, however, we've picked only the key moments from the process to illustrate. Remember, it may well be that your first idea is the best idea, but you should learn to exhaust the possibilities of these briefs by making good use of both research and intuition.

Tips

- Your advertisements must grab people's attention in a landscape full of ads attempting the same thing.
- Base your early thoughts around the product's USP. What is its unique selling proposition?

Advertising Assignment
Client: High & Mighty
Medium: Poster
Campaign and design requirements:
Communicate to outsize males that High & Mighty is the specialist clothing retailer just for them. Produce both press ads and posters.
Hints: It's essential that you don't imply to the audience that you are judging them in any way, or that they should be judged at all. This brand's inspirational USP is a gift, so work with that.

HIGH & MIGHTY
Quality Clothes for large men

We can clothe a man up to a 60 inch chest

⬆️ ➡️ **Initial concept sheets** The initial concepts for this campaign go straight to the point, using copy and imagery that immediately communicate the nature of the business. The USP of the retailer — that they sell big clothes for big men — is immediately obvious from these early visuals.

Visualizing
Once your ideas have begun to take shape, the next stage is giving them visual form in a campaign. A campaign is a series of advertisements presented to the public either in different locations (press ads, posters, billboards, buses) or as the same concept presented in different ways — a themed series of press ads, perhaps. Often it's both. "Campaignability" is crucial in determining the strength of a concept, and this is where the design process begins. Campaigns succeed when readers spot the common theme and respond to it. The phrase "Have you seen the latest ad for…" is music to advertiser's ears, and it is a commonality of design that ensures this "brand building" happens. To achieve this, your design layouts must be bold, clear, and memorable.

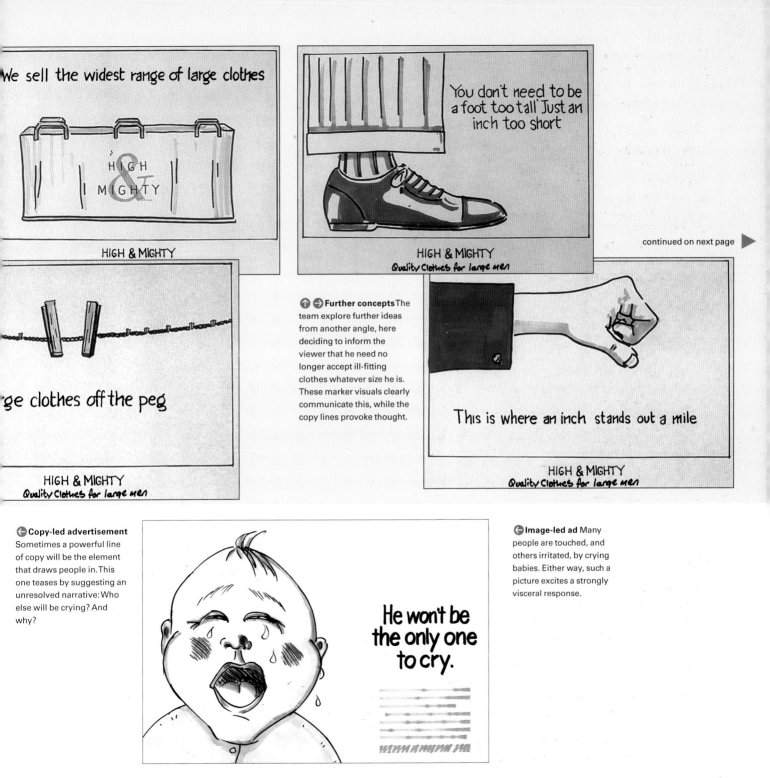

continued on next page ▶

Further concepts The team explore further ideas from another angle, here deciding to inform the viewer that he need no longer accept ill-fitting clothes whatever size he is. These marker visuals clearly communicate this, while the copy lines provoke thought.

Copy-led advertisement Sometimes a powerful line of copy will be the element that draws people in. This one teases by suggesting an unresolved narrative: Who else will be crying? And why?

Image-led ad Many people are touched, and others irritated, by crying babies. Either way, such a picture excites a strongly visceral response.

Final visuals Having explored possibilities, the team have decided that the posters should take a form that expects the viewer to interpret them. This "conspiracy" between the product and the viewer will create a lasting resonance. The written puns from the earlier concepts have been dropped, and the company name and subheading now take the dominant position (which the client will like). The visual puns of the oversized appliances convey their own simple message. These sophisticated final marker roughs present the concept in a convincing way.

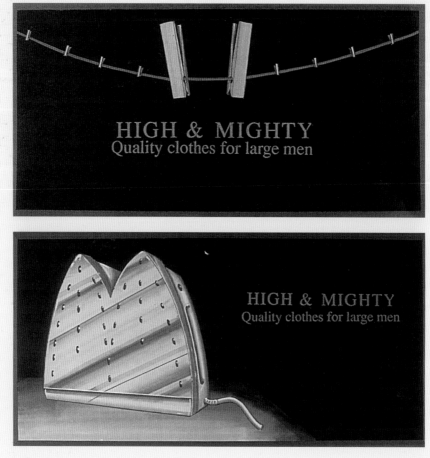

HIGH & MIGHTY
Quality clothes for large men

HIGH & MIGHTY
Quality clothes for large men

Tips

- Be brilliantly creative, but never at the expense of the main purpose of an ad: To sell the product.
- Your ad must make sense, and ring true. Good advertisements create a "conspiracy" between the product and the audience.
- Design exists only to convey information effectively. Good ideas come first.

In very basic terms, most advertisements are either copy-led (where the words of the ad take the dominant position on the page and are supported by an image); image-led (where the image is dominant and supported by the copy); or something in between that plays on both elements. Look through awards annuals and see if you can identify which are which. Making such a decision is where the relationship between the art director and the copywriter is tested. A powerful copyline may be the best way to sell the product, so it should be the first thing people see. Equally, a powerful picture may be the more effective tool, so you may decide that your advertisement should be image-led.

For visualizing press ads you should use large layout pads that will enable you to render the ad at full size. Once you've completed the layout, you can paste it into an actual newspaper to demonstrate the ad in context. TV ads can be visualized using storyboard pads, the pages of which are segmented into screen-shaped boxes for you to draw in. Each box represents a scene in the ad, underneath which you can write down any dialog, sound effects, or stage directions.

The key skill for both these tasks is mastery of the marker pen. They are good for both rough layouts and more finished renderings, as they come in a wide range of colors and thicknesses.

Computers will eventually play a very large part in the final stages of a campaign. Still, it is only in the final stages of a developing campaign that they become necessary. Remember that in the advertising industry, the most highly valued skill is an ability to generate great ideas. Consequently, any young designer working

Advertising Assignment

Client: RNID–Don't Lose The Music
Medium: Direct Mail

Campaign and design requirements:
The Royal National Institute for the Deaf wish to communicate to 18–24-year-old music fans that exposing their ears to loud music can cause permanent hearing damage. Your message should be that if people take care of their hearing now, they will be able to enjoy music for years to come.

Hints: You may think that a health-awareness campaign has no identifiable USP. However, we are bombarded with a wide variety of health warnings all the time, and people don't like to think too heavily about them as it can be distressing. This is your competition and your challenge.

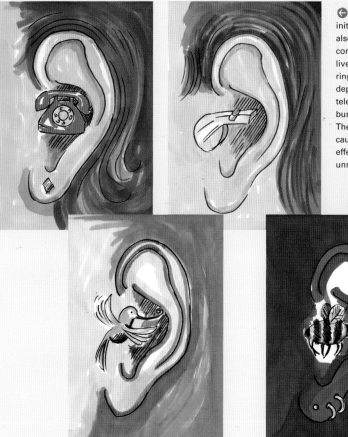

⬅ ⬇ Initial concept sheets: The initial concepts for this campaign also go straight to the point by considering what it would be like to live with tinnitus. The constant ringing or buzzing in the ears is depicted by imagining a tiny telephone, hummingbird, bumblebee, or whistle in the ear. The sense of irritation this would cause is communicated simply and effectively, making a copy line unnecessary.

continued on next page ▶

on a Mac without a huge pile of accurate renderings under their arms has missed the point.

What now?

Learning to develop good ideas and then visualizing them accurately comes only with experience, which in turn comes only with lots and lots of practice.

This is where art schools, and books like this, come in. They will offer you invaluable advice and, most importantly, an opportunity to hone both your instincts and your judgment, thus enabling you to produce the kind of art likely to get you work. Very few people attain jobs in advertising today without some kind of art-school training.

As a junior designer or art director joining an agency,

you will most likely be teamed with a copywriter and work under the supervision of the creative director. Get used to working with a partner early on, perhaps on these assignments. Many students team up when looking for work, as a sympathetic creative partnership is worth its weight in gold.

Assuming that you're already at art school, entering international student awards schemes like D&AD and Young Creatives is a particularly good way of getting valuable exposure. A great portfolio augmented with an award or two is an incredibly persuasive testament to your ability. It can also mean that, instead of having to knock on doors for a place with an ad agency, they will be knocking on yours!

When looking for a job, the three most important things you can possess are a stunning portfolio (or

Tips

- Make sure your ads work across a complete campaign.
- Learn to visualize your concepts by mastering the art of working with marker pens.
- Work up ads at full size, or as near to it as possible.
- With the exception of research, don't go near a computer until the final stage of the whole process.

Further concepts The team decide that while the initial ideas convey the irritation caused by tinnitus, they don't convey the message that people should protect their ears against it. These visuals use a witty solution to solve this problem. Tags stitched into clothes tell us how to care for them so that they will last—shouldn't ears come with the same instructions? Turning them from portrait to landscape also allows us to see more of the models' heads, making each ear less "generic."

"book"), determination, and nerve. Lots of people can help you with the first—but the last two are up to you. Some tips on presenting your work:

Keep your book short and sweet, with an emphasis on press and poster work. It's a good idea not to fill it with art that rests on absolute creative freedom. Ferraris sell themselves, but hemorrhoid cream is another matter. Restrictive briefs force creativity, and demonstrate your ability to sell products of all kinds.

When presenting your book, remember that good work speaks for itself—it shouldn't need you to explain it to make sense. If it does, either don't show it or improve on it before you do. Always ask for criticism, too, and push for it if it's not immediately forthcoming. Then adapt your book accordingly.

When arriving for an interview, don't imagine that dressing in a gorilla suit will mark you out as "creative." It won't—it will mark you out as an idiot who doesn't take the work seriously. Try being clear, concise, punctual, and well-mannered instead. People in Adland have not only seen it all before, they're always in a hurry. Just get to the point, and help them to help you.

There's always room for good, enthusiastic, and conscientious people. But if you've had a run of unsuccessful applications, remember that finding work and obtaining a satisfying career is the result of two factors: luck and slog. Stick with it, act on criticism, and keep your chin up. If this still doesn't help, remember that Jack Kerouac wrote fifteen novels before *On the Road* was published. If you're still in the doldrums and thinking of giving up, it may be that it's not for you.

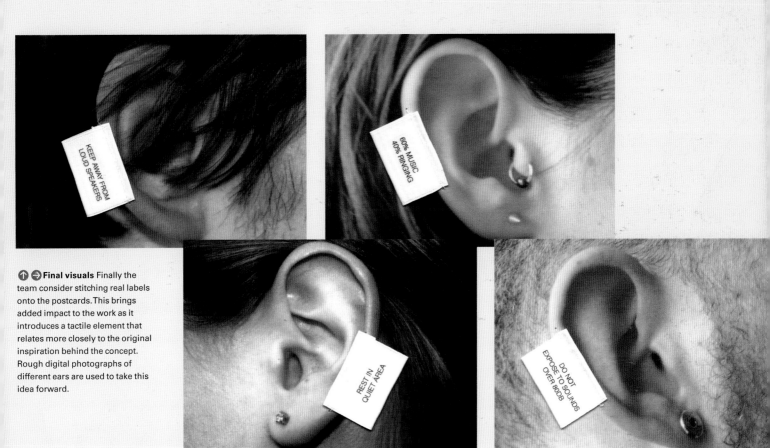

Final visuals Finally the team consider stitching real labels onto the postcards. This brings added impact to the work as it introduces a tactile element that relates more closely to the original inspiration behind the concept. Rough digital photographs of different ears are used to take this idea forward.

Finally, remember that no one is comfortable in interviews, either side of the table. It's a false situation and everyone knows it. So be yourself, and make points effectively and quickly. If you don't get the job, ask for criticism, then move on and call it practice. If you do, feel free to skip all the way home.

Tips

- Get used to working as part of a team that makes the most of each person's skills.
- Winning a student awards scheme will give your career a major boost.
- Your portfolio (or "book") should be short, strong from front to back, and contain nothing but excellent work relevant to the industry.
- A book that contains well-executed marker roughs shows that you put a premium on ideas.
- Real-life advertisements don't have someone to explain them. If your work needs explaining, it's not good enough.
- Don't be afraid to point out things in your work you'd now do differently.
- Always ask for criticism, and act upon it.
- In interviews, be clear, concise, direct, well-mannered. Take yourself, and the business, seriously.
- Don't give up.

Advertising Assignment

Client: Sanderson's stationery

Campaign and design requirements: Update the current Sanderson's range of pads and notebooks. Products in the range include standard A4 wide ruled refill pads; A4 ⅕-in square (5-mm square) ruled pads; A5 plain sketch pads; A5 wide ruled notebooks. The treatment should be concept-driven and visually appealing, and succeed in persuading people to return to Sanderson's for their stationery.

Hints: Discovering such an everyday product's USP can be difficult, as the product is readily available just about everywhere. Perhaps its USP could be the intriguing design of the packaging?

⬇ ➡ **Initial concept sheets**
The team first consider the basic nature of the products — that they are things to make marks in — and decide to look for parallels in the world around them. Road markings are a neat solution to this, as they are both made marks and part of our daily landscape. The group collect images.

Further concepts Having collected a number of images, the team then decide which road marking relates most strikingly to each product—double yellow lines for wide ruled paper; a bicycle from a cycle path for the sketchbook. They then visualize the layout of each pad. This witty pairing of ideas makes for an effective concept.

Final visuals The black-and-white photos are both strikingly effective and economic to print. It transpires that the original research photographs taken by the group in the initial stages are of such a quality that they are perfect for final artwork. And due to the fact that they've already been taken, the designers decide to produce fully finished artwork to present to the client.

A4 Standard Refill Pad

A5 Sketch Pad

A5 Notebook

A4 Squared Paper

S A4 Standard Refill Pad
Wide ruled with margin
150 sheets

S A4 Squared Paper
Square ruled 5 mm
50 sheets

S A5 Notebook
Wide ruled
44 sheets

S A5 Sketch Pad
44 sheets
90 gsm

It is very important to realize that the design of an identity program is much more than the creation of a logotype. Identity is total design. Every way in which an organization manifests itself is a part of its corporate image. The logotype is only one small part of that image, and although important, it is nothing without the support of the rest.

"

To be a good designer in the corporate sphere you must fully understand what identity systems are and what they seek to do. Many designers fail to achieve successful results because their initial premises are false; they focus on the wrong things. Often this involves far too much attention being paid to other brands in a similar market. The presumption that earlier designers got it right perpetuates poor solutions and produces uninspired, derivative work. Observation is important, however; but understanding is vital. It is an attention to detail, determination, the ability to keep asking what and why—these qualities are what make a good corporate designer.

I believe it is vital to remember that design is a verb; it is a process, and one that is generally misunderstood. Students, and even some professionals, often see design as the addition of something, a cumulative activity. In fact, it is nearly always the opposite, concerned with discovery much more than with invention. The answer to most design problems is usually to be found in asking the right questions. True, the solution is rarely evident at first, but once revealed it all too often appears obvious. Effective design is not possible without research, investigation, and analysis.

Early in my career a large design company I was working for was asked to develop an identity program for a newly privatized power utility company. The lead designers did not at first brief the junior designers with all the information they had gathered about the company. Instead they gave us a list of around twenty key words that summed up the activities, aspirations, and environments in which the organization operated. Words such as: power, energy, responsibility, national, care, service, and so on. Three or four designers were asked to make as many A4 black-and-white drawings as they could over two days, each drawing to depict one, two, or more of the words as visual images.

These drawings were to be quick, first-reaction sketches, produced one after another. At the end of this drawing period we each had between 100 and 200 drawings. We then began to sort them into types and themes. It was very interesting to see that although we had worked in isolation from each other we had made many identical drawings. These drawings provided us with a valuable insight into imagery that exists in the collective consciousness. Other drawings were unique and valuable for the opposite reason: because they revealed totally original insights into the subject matter. Once the subject was revealed we were no longer able to engage in this uninhibited process of discovery, for our knowledge always got in the way. Creative thinking becomes limited once specifics are imposed.

This brainstorming process very quickly produces a broad range of visual material appropriate to a project's development. Final results can often be traced back to these early research exercises. The material produced at this stage must be carefully sifted so as to allow its nature to become evident. Don't be too quick to reject anything, for whether ideas are relevant or not may not be clear until very much later in the process.

This way of working has over the years proved again and again to be a valuable starting point. Often it is impossible to discount what you know about a subject; instead develop initial ideas by defining the keywords, then concentrate on them without reference to any other research material.

Another important aspect of the designer's work, often overlooked, is examination of the brief. Too often designers accept briefs, without question, and seem to think that a correct solution will simply be a reflection of that brief. In practice most clients rarely know exactly what they want, and regard design as an extra, something you add at the end to make things pretty. This is, of course, an enormous mistake, and so in most cases your first job is to educate your client about the role and value of design.

Gaining clients' trust is essential for a fruitful working relationship. They must have total confidence in you and your abilities. You are providing a professional service, and you are a partner in the future success of the organization that employs you.

When presenting ideas I believe it is never wise to show more than one different idea. Two solutions can make the client feel that you have some doubts about one or even both of your designs. Even if you feel you have two effective solutions, you should make a choice. If the client does not like it you can always present the other at the next meeting.

Make sure you know who your client is. This may sound strange, but often the person you deal with day to day is not the person with whom the final decision rests. Often it is a committee that comes to a collective conclusion; these are the hardest presentations to make. Don't forget it is your meeting; you must present your work to the entire group and respond to their questions without losing control. Each will have personal prejudices that will influence their response to the work you present. Allow them to say, "I don't like blue," but don't allow this to distract you from your clearly argued explanation that this is the correct solution for the job at hand.

I never consider a project finished; identity programs are always evolving. Each year you will need to revisit aspects and see if they are still appropriate, and literature will need to be continually maintained and occasionally invigorated to keep the identity fresh.

David Phillips

⬆ **Points east** The corporate identity devised by Rick Eiber Design for upmarket florist Zen manages to combine natural touches (pale tinted leaves and undyed string) with a sophisticated use of white space. In particular, the generous letter spacing in the company name fosters a mood of calm restraint.

Woolmark

Quaker

Lufthansa

UPS

Nissay

⬆ ❷ **Classic logos and trademarks** are ones that have stood the test of time. They serve as a way of condensing complex reality into a single simple statement, one that can be controlled and modified over time.

SECTION 3 | COMMERCIAL PRACTICE

MODULE 12 | Corporate Design

UNIT 2 | **The Business of Corporate Design**

The creation of corporate identities and their associated elements is an important part of contemporary graphic design practice. Identity is difference — if we were unable to differentiate one person, product, or company from another we would be lost. Difference helps us to define the nature of things.

Long-term thinking

When creating an identity program it is essential that you seek to create something that has the ability to grow. Your designs should always be truthful, simple, and direct.

Research

The design of corporate identity programs requires you to become completely familiar with all the activities of the organization that has commissioned you. To achieve this you must ask questions, make observations, and investigate. Take photographs, make drawings, and collect similar materials. You must look at both the organization and the environment in which it operates. Talk to everyone you can, from the top of the company to the bottom. You never know where the spark for your idea will come from. Ask questions like: What functions does the company perform? Where do they perform them? Who are their customers? Why do they operate in this way? What does the future hold? What does the organization mean to you? All these questions will help

you build a picture of the organization for which you are designing.

It is important to think about the medium in which your identity is most likely to be seen; for example, an airline's logo is most prominently displayed on the tail of its aircraft, not its letterhead.

Spider diagrams

These are very useful tools for developing ideas. Starting from the center, write down all the words and ideas that you associate with the organization, its name, and its services. Then expand on these words and create more links so as to create a network of cross-related themes. These diagrams often throw up ideas or demonstrate relationships between different ideas that are not initially evident.

Corporate Image

Corporate image is more than just a mark or a typographic style. It is the total image of an organization, from the largest to the smallest part. Each part builds an image and defines that organization's presence in the world. How a company answers the telephone is as important as the color of its vehicles. In the past, to maintain their image consistently, companies issued corporate-design guidelines in the form of large books. These manuals are now less popular, as artwork and design information can be controlled and distributed on CD.

When you design a corporate image you are defining what an organization is or seeks to be. It is therefore vitally important that your design is truthful, an accurate reflection of reality.

Developing design concepts

As you gather together material about the organization and associated areas it is best in the

initial stages to make your research as broad as possible. Don't edit your material at this stage, just gather it together. Equally, don't reject any of your ideas as being too outlandish or experimental; it is too early to know yet. If your company has an existing identity, collect every use of it that you can.

Developing visual concepts

When you start to develop visual imagery you will already have some idea what to plan to do. You should, however, leave yourself open to every and any potential source of imagery. Photographs, fine art, pictures from papers and magazines, textures, colors, sounds, and even smells—they are all useful stimuli. Think about making mood boards or scrapbooks. Make reference sheets of other identities from rival firms.

Think about the organization and its purpose; try to capture its spirit. Can this be done with a mark, an object, or a color? Don't start using the computer too

⬆ **A spider diagram** is, in essence, lateral thinking in diagrammatic form. The resulting web of words enables you to make connections between apparently unconnected ideas.

Logo evolution The John Deere logo is a simple visual pun. It has changed remarkably little over the years, although the tail started to creep up fairly early on. Note that as the company became better known, it was able to pare down the amount of information incorporated into the logo.

⬅ An early-days logo.

➡ The pictorial elements are simplified.

⬅ Branding no longer states the company's location.

➡ A highly stylized treatment.

⬅ A more realistic version.

early; pen, paper, pencil, and paint are all much more direct and useful tools at this stage. Explore scale and different media, but don't think about applications yet. Don't clutter your mind with too much detail.

Presentation

When presenting an idea it is important to clearly show your development process from first concept to final design. Indeed, narrative is a useful tool, providing an immediate structure to your presentation. If you tell a story about how your design came into being it will be much more memorable. Your story should have a beginning, middle, and end. In order to appear confident, and for the thoughts to flow smoothly from one to another, make sure you practice your presentation as much as possible. Keep it short: you don't have to talk about everything you did to arrive at the finished design. A useful rule of thumb is that work should be capable of being shown on between two and six A3 boards.

Tips

Design points:
- Putting your design on to real objects is a very effective way of fixing an idea in a client's mind.
- Complex designs rarely work.
- Don't use too many colors (3 max).
- Make your design work in black and white first.

Application

Company literature should all be clearly identifiable as being from the same source. You should make a choice of a range of company fonts; these can either be a few different weights of the same font or two different fonts that work well together. More than two fonts should in general be avoided.

Software

Adobe Illustrator and Macromedia Freehand are both excellent programs for the development of identity graphics. They are excellent tools for exploring themes such as the manipulation and mutation of geometric forms.

Letterhead design and layout

The standard letter size in the United States is expressed in imperial measures: 8½ x 11 in (216 x 279 mm). In Europe, the standard letter size is nearly always laid out on an A4 sheet of paper (8¼ x 11¾ in, 210 x 297 mm). These are the standard sizes for all business correspondence in the West. When designing a letterhead it is important to remember that these sheets will always be seen by the organization's customers with text on it. Often students design a letterhead without ever checking how normal word-processed text looks in combination with it, or considering where such text might be placed.

It is typical to fold a letter into thirds before placing it into an envelope. Think how this will affect the positioning of your letterhead. The body of the letter should not begin until a third of the way down the sheet of paper. Above that first fold is usually the most appropriate location for the company name and logotype. The company address and the address of the person for whom the letter is intended should also be placed in this area.

The margin on the left of the page should be at least 1⅛ in (30 mm); this is to allow space for the letterhead to be hole-punched for filing. Business details that are required by law, such as company registration numbers and names of directors, can be accommodated at the base of the page.

Other than adhering to the above there is no absolute fixed format, and indeed it is perfectly possible to run a letterhead up the side of a page—this might be particularly effective if the company was trying to promote a funky, design-conscious image. But it is also worth thinking about the length of letter a particular organization might produce. Lawyers often write long letters that cover many pages, whereas stores rarely write more than a few paragraphs.

EXERCISE

Logo design

Design a corporate logo for "Tiger Security Systems." First, jot down words that you associate with "Tiger" and "Security," or construct a spider diagram. Do some quick sketches and search for the essence of the brand. Apply your logo to a letterhead, uniform, and livery.

Corporate Assignment

Client: Elephant Plant Hire

Elephant Plant Hire hires mechanical plants for use on building sites and other construction projects. The items they hire range from hand power tools and compressors to earth-moving machinery and large cranes. The environment in which the company works is dirty and tough. The company is a new creation formed from the merging of two existing companies. The name has many strong positive associations, and it is unlike its competitors.

Remember, elephants are strong, trustworthy, dependable, cute, and they never forget. Although there is an obvious temptation to depict the animal it may not be necessary or desirable.

Design requirements: The identity program should be suitable for use on all the machines that the company owns. In addition it should also work on letterheads, business cards, and other items of business stationery. The identity program is required both to identify ownership and promote the company.

Technical requirements: The program should be suitable for reproduction in both color and black and white. Applications to vehicles and other three-dimensional objects should take technical restrictions into account.

⬆️ ➡️ **Bare essentials** The challenge in developing logos is to edit out extraneous details and capture the essence.

⬅️ **Existing imagery** As a source of inspiration it is worthwhile to create a mood board, pinning up elephant pictures from as many different sources as possible.

continued on next page ▶

Tips

- Think about the nature of the service the company provides.
- Picture where the identity is most likely to be seen.
- Plan which methods of application might be used.
- Whatever method you employ the cost will have implications.
- The best designs are simple and unique.
- If you take away an element of your design the core message should still be discerned.
- Don't go straight to your computer.
- Drawing is a valuable development tool.

The abstract
approach—in which the
geometry of machine
parts serves as the basis
for logo development—
contrasts with those that
see the Elephant name as
the company's USP.

This neat graphic solution
works well in two dimensions.
Coloring the elephant pink is a
clever way of linking the design
to an image that already exists
in people's minds in relation to
"elephant."

ELEPHANT

elephant E

ELEPHANT PLANT HIRE LIMITED

23/10/02

our reference 0987654/wr
your reference 23456/04/ty

Elephant House
6 Tusk Street
London W1 7BB

t +44 (0)20 1234 5678
f +44 (0)20 1234 8765

elephant

Elephant House
6 Tusk Street
London W1 7BB

t +44 (0)20 1234 5678
f +44 (0)20 1234 8765

Ronald Brown-Smith   23/10/02
Big Building plc

elephant

Elephant House
6 Tusk Street
London W1 7BB

t +44 (0)20 1234 5678
f +44 (0)20 1234 8765

23/10/02   Ronald Brown-Smith
                Big Building plc
                125 Brick Lane
                London EC2 7XV

Dear Ronald

Foemata reddit, scire velim, chartis pretium quotus arroget annus. scriptor abhinc
annos centum qui decidit, inter perfectos veteresque referri debet an inter vilis
atque novos? Excludat iurgia finis, "Est vetus atque probus, centum qui perficit
annos." Quid, qui deperit minor uno mense vel anno, inter quos referendus erit?
Veteresne poetas, an quos et praesens et postera respuat aetas?

"Iste quidem veteres inter ponetur honeste, qui vel mense brevi vel toto est
iunior anno." Utor permisso, caudaeque pilos ut equinae paulatim vello unum,
demo etiam unum, dum cadat elusus ratione ruentis acervi, qui redit in fastos et
virtutem aestimat annis miraturque nihil nisi quod Libitina sacravit.

Ennius et sapines et fortis et alter Homerus, ut critici dicunt, leviter curare videtur,
quo promissa cadant et somnia Pythagorea. Naevius in manibus non est et
mentibus haeret paene recens? Adeo sanctum est vetus omne poema. ambigitur
quotiens, uter utro sit prior, aufert Pacuvius docti famam senis Accius alti, dicitur
Afrani toga convenisse Menandro, Plautus ad exemplar Siculi properare Epicharmi,
vincere Caecilius gravitate, Terentius arte.

Hos ediscit et hos arto stipata theatro spectat Roma potens; habet hos numeratque
poetas ad nostrum tempus Livi scriptoris ab aevo.

Looking forward to getting your cheque.

Yours sincerely

Fred Smith

Elephant Plant Hire Limited
Registered in the UK
Company number 12345678
vat registration 976 54321

23/10/02

our reference 0987654/wr
your reference 23456/04/ty

elephant

Elephant House
6 Tusk Street
London W1 7BB

t +44 (0)20 1234 5678
f +44 (0)20 1234 8765

Ronald Brown-Smith
Big Building plc
125 Brick Lane
London EC2 7XV

Dear Ronald

Meliora dies, ut vina, poemata reddit, scire velim, chartis pretium quotus
arroget annus. scriptor abhinc annos centum qui decidit, inter perfectos
veteresque referri debet an inter vilis atque novos? Excludat iurgia finis,
"Est vetus atque probus, centum qui perficit annos." Quid, qui deperit
minor uno mense vel anno, inter quos referendus erit? Veteresne poetas,
an quos et praesens et postera respuat aetas?

"Iste quidem veteres inter ponetur honeste, qui vel mense brevi vel toto
est iunior anno." Utor permisso, caudaeque pilos ut equinae paulatim
vello unum, demo etiam unum, dum cadat elusus ratione ruentis acervi,
qui redit in fastos et virtutem aestimat annis miraturque nihil nisi quod
Libitina sacravit.

Ennius et sapines et fortis et alter Homerus, ut critici dicunt, leviter curare
videtur, quo promissa cadant et somnia Pythagorea. Naevius in manibus
non est et mentibus haeret paene recens? Adeo sanctum est vetus omne
poema. ambigitur quotiens, uter utro sit prior, aufert Pacuvius docti
famam senis Accius alti, dicitur Afrani toga convenisse Menandro,
Plautus ad exemplar Siculi properare Epicharmi, vincere Caecilius
gravitate, Terentius arte.

Hos ediscit et hos arto stipata theatro spectat Roma potens; habet hos
numeratque poetas ad nostrum tempus Livi scriptoris ab aevo.

Looking forward to getting your cheque.

Yours sincerely

Fred Smith

Elephant Pla
Registered i
Company nu
12345678
vat registrati

Dear Ronald

Welim, chartis pretium quotus arroget annus. scriptor abhinc annos
centum qui decidit, inter perfectos veteresque referri debet an inter vilis
atque novos? Excludat iurgia finis, "Est vetus atque probus, centum qui
perfict annos." Quid, qui deperit minor uno mense vel anno, inter quos
referendus erit? Veteresne poetas, an quos et praesens et postera
respuat aetas?

"Iste quidem veteres inter ponetur honeste, qui vel mense brevi vel
toto est iunior anno." Utor permisso, caudaeque pilos ut equinae paulatim

Ronald Brown-Smith
Big Building plc
125 Brick Lane
London EC2 7XV

Dear Ronald

Peliora dies, ut vina, poemata reddit, scire velim, chartis pretium
quotus arroget annus. scriptor abhinc annos centum qui decidit,
inter perfectos veteresque referri debet an inter vilis atque novos?
Excludat iurgia finis, "Est vetus atque probus, centum qui perficit
annos." Quid, qui deperit minor uno mense vel anno, inter quos

ELEPHANT PLANT HIRE LIMITED

23/10/02   Ronald Brown-Smith   Elephan
                Big Building plc   6 Tusk
                125 Brick Lane   Londor
                London EC2 7XV
                                          t +44 (0
                                          f +44 (0

Dear Ronald

Gneliora dies, ut vina, poemata reddit, scire velim, chartis pretium
quotus arroget annus. scriptor abhinc annos centum qui decidit,
inter perfectos veteresque referri debet an inter vilis atque novos?
Excludat iurgia finis, "Est vetus atque probus, centum qui perficit
annos." Quid, qui deperit minor uno mense vel anno, inter quos
referendus erit? Veteresne poetas, an quos et praesens et postera
respuat aetas?

"Iste quidem veteres inter ponetur honeste, qui vel mense brevi vel
toto est iunior anno." Utor permisso, caudaeque pilos ut equinae
paulatim vello unum, demo etiam unum, dum cadat elusus ratione
ruentis acervi, qui redit in fastos et virtutem aestimat annis
miraturque nihil nisi quod Libitina sacravit.

Ennius et sapines et fortis et alter Homerus, ut critici dicunt, leviter
curare videtur, quo promissa cadant et somnia Pythagorea. Naevius
in manibus non est et mentibus haeret paene recens? Adeo sanctum
est vetus omne poema. ambigitur quotiens, uter utro sit prior, aufert
Pacuvius docti famam senis Accius alti, dicitur Afrani toga convenisse
Menandro, Plautus ad exemplar Siculi properare Epicharmi, vincere
Caecilius gravitate, Terentius arte.

Hos ediscit et hos arto stipata theatro spectat Roma potens; habet
hos numeratque poetas ad nostrum tempus Livi scriptoris ab aevo.

Looking forward to getting your cheque.

Yours sincerely

Fred Smith

A selection of finished letterheads The most
successful are those that combine loose sketch
drawings with cool modern type. This makes the
company seem trustworthy and reliable, as well as
fun and innovative.

UNIT 1 | **Seminar: Professional Pointers**

The world of web design is a varied place occupied by all sorts of artists, designers, and programmers. As someone with an interest in web design, you should, at first, try not to be put off by all the jargon and complicated language—you will learn this as you go along, and overall it is very much a case of learning to crawl, walk, and then run. Creating a website can be very straightforward, and if you follow the assignment on pages 172–5 you will learn to do just that.

"The industry ranges from those who are part of large teams of developers and designers, looking after, for example, the huge BBC Online site(s), to individuals wanting to create their own site. Obviously a huge space exists in between these extremes. The skills you need to develop as a designer will be determined by where you want to sit within this range. Assuming you are working on a large site you may have a very particular role within the team—perhaps editing and uploading images with minor text changes. If this is the case, a basic understanding of software such as Dreamweaver and Photoshop would probably suffice. On the other hand, you might end up developing online shopping applications, in which case a much more extensive knowledge of programming languages would be needed.

The key to any successful website has to be understanding your audience. All too often websites showcase a designer's software skills and cutting-edge graphics, with precious little thought to which people are using the site and what for. There is nothing wrong with pushing those boundaries, just don't forget to consider the end user: design for the audience and not for yourself. Over the next few pages we will consider some of the key issues, followed by an assignment that you can work through to design your own website.

www.giraffecards.com
Certain sections of the site allow users to download related information in PDF format.

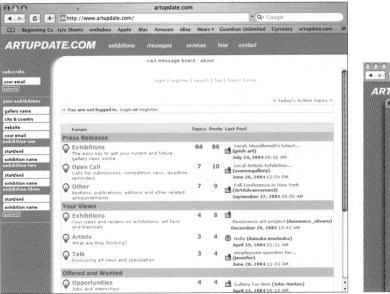

 **www.artupdate.com**
Existing users employ
"forms" to subscribe. A CGI
script handles the delivery of
the information to the
artupdate office.

Programming language

My first involvement with web design
came when a friend who had been studying computer
programming asked if I could design the interface to a
website. At the time, the Internet was relatively new,
and for me the challenge was all about getting
something to look great using a very limited palette of
colors across a very small pixel area. The project went
well and we collaborated on other things. Then along
came software such as Macromedia Dreamweaver,
which made the idea of learning a programming
language such as HTML achievable to those who, like
me, lacked a traditional computer science or
programming background.

I now spend most of my time on arts- and design-
based websites. One example, www.giraffecards.com,
is a simple site, pitched at all users accessing the site
from a range of computers (it works on all main
browsers with a slow connection). The site functions as
an information point for those users wanting to find out
more about www.giraffecards.com's printing services.

Navigation

Clients have recently been requesting
database-driven sites, which typically allow for
updating in house. A current example is
www.artupdate.com. At the time of writing, I am giving
the site a complete makeover. From very humble
beginnings, it has grown enormously and now
provides artworld information to thousands of
subscribers fortnightly. This is ideal for a database
website. Users will be able to log in and access relevant
information; meanwhile, artupdate staff will be able to
avoid many repetitive and mundane data-entry tasks.
The site makeover is at an early stage at the moment, so
above are some existing screen shots. Have a look at
www.artupdate.com and perhaps by the time you see
it, the site will be database-driven. See if you can figure
out the differences and, I hope, benefits of the changes.
After all, once you have learnt the basics of making a
site you will most probably want to move to database-
driven sites yourself.

Chris Jones

UNIT 2 | **Planning a Website**

Web design is no different from any other design process: the more organized you are the more successful you will be. In the first instance you should begin to plan your site on paper (or computer). Careful planning will save you considerable time. The main purpose of this planning is to carefully map out the site architecture. Understand how the site will allow the user to try to move around the content, and then anticipate how the user might like to move through the site. An easy-to-navigate site is essential to success.

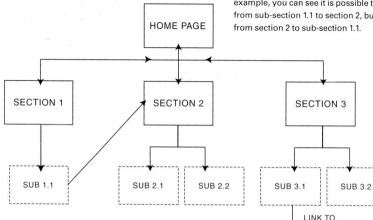

Website map The diagram illustrates the website sections, main subsections and the routes of navigation between pages. So, for example, you can see it is possible to travel from sub-section 1.1 to section 2, but not from section 2 to sub-section 1.1.

Logistics
• Ensure that you fully understand what the website is required to do and that you have access to all relevant content to build your site.
• Consider the hosting of the site early on, as this may well affect certain aspects of how you build it.

Aesthetic considerations
• Screen size: Who is the audience, and thus on what size screen will the site need to be seen?
• File types: Are plug-ins available for the audience to allow Flash or Quicktime?
• Font size: Are there any special requirements for larger font sizes?
• Browser compatibility: consider the target audience and the browsers from which they will most likely be visiting the site.

Consider the following:
• Hierarchy: How many levels will the site have?
• Navigation: How will the user move between pages?
• Assets: What images and text will need to be generated to populate the site?
• Domain: Will a domain name need to be registered?
• Host: Where will the site be hosted?

Aesthetics: screen size
Keep in mind the fact that different viewers will visit your website using monitors with different screen resolutions. There are many different screen resolutions but the most widely available are 640 x 480 pixels, 800 x 600 pixels, and 1024 x 768 pixels. Most "mainstream" sites are designed for viewing on an 800 x 600 pixel screen.

Don't forget, while you might be designing your website around the standard screen pixel resolutions, you still need to allow for the browser—toolbar, address bar, scrollbars—and different browsers have different dimensions for each of these elements.

Safe recommendations that allow for the browser attributes are (in pixels): 640 x 480 = 599w 290h; 800 x 600 = 759w 410h; and 1024 x 768 = 983w 578h.

Image formats: JPEGs and GIFs
Various image formats are available for use on the web, the most widely used being JPEGs and GIFs. But a major consideration in choosing the file type is the type of information you are saving. JPEG files can contain millions of colors and are therefore good for saving photographic information. But one thing to remember is that some loss of quality is inevitable when saving, because color information is reduced in order to make the file size smaller.

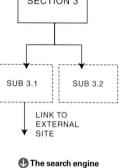

The search engine www.google.com is a good illustration of a site viewable by all, but with different screen resolutions you see more or less white space.

640 x 480px

800 x 600px

1024 x 768px

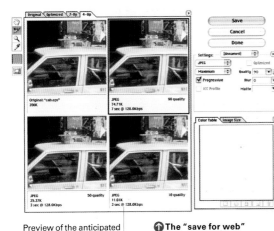

Preview of the anticipated download time, based on modem speed.

↑ **The "save for web" function** in Adobe Photoshop allows you to see the image based on a range of quality settings.

Image saved as a JPG

Image saved as an 8-color GIF

⬇ **Which type?** Within the families of serif, sans serif, and monotype, the fonts listed below are those recommended for web graphics: almost all computers have them. Serif fonts are generally used within print—the serifs at the end of each character help your eye move across the page. Sans serif type is generally more legible for screen viewing as it has no serifs, and is therefore less distracting to the eye.

Serif
Times
Times New Roman
Georgia

Sans Serif
Arial
Helvetica
Verdana

Monotype
Courier
Courier New

GIF files have a reduced color palette by comparison and so are particularly good for recording solid areas of color information such as single-color logos or buttons. GIF can also be used to record transparency and animation sequences.

In both cases, it is very important to try and keep file size to a minimum. Much depends on the audience for your website. If, for example, you are designing a site that will be accessed by a wide variety of people from all over the world you will need to consider that not everyone will be on a high-speed Internet connection using the latest PC or Mac. Using the Photoshop "save for web" option is a very good way of visualizing the final image quality and anticipated download time for a variety of internet connection speeds. Generally speaking, images should be saved at 72 dpi at the final pixel dimension (don't resize images from within programs such as Dreamweaver).

Fonts

The main thing to bear in mind here is that viewers will only be able to see your website in the typeface you have chosen if they have that particular font installed on their computer. For this reason, when designing your site you are advised to stay within certain font families: serif, sans serif, or Monotype.

So what happens if you include a font that the viewer does not have installed? As most web browsers have the default setting of Times or Times New Roman, if a specified font is not available, or if you do not specify a different font within the HTML code, type will be displayed in Times or Times New Roman.

There are numerous ways of specifying the font size; perhaps the most common method is to give a value of between 1 and 7, where 1 is the smallest and 7 the largest, with size 3 being equivalent to 12 pt. Over the last couple of years a system called Cascading Style Sheets has become widely adopted by web designers as a way to control fonts, among other things.

Cascading style sheets

A style sheet is a set of instructions that tells the web browser how to present a page. Style sheets can control many elements of the website design, including font, background images, image positions, and text alignment. This is not the place to explain every aspect of using Cascading Style Sheets so we will just look at some of the basic typographic control elements at the end of our assignment (see page 173). Should you require further reading check out the resources in the bibliography (page 187).

Designing for different browsers and platforms

Unlike designing for print, designing a web page is never a completely controllable process. Different computers and different browsers will all affect how the web page is displayed. One of the first issues to be aware of is Gamma (the brightness of the screen). Simply put, information appears darker on PCs than on Macs, so any graphic you design on a PC will look rather washed out on a Mac. In addition, Macs and PCs have different default character-width size, meaning that text and images tend to look slightly larger on Macs.

There are many ways of surfing the Internet, most typically using a computer and a browser such as Internet Explorer or Netscape Navigator. But there are many other browsers—Safari, Opera, and Mozilla are just a few—and devices other than a regular computer: WebTV, smart phones, and PDAs. Ideally you want your site to work across all browsers and devices, but in practice you may have to construct different sites for use by different browsers or devices. You should continually check your site as you design it by viewing it on different browsers and have a thorough understanding of the audience for which the site is being built. For example, a home shopping website that does not take into account the needs of the WebTV user will certainly lose custom.

American Airlines reservations — as seen by Internet Explorer.

American Airlines reservations — as seen by Opera.

American Airlines reservations — as seen by Safari.

Browser variables Notice how different browsers render the form. Some differences are quite subtle such as the box to enter the city & airport, varying in width and height on all browsers. Other differences are more apparent such as how 'Opera' renders the background.

Static versus dynamic

Websites and web pages can be written in numerous languages, but HTML is a good place to start. HyperText Markup Language is the most popular language used on the Internet. Using HTML, you are able to build documents (web pages) with text, images, sounds, and links to other pages—in short, a website.

The Internet has come a long way since its first emergence, one major difference in many of today's websites being that they are dynamic rather than static. The principal difference is that in a dynamic site, the web server creates the page on demand. Amazon.com is a good example. When you search for a book within Amazon the page you get delivered is generated on the fly, based on your search criteria. Text and images are pulled into a pre-programmed template, delivering you the relevant information. Compare this with a static website, in which each page is required to be designed and exist on the server before the information for a particular book can be presented.

Interfaces and navigation

Designing for the web is not the same as designing for print: pages not only have to look great, but work across a range of devices and browsers; they must also be straightforward to navigate and intuitive—that is, you should know what to click on and where to look without being told. This is where the interface design becomes extremely important and you, as the designer, can make a big difference.

One standard feature within most sites is the menu, presented normally as either a row across the top of the

page (www.apple.com), or maybe a column down the page (www.cnn.com). Either way, it must be prominent.

Another option is to use frames that allow two or more pages to be presented at the same time, with the menu remaining visible while the "content" area scrolls. Alternatively, you can employ drop-down or fly-out menus, as demonstrated on the American Airlines website (www.aa.com).

Making your page layouts consistent will help the user navigate through your site. Navigation menus should always be in the same place and follow the same format. And make sure you are aware of the conventions that already exist: underlined blue text, for example, is frequently used to indicate a link, so it would not be a good idea to use underlined blue text for decorative reasons—the user will mistakenly assume your links don't work.

⊙ **Drop-down** or fly-out menus are a popular option, as indicated on the American Airlines website.

⊙ **Site using frames** A framed site allows, in this example, the forms on the left and the menu at the top to remain in place whilst the "content" scrolls.

⊙ **Notice the URL** Unlike the usual "www.domainname.com" the URL contains many numbers and characters, which is a good indicator that the site is dynamic.

⊙ **Horizontal menu** On the Apple website (www.apple.com) the menu bar runs along the top of the page.

⊙ **Vertical menu** The CNN website (www.cnn.com) employs a menu running down the left-edge of the screen.

Web-Design Assignment

Project: Basic portfolio website

Software specifications: In this assignment we are going to produce a basic portfolio website for your images. The methods described are based on using Macromedia Dreamweaver MX2004 on a Mac running OS10.3. Macromedia Dreamweaver is available as a 30-day free download from macromedia.com. Much more extensive tutorials are also provided on the Macromedia website.

The example presented here is a very basic beginning and should be used as more of a starting-point than an end-product. You might want to consider adding information to each page about the images presented. The navigation also needs work, so that the viewer can go back to the index page.

1 Create a folder on your desktop, naming it "website." Inside this folder, make two more folders named "images" and "css." If you already have some images these should be saved at the relevant size and placed into the "images" folder. Now make a thumbnail (smaller) version for each image, and save them with the following naming conventions:
image1.jpg thm_image1.jpg
image2.jpg thm_image2.jpg
image3.jpg thm_image3.jpg
Repeat the process for six images.

2 Open Dreamweaver and select SITE > NEW SITE. Press the ADVANCED tab and enter as "My First Site." Below this you will see "Local Route Folder" and a folder icon. Click on the folder icon and navigate to the folder (website) you made in Step 1. Once you choose this folder a website caché will be created (press OK), and you are now ready to build your website.

3 Create a new page NEW > DOCUMENT and choose BASIC HTML. This will generate an empty page. The first page of your site must be saved as index.html, or index.htm, because almost all web hosts are set up to recognize the first page as index.html. So go to SAVE AS, and save the file into your folder WEBSITE as index.htm, or index.html. Now create six more new documents and save them as 1.htm (or 1.html), 2.htm. 3.htm, etc. These should also be saved into your folder named "website."

4 We are going to start by inserting a table into the index page. Open index.htm and go to INSERT >TABLE. Choose six columns and three rows with a width of 500 pixels. Set the cell pad, space, and border to 0 and press OK.

5 Click in the top left cell and go to INSERT > IMAGE and browse your folders to find the thumbnail images you saved earlier. Insert thm_image1.jpg. Move to the second cell and insert thumbnail 2, and so on, until you have inserted all thumbnail images.

website ▶		css ▷
		images ▷

1

website			
	1.htm	image1.jpg	
	2.htm	image2.jpg	
	3.htm	image3.jpg	
	4.htm	image4.jpt	
	5.htm	image5.jpg	
	6.htm	image6.jpg	
	css ▷	thm_image1.jpg	
	images ▶	thm_image2.jpg	
	index.htm	thm_image3.jpg	
		thm_image4.jpg	
		thm_image5.jpg	
		thm_image6.jpg	

3

4

5

6 Clicking in the bottom left cell, drag across the bottom row, highlighting the bottom set of cells.

7 Then go to MODIFY >TABLE > MERGE CELLS. This will merge the cells into one cell allowing you space to type some words about your work.

8 You now need to turn each image into a link to the relevant page. Thumbnail image 1 will link to 1.html, thumbnail 2 to 2.html, etc. To do this, click on thumbnail image. In the properties box (WINDOW > PROPERTIES) click on the folder and navigate to 1.htm, thereby creating a link between the small thumbnail image and the page. Repeat the process for each image. Save the document, FILE > SAVE.

9 Open 1.htm and insert the large image: INSERT > IMAGE and browse your folders to find image1.jpg. Save the file and repeat for 2, 3, 4, 5, and 6.htm. If it is not already open, then open index.htm and go to FILE > PREVIEW IN BROWSER, choose a browser and test your site. Assuming everything has been set up correctly, you will have a simple website.

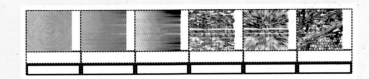

6

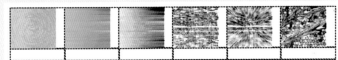

Add a few words all about the images above.
There are options to modify the font and size available in the PROPERTIES window (WINDOW, PROPERTIES).
Pressing a RETURN creates a

double space.

Pressing SHIFT, RETURN
creates a single space

7

Src	ges/thm_image1.jpg	⊕ 📁
Link	1.htm	⊕ 📁

8

Try this

Open 1.htm and click below the image.
Type BACK
Now highlight the
word BACK and in the properties box click on the folder and navigate to index.htm. The word BACK should now appear underlined (as above), and link directly to the index.
Repeat this step on 2, 3, 4, 5, and 6.htm

BACK

One final thing

Dreamweaver comes with pre-built Cascading Style Sheets (CSS). To add a style go to FILE > NEW and choose CSS STYLE SHEETS > BASIC ARIAL. Save the file into the CSS folder you made in Step 1. To attach the style to your page, open index.htm and go to WINDOW > CSS STYLES. Click the top right tab and select ATTACH STYLE SHEET. Open index.htm and ensure LINK is pressed. Then select OK. The text on the index page should now be in Arial font.

```
▼ Design
CSS Styles | Layers
[no styles defined]
```

Go to Code
New...
Edit...
Duplicate...
Rename...
Apply
Delete

Use External Editor

Attach Style Sheet...
Export...
Design-time...

Help

Group CSS Styles with   ▶
Rename Panel Group...
Maximize panel group
Close panel group

Add a few words all about the images above.
There are options to modify the font and size available int the PROPERTIES window (WINDOW, PROPERTIES).
Pressing a RETURN creates a

double space.

Pressing SHIFT, RETURN
creates a single space

UNIT 1 **Seminar: Professional Pointers**

Encounters with packaging are, for most of us, an everyday experience. A typical grocery store stocks about 30,000 to 40,000 packaged items, and it is in this environment that competition for consumer attention is most intense. If you are, or aspire to be, a packaging designer, this is where your work is likely to be found. The grocery store has become the packaging design gallery where horrors and delights abound. Go and look—what works and what does not?

"If it's not seen, it won't be bought"

" I am fortunate to work in an occupation that continues to fascinate me, as a teacher and consultant. During my time at the international design consultancy, Siebert Head, we worked with some of the world's leading brands, an enviable portfolio of clients in a competitive business. Big brands, however, inevitably require a delicate touch, design subtleties that move the brand forward in an evolutionary, rather than revolutionary, way. This was evident in our redesign of the Mars logo. It needed increased standout to compete against growing competition yet could not incorporate radical changes that might confuse brand loyal consumers. Smaller companies and new brands, by contrast, often allow the designer to have greater creative freedom.

Identifying target markets can lead into unfamiliar areas. A pan-European project for Proctor & Gamble's Camay shower gel revealed national differences that had to be reflected in the packaging, while still presenting an integrated Camay family. In Italy shower gel was precious—the container selected was only 110ml. In Germany, however, they needed a big 1-litre container.

As a marketing tool, packaging design is a cost-effective method of gaining market share and explains why many packs are frequently revised in addition to introducing new concepts. This fast turnaround is good news for designers seeking a career in packaging. "

Bill Stewart

◀ **Take account of the curves**
Typography and graphics are designed to work in harmony with the tub shape.

In the FMCG (fast-moving consumer goods) sector, represented by the bulk of products stocked by grocery stores, many packaged products represent a low-cost purchase. Here, consumers can experiment with products and brands with little risk. Unlike buying a DVD player, for example, where the higher cost demands our higher involvement in comparing specifications and appearance between brands, we have a lower involvement with grocery goods. In addition, the DVD player is a long-term purchase, unlike groceries, which are bought frequently, often on a daily or weekly basis. This means that in the grocery store, brands have to work hard to gain our attention—to sell themselves from the shelves with or without advertising support.

In designing packaging, the crucial factor is to create standout appeal. If you do not see the brand or product as you scan the shelves, you are unlikely to buy it.

Integrating shape with graphics creates powerful branding

A key packaging design opportunity is the ability to achieve product differentiation and brand recognition through the use of shape. The triangular Toblerone carton, Perrier mineral water bottle, Ben and Jerry's ice-cream tub, and the waisted Coca-Cola bottle, are examples where the shapes are so distinctive that they instantly identify the brand without recourse to reading the label. Through the manipulation of shape and selection of materials we can also build in consumer benefits, creating features that may, for example, assist product dispensing, handling, or storage. These, in themselves, may make the pack stand out, encouraging initial and repeat purchase, perhaps, as was the case with the Toilet Duck pack, establishing a product sector standard that competitors were forced to address.

Strong brand identity
Clear, graphic branding, which has changed very little over the years.

Build a profile of the target audience

Success in packaging design is not about winning design awards, although, for a student in particular, that is certainly a rung on the ladder to a design career. Packaging is really concerned with increasing product sales through effective promotion of products and brands, while still maintaining the basic functions of product protection and containment. For FMCG goods, in particular, clients are increasingly looking for innovative packaging solutions, combining technological advances in materials and techniques with graphics designed to target niche markets. For example, one of the fastest-growing market sectors is ready-to-cook meals, where packaging of increasingly varied product offerings is a key factor in expanding the market, recognizing the needs of a time-poor/cash-rich market sector. The drivers behind this are demographic, social, and cultural changes. Any design student should engage with such changes, for the ability to understand changing lifestyles is a key factor in the design process. Society today increasingly moves seamlessly across previously taboo barriers of age, race, gender, religion, and class. We live in a world where we aspire to dreams that are, in part at least, attainable. As designers, we should recognize that, for example, the majority of Harley Davidson motorcycle buyers are 50-plus males. Their motivation is aspirational, seeking freedom, rebellion, and power perhaps denied to them in their youth through cultural taboos or financial pressures. Translating this into graphic imagery, we are not portraying old folk on motorcycles but selling a dream of rebellion. No matter how slick or skillful graphic presentation may be, successful packaging design requires this level of understanding to underpin communication of the big idea to the target audience.

Brands seek innovation

Technological advances are now playing an important role in packaging design. We have to consider how packaging will sell from the screen as well as the shelf, recognizing the impact of Internet-based home shopping. The use of thermo-chromic inks and color-changing pigments extend graphic possibilities, and soon packs will incorporate moving images and sound. While graphic-design students need to immerse themselves in all aspects of design, for packaging applications, new developments in materials and methods also have to be monitored in response to the demands of brand innovation.

Packaging as a career

Above all, packaging designers need to have a passion for design. That entails reading books, magazines, and web-based information. It means being curious, critical, and observant. All design disciplines involve an interaction with people, so it follows that designers need to achieve an understanding of people and their lifestyles. Most commercial design agencies will assign a team to a project, under the supervision of a studio manager. It would be normal practice for the team to briefed together before breaking to work individually on concepts. Team meetings will then be held to critique the ideas that each designer is proposing. Remember that there is seldom just one design solution to a problem and the studio will be seeking a breadth of conceptual thinking.

Packaging with personality
Packaging for a range of noodles uses the shape of the tub to create a memorable example of branding.

UNIT 2 | **Developing Brands**

The assignments that follow are typical of those undertaken commercially by packaging designers, but whatever the project might be, the approach remains the same, working on a stage-by-stage basis.

The brief

All projects begin with a brief provided by the client, often by the marketing department or brand manager. Frequently, a client's written brief will be expanded upon verbally. As your work will be judged against the agreed brief, it is essential that all aspects are fully documented. Keep detailed notes.

Tip

Read and reread the brief. Keep checking your design work to ensure it meets the brief.

Research

Before design work starts, an in-depth understanding of the target audience is required. This usually means going beyond the information outlined in the brief, and involves the designer in researching target audience lifestyles. The objective is to identify with and relate to the group of consumers in question in order to understand their habits, wants, desires, and motivations. It is a matter of "getting under the skin" of the target to the extent that their behavior can be predicted. Typically, it can be helpful to know:

- Brands that they buy
- Where they live—apartment/house
- What cars they drive
- What food they eat
- What fashions they follow
- What type of vacations they take
- What sort of relationships they may have
- What TV/magazines they might see/read
- What drinks they prefer

Packaging Assignment

(Brief set by Nicola Miller, Smirnoff Ice, for the D&AD student competition, Corus Steel Packaging-Design Awards)

Client: Smirnoff Ice

Brief: Design a new container for Smirnoff Ice that will appeal to males aged 18–24 years. The design needs to reflect Smirnoff Ice's positioning as a drink that is ahead of the game and edgy—unexpected, masculine, and with a "dark" excitement value.

Background: The original Smirnoff Ice has a classic taste of lemon, and Smirnoff Black Ice is a citrus blend with a crispier, drier bite. Both are lightly carbonated and served chilled. Currently, Smirnoff Ice comes in two different formats: bottle and can. Although Smirnoff Ice is a market leader and considered the most masculine of the RTD market there is a need to broaden the category and attract new consumers, particularly males.

Brand proposition: A crisp, refreshing drink with a sharp edge due to the pure triple-distilled Smirnoff Vodka.

Target audience: Males aged 18–24 years. They accept Smirnoff Ice as a brand that they have tried but do not drink regularly. They currently think Smirnoff Ice is like every other sweet drink in a bottle, and at present will only drink Smirnoff Ice at the end of a night when they are full with beer. This group respects innovation and differentiation.

Technical design considerations:
- The design should be for a new container for Smirnoff Ice.
- Smirnoff Ice is consumed at home or in a bar while standing/dancing and therefore must be easy to hold.
- The design needs to be significantly different from what is currently available in the RTD market.
- The packaging needs to communicate Smirnoff Ice's positioning as a premium brand with a refreshing taste.
- The structural and functional aspects of the design should be the focus rather than just the graphics.
- Smirnoff Ice has a shelf life of nine months.
- Steel offers advantages such as formability, a metallic look, conducts cold, and is fully recyclable.

Mandatories:
- The design can be either for a container that holds 275 ml (for bar/pub consumption) or 300 ml (for home consumption).
- The current logo must be included.
- The primary material must be steel.

Hints: The key task in this assignment lies in understanding how and where 18–24-year-old men would drink Smirnoff Ice. This audience has to appear "cool" both to their male companions and, importantly, to the females they seek to impress. At the same time, it cannot be too sophisticated or exclusive. It is about "street cred" and urban fashion. Get this right and the design will begin to form.

The list is by no means exhaustive but by the time the questions have been addressed and answered, a profile will emerge. As designers are working primarily in visual media, it is often preferable to illustrate lifestyles through images rather than text. Tear-sheets from magazines and photographs capture lifestyles in a succinct and meaningful way, and make good material for showing to the client.

In the Smirnoff brief included here, students could readily identify with the target.audience. Their dedication to research was amply illustrated by photographic evidence obtained at nightclubs, which, for the sake of privacy, is omitted.

Research should also consider competitor products and point-of-sale conditions.

Working in three dimensions

It is good practice to develop container shape and graphics together rather than go too far down the road of independent development. This avoids forcing graphics onto an unsympathetic shape later on. So for each structural shape you may propose that there should also be some accompanying suggestion of how graphics may be applied to it. While thumbnail-sized sketches may be fine for initial ideas, all serious design candidates should be drawn full size. Structural design, particularly where molded plastic or glass containers are involved, is highly influenced by the choice of curves and radii. Subtle changes in curvature have dramatic effects upon appearance and so it is important that this is accurately captured in any sketches. Some students feel compelled to rush to the Apple Mac from the outset. For the sake of speed (important in a commercial project) and to avoid creativity being dominated by technological limitations, it is both much faster and less inhibiting to generate a wide range of initial concepts in sketch format. Favored design candidates can be worked up later.

It is useful, particularly for designers new to three-dimensional work or packaging design, to collect

Tip

Draw serious design candidates at actual size. Use French curves for accuracy. Show front elevation and base "footprint."

Research This mood board, just one of several developed for this project, communicates the target audience in an immediate and highly visual way, needing little additional explanation. The designer has included lifestyle information about the target audience here, showing fashion, attitude, and the motivating interest in fast cars and motorbikes.

Initial concepts Showing the existing container in sketch work is a good way of creating both a benchmark to work from and indicating scale. While these are roughs, consideration of both shape and graphics is already taking place as integrated design features. This is the preferred technique rather than trying to force the branding onto an unsympathetic shape later.

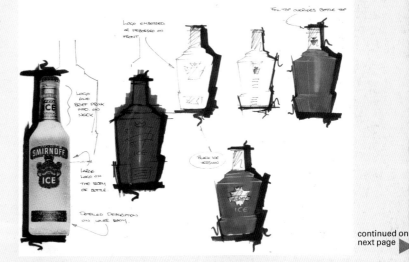

continued on next page ▶

examples of packs produced in the materials you are considering for the project. So if the pack is going to be a glass bottle, for example, have a good look at bottles to see how curves work in glass, what radii are used around the base and top, how closures are added, etc. There are usually good reasons, which involve the limitations of the materials and production processes, why containers appear as they are. Borrowing these features will make your design work more realistic and visually more convincing.

Your research should have indicated how products are displayed at the point of sale. From this you can decide what is the main panel of the pack, that is, the panel that the purchaser is most likely to see. It may not be the most obvious or largest surface. An ice cream tub, for example, may be displayed in a chest freezer in-store where it is the top that is seen. Clearly, in this instance, it would be a mistake to concentrate design work on the body of the tub when the top is actually performing the initial task of communicating branding

Tip

Mock up your container in any material—card or foam is often useful—to check visible panel sizes.

Explore all material options from the outset. It helps stimulate thinking and even impractical ideas may later be modified to work in another format.

and product information. Having selected the main panel, concentrate on designing for that, checking to see how much of it will be visible. If the container is curved, as would be the case for a can of beans, for example, graphics will have to work within the line of sight and not partially disappear around the circumference of the container.

Full-size mock-ups are useful, especially for any type of molded container. These are not models but simply tools to help you see how curves or molded areas will work in three dimensions.

Materials and pack forms

In some packaging design briefs, the choice of materials is open, so, for example, if the brief concerned is designing a container for honey, it would be reasonable to consider glass jars, plastic tubes, plastic jars, metal tins, or even, perhaps, ceramic pots. Each material brings its own character to the study but also its own advantages and disadvantages. Glass jars

⬆ **Refinement** While still working in sketch format and using the same basic shape, the designer begins to explore more subtle design features, in effect developing the theme of this concept. Foam models of this and other design candidates were produced to actual size to test how the container would "feel" when

being handled. Referring back to the brief, would it be credible for "cool" guys to be seen drinking from this bottle? Is it masculine enough? During the design process, we need to constantly review the requirements of the brief, testing each design proposal against the specified objectives.

⬇ **Final proposals** The earlier concepts have been refined and the shape modified to improve stability. Both product varieties have been considered, the designer producing vacuum-formed plastic models on which bottle color and graphics have been applied.

provide quality and heritage and allow sight of the product. Ceramic pots have a distinctive "home-made" feel and, if the design is attractive, consumers may reuse the containers—particularly significant if the containers carry branding that is constantly seen in its after-use role. Such brand reinforcement is a powerful tool in maintaining brands at the front of mind. Alternatively, if plastic tubes were considered, honey could be squeezed directly onto toast, positioning honey in a less traditional role, offering convenience and an element of fun rather than focusing on heritage.

For designers with a graphic design background, it is useful to think of material selection as an extension of the graphic palette. Not only are the usual graphic tools available, but now there is also a new toolbox to use, containing materials with differing properties and emotional meanings—surface finishes, textures, and, in some cases, the ability to emboss/deboss text and graphic devices.

The initial stages of a study are the time to explore these options, thinking widely and considering all materials. Later you can reject some design candidates on the grounds of practicality, cost, filling problems, etc. For now, however, commit all ideas to paper because there is likely to be a germ of an idea that can be used or adapted. In the honey example, ceramic jars may ultimately be too expensive but this imagery might be used to create a plastic container that incorporates the shape, texture, or colors of the original.

Graphic and structural development

Having established a thorough understanding of the brief, conducted research to the stage where you know the target audience, the market, and competitor products, designing can begin. In practice, this will likely have been in progress, at least mentally, as research progressed. Now, these initial thoughts need to be visually captured to allow exploration in greater detail and to reveal your thinking to other design team members. This is not the time for highly finished renderings. It is the time, however, for showing a wide range of ideas and for providing the underlying rationale behind each of them. This rationale should address how your concepts meet the brief and how it will help sell products. While creativity should not be dampened by practical considerations at this point, be aware that creativity alone is not enough.

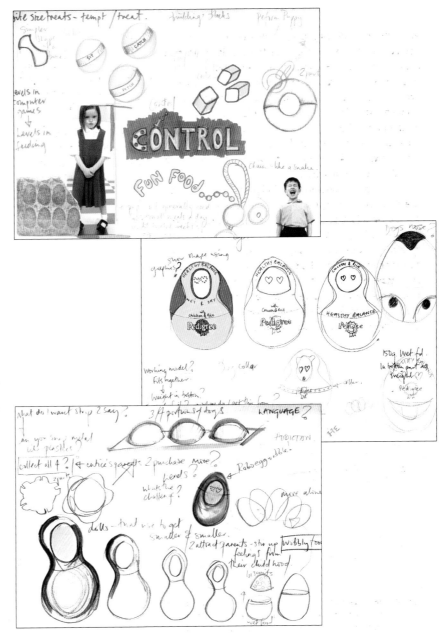

⬆ **Initial concepts** should be in sketch format, encapsulating your thinking. The sketches shown here illustrate the point. This project, for a brand of pet foods, concerned the design of packaging that would engage children with caring for their pets.

The designer has concentrated on getting initial ideas onto paper, annotating this with notes to explain the thinking behind the design work. Little more is needed at this stage. Note that, while shape has been a major design consideration, graphics and branding have been considered from the outset. From these initial concepts, further structural and graphic development took place, combining foam models and graphics worked up on the Apple Mac.

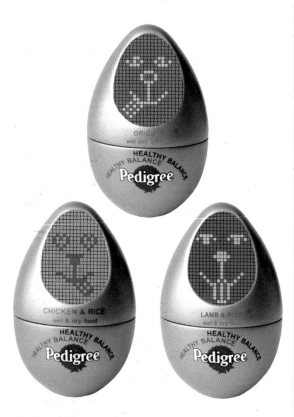

↑ Three-dimensional models
In this example, models have been vacuum-formed from plastic, paint-sprayed with metallic silver and decorated with computer-generated graphics to give a realistic appearance. Three product varieties are shown here, indicating how the basic pack shape can work across a product range. The results are realistic and believable, allowing the models to be placed on shelf and viewed against competitor products.

Packaging design is a strictly commercial activity and ultimately, creativity and innovation must be directed towards solutions that meet the brief.

Presenting work

Presenting your ideas to a client is an exercise in communication, and while techniques using photography or computer-generated images have a role to play, for packaging design, where the end result will be a three-dimensional object, pack models with applied graphics provide the ideal medium.

Packaging Assignment
(Brief set by Mike Nicholls, Toni & Guy Media, for the D&AD student competition, Corus steel packaging design awards)

Client: Toni & Guy
Brief: Create structurally unusual packaging for a new range of male hair care products that focus on the "Generation-X" attitude—geared towards up-and-coming, youth-orientated, non-conformist, fashion conscious image makers and trend-setters. The design should utilize the aesthetic and structural qualities of steel to create packaging for a new range of male hair care products, uniquely combining this masculine identity with the unexplainable X-factor. The design should also differentiate Toni & Guy products from its competitors.
Background: The Toni & Guy philosophy is that each client's hairstyle should be personalized. We take into account facial features, hair type, fashion taste and lifestyle to create an individual approach to nurturing hair. Toni & Guy's Core products are sold in the Toni & Guy salons and main-street stores, and are liked for their funky packaging and in-your-face colors. A mixture of foil, metal, and plastics achieve a dynamic that is seen as contemporary and stylish, thus standing out on-shelf.
Target audience: There are two Toni & Guy ranges: Core and Insights. Both are mass-market products, but whereas Core appeals to the younger end of the market, Insights appeals more to older clients, and have a more upmarket feel. For this brief the men's range is to be mass market but definitely exclusive—aspirational, expensive, bold, and unusual. At present, only 4 percent of the Toni & Guy products market is male. For this brief, the target audience is:

- 20–30-year-old males who would buy the product for personal use
- Professional salon hairdressers

Technical design considerations:
- The products should be: a 2-in-1 shampoo and body gel, conditioning treatment, volumizing or thickening treatment, wax or clay styling product, shaving or skin treatment.
- The multi-benefits concept—less fuss and effective performance—should be incorporated, e.g. shampoo and body gel in one gives a simple choice and an efficient application.
- Steel offers advantages such as strength, safety, formability, printability, and is fully recyclable.

Mandatories:
- The form must be used to achieve shelf standout and incorporate the "Generation-X" element.
- Toni & Guy branding must be used.
- Steel needs to be the primary component.

Hints: Toni & Guy are (in male hairdressing terms) expensive. What male groups are likely to go to their salons? Others, perhaps with less disposable income, may still wish to buy a quality brand for styling at home, so how can they be made to feel confident about a product which has had, up until now, a largely female client base? Although this range is aimed at young men, these are people concerned with style rather than machismo. What mobile phones, MP3 players, and other gadgets would you find in their homes and what would your pack design be sitting alongside in their bathrooms?

Initial concepts The sketches show some of the concepts being considered. Shapes have been kept simple and elegant, avoiding masculine clichés. Consideration of branding and colors are incorporated even in these early sketches.

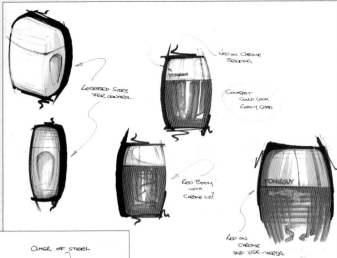

RECESSED SIDES FOR CONTROL.

RED ON CHROME BRANDING

CONTRAST COULD LOOK REALLY GOOD

RED BODY WITH CHROME LID?

TONI&GUY

RED ON CHROME AND VISE-VERSA.

Research This student has prepared a mood board from many sources, distilling it down to show young men who want to look good and for whom style is really important.

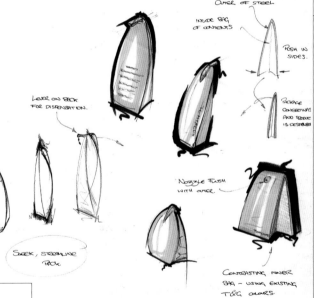

OUTER OF STEEL

INSIDE BAG OF CONTENTS

PUSH IN SIDES.

PACKAGE CONCERTINAS AND PRODUCT IS DISPENSED

LEVER ON BACK FOR DISPENSATION.

NOZZLE FLUSH WITH OUTER.

SLEEK, STREAMLINE PACK.

CONTRASTING INNER BAG - USING EXISTING T&G COLORS.

Style and function Here, both style and function are considered. You may think about comparing the average PC with an iMac. Their function is broadly similar but the difference lies in the detail, how they operate, and, importantly, how they look. This provides a clue about approaching this study.

BALL SHAPED NOZZLE

Final proposal The final proposal has been mocked up and photographed, demonstrating a spring steel shell and flexible pouch, with product being dispensed through a non-return valve on the front panel. Graphics have been kept simple, showing the logo only, using gloss varnish on a matte silver base. While the idea is strong, the designer has not fully explored all the practical implications, particularly the messy dispensing system—the design as proposed could have problems and might require modifications. The point is that a design process has been followed, resulting in an innovative pack design that has the potential for further development.

Concept development The favored concept in this instance is a collapsible pouch, offering a method of dispensing the product together with a very different appearance to other products. The concept was worked up in sketches and in physical mock-ups.

FAR MORE MASCULINE APPEARANCE

Resources

The International Organization for Standardization (ISO) 'A' series is a system for sizing paper that was first used in Germany in 1922 where it is still called "DIN A" (Deutsche Industrie Norm). Each size is derived by halving the size immediately above it. Each size is the same as another geometrically as they are halved using the same diagonal. A0 is the first size and is 10¾ square feet (one square metre, approximately) in area. A series sizes always refer to the trimmed sheet. The untrimmed sizes are referred to as "RA" or "SRA." About 26 countries have officially adopted the A series system and it is commonly used everywhere in the world except Canada and the United States.

The 'B' series is used when a size in between any two adjacent A sizes is needed, which is relatively rare. The British and American systems, unlike the metric A system, refer to the untrimmed size of the sheet. As quoting just the A or B number can cause confusion, both the A or B size and the size in inches or millimeters should be given when specifying paper.

Paper usage formulae

To calculate the number of sheets of paper required to print a book (excluding covers):

$$\frac{\text{Number of copies to be printed} \times \text{Number of pages in book}}{\text{Number of pages printing on both sides of sheet}} = \text{Number of sheets required}$$

To calculate the number of copies obtainable from a given quantity of paper:

$$\frac{\text{Number of sheets} \times \text{Number of pages printing on both sides of sheet}}{\text{Number of pages in book}} = \text{Number of copies}$$

ISO A series

	Inches	mm
A0	13.11 x 46.81	841 x 1189
A1	23.39 x 33.11	594 x 841
A2	16.54 x 23.39	420 x 594
A3	1.69 x 16.54	297 x 420
A4	8.27 x 11.69	210 x 297
A5	5.83 x 8.27	148 x 210
A6	4.13 x 5.83	105 x 148
A7	2.91 x 4.13	74 x 105
A8	2.05 x 2.91	52 x 74
A9	1.46 x 2.05	37 x 52
A10	1.02 x 1.46	26 x 37
RA0	33.86 x 48.03	860 x 1220
RA1	25.02 x 33.86	610 x 860
RA2	16.93 x 24.02	430 x 610
SRA0	38.58 x 50.93	980 x 1280
SRA1	25.02 x 33.86	610 x 860
SRA2	17.72 x 25.20	450 x 640

ISO B series (untrimmed)

	Inches	mm
B0	39.37 x 55.67	1000 x 1414
B1	27.83 x 39.37	707 x 1000
B2	19.68 x 27.83	500 x 707
B3	13.90 x 19.68	353 x 500
B4	9.84 x 13.90	250 x 353
B5	6.93 x 9.84	176 x 250
B6	4.92 x 6.93	125 x 176
B7	3.46 x 4.92	88 x 125
B8	2.44 x 3.46	62 x 88
B9	1.73 x 2.44	44 x 62
B10	1.22 x 1.73	31 x 44

ISO C series envelopes

	inches	mm
C0	36.00 x 51.20	917 x 1297
C1	25.60 x 36.00	648 x 917
C2	18.00 x 25.60	458 x 648
C3	12.80 x 18.00	324 x 458
C4	9.00 x 12.80	229 x 324
C5	6.40 x 9.00	162 x 229
C6	4.50 x 6.40	114 x 162
C7	3.20 x 4.50	81 x 114
DL	4.33 x 8.66	110 x 220
C7/6	3.19 x 6.38	81 x 162

US book sizes

inches	mm
5 1/2 x 8 1/2	140 x 216
5 x 7 3/8	127 x 187
5 1/2 x 8 1/4	140 x 210
6 1/8 x 9 1/4	156 x 235
5 3/8 x 8	136 x 203
5 5/8 x 8 3/8	143 x 213

British standard book sizes

	Quarto		Octavo	
	inches	mm	inches	mm
Crown	9.69 x 7.44	246 x 189	7.32 x 4.84	186 x 123
Large Crown	10.16 x 7.91	258 x 201	7.8 x 5.08	198 x 129
Demy	10.87 x 8.62	276 x 219	8.5 x 5.43	216 x 138
Royal	12.28 x 9.33	312 x 237	9.21 x .14	234 x 156

Inches	mm	Bible	Bond/writing	Book (coated and uncoated)	Cover (coated and uncoated)	Gravure	Ledger	News print	Offset (coated and uncoated)	Onionskin and manifold	Opaque circular	Text	Wedding
16 x 21	406.2 x 533.4						♦						
17 x 22	431.8 x 558.8		♦				♦			♦	♦		♦
17 x 28	431.8 x 558.8		♦				♦			♦	♦		
19 x 24	482.6 x 609.6		♦				♦			♦			
20 x 26	508.0 x 660.4			♦	♦								
21 x 32	533.4 x 812.8							♦		♦			
22 x 24	558.8 x 609.6		♦										
22 x 34	558.8 x 863.6						♦	♦		♦	♦		♦
22.5 x 35	571.5 x 889.0			♦					♦				
23 x 35	584.2 x 889.0				♦								
24 x 36	609.6 x 914.4			♦				♦					
24 x 38	609.6 x 965.2		♦				♦			♦			
25 x 38	635.0 x 965.2	♦		♦		♦			♦		♦	♦	
26 x 34	660.4 x 863.6									♦			
26 x 40	660.4 x 1016.0			♦	♦							♦	
26 x 48	660.4 x 1219.2			♦									
28 x 34	711.2 x 863.6		♦				♦	♦		♦	♦		
28 x 42	711.2 x 1066.8	♦		♦		♦		♦	♦				
28 x 44	711.2 x 1117.6			♦		♦			♦				
32 x 44	812.8 x 1117.6	♦		♦		♦			♦				
34 x 44	863.6 x 1117.6		♦					♦					
35 x 45	889.0 x 1143.0	♦		♦		♦			♦		♦	♦	♦
35 x 46	889.0 x 1168.4				♦								
36 x 48	914.4 x 1219.2			♦				♦	♦				
38 x 50	965.2 x 1270.0	♦		♦		♦		♦	♦		♦		
38 x 52	965.2 x 1320.8								♦				
41 x 54	1041.4 x 1371.6			♦					♦				
44 x 64	1117.6 x 1625.6								♦				

Glossary

Airbrush A mechanical painting tool producing a fine spray of paint or ink, used in illustration, design, and retouching.

Art(work) (a/w, A/W) Any illustrative matter prepared for reproduction, such as illustrations, diagrams, and photographs. Usually distinct from text.

Bar code A pattern of vertical lines identifying details of a product, such as country of origin, manufacturer, and type of product, conforming to the Universal Product Code (UPC)—there are several different formats for product coding.

Base artwork/black art Artwork requiring the addition of other elements such as halftone positives before reproduction.

Baseline grid In some applications, an invisible grid to which lines of text can be locked so that their baselines align from column to column.

Bézier curve In object-oriented drawing applications, a mathematically defined curve between two points (Bézier points). The curve is manipulated by dragging, from an anchored point, control handles which act on the curve like magnets.

Bit map A text character or graphic image comprised of dots.

Bleed The part of an image that extends beyond the edge of a page. Images which spread to the edge of the paper allowing no margins are described as "bled off".

Box feature/story Information in a publication presented separately from the running text and illustrations and either surrounded by a box rule or underlaid with a tint patch.

CAD/CAM *abb*: computer-aided design and manufacturing, where computers are used to control, in many cases, the entire production process from design to manufacture.

CAG *abb*: computer-aided graphics, as in graphic design.

CD-ROM *abb*: compact disk read-only memory. Non-erasable storage systems of huge capacity— around 650MB, which is enough space for a type foundry's entire font library.

CMYK Acronym for the process colors of cyan, magenta, yellow, and black inks used in four-color printing.

Color correction The adjustment of the color values of an illustration either (1 *pho*) by the original photographer using color-balancing filters, or (2 *rep*) by adjusting the color scanner to produce the correct result. Subsequently, corrections can be made on the color-separated films or on a computer by means of an image-manipulation application.

Color model In graphics applications, the way in which colors can be defined or modified. The most common color models are RGB (red, green, and blue); HSB (hue, saturation, and brightness) or HLS (hue, lightness, and saturation); CMY; CMYK (process colors); and PANTONE (spot colors).

Color transparency/tranny (pho.) A photographic image produced on transparent film as a color positive.

Copyright The right of the creator of an original work to control the use of that work. While broadly controlled by international agreement (Universal Copyright Convention), there are differences between countries. In the U.S. copyright of an intellectual property is generally established by registration, whereas in the U.K. it exists automatically by virtue of the creation of an original work. Ownership of copyright does not necessarily mean ownership of the actual work (or vice versa), nor does it necessarily cover rights to that work throughout the world (the rights to a work can be held territory by territory).

Copywriting A term applied to the writing of copy specifically for use in advertising and promotional material.

Corporate identity The elements of design by which any organization establishes an appropriate, consistent, and recognizable identity through communication, promotion, and distribution material.

Crop To trim or mask an illustration so that it fits a given area or to discard unwanted portions.

Cutout (1 *rep*) An illustration from which the background has been removed to provide a silhouetted image. (2 *fin*) A display card or book cover from which a pattern has been cut by means of a steel die.

Desktop publishing (DTP) Used to describe the activity of generating text, page layout, and graphics on a computer and then printing, or publishing, the result.

Dots per inch (dpi) The unit of measurement that represents the resolution of a device such as a printer, imagesetter, or monitor. The closer the dots are together (the more dots per inch) the better the quality. Typical resolutions are 72 dpi for a monitor, 300 dpi for a LaserWriter, and 2450 dpi (or much more) for an imagesetter.

Dropping-out The repro house term for the replacement of a low-resolution scan by a high-resolution scan, prior to final output.

Drop shadow An area of tone forming a shadow behind an image or character, designed to bring the image or character forward.

Dummy (1) The prototype of a proposed book or publication in the correct format, binding, paper, and bulk, but with blank pages. (2) A mock-up of a design showing the position of headings, text, captions, illustration, and other details.

Duotone (*rep*) Technically, two halftones made from the same original to two different tonal ranges, so that when printed — in different tones of the same color — a greater tonal range is produced than is possible with a single color.

Edition (*pri*) The whole number of copies of a work printed and published at one time, either as the first edition, or after some changes have been made (revised edition, second edition, etc.)

End/back matter The final pages of a book, following the main body, such as the index. Also called "postlims."

Final film (*rep*) The positive or negative used for plate making, incorporating all corrections and in which the halftones are made with a hard dot.

Flat plan A diagrammatic plan of the pages of a book used to establish the distribution of color, chapter lengths, etc. Also called a flowchart.

Font/fount Traditionally a set of type of the same design, style and size. On the Mac, a font is a set of characters, including letters, numbers and other typographic symbols, of the same design and style.

Four-color process (*rep / pri*) The printing process that reproduces full-color images by using three basic colors — cyan, magenta, and yellow, plus black for added density.

Front matter The pages of a book preceding the main text, usually consisting of the half-title, title, preface, and contents. Also called "prelims."

GIF *abb:* graphic interchange format. A file format used for transferring graphics files between different computer systems via the CompuServe information service.

G/m2/gsm/grams per square meter (*pap*) A unit of measurement indicating the substance of paper on the basis of its weight, regardless of the sheet size.

Graphic (1) A typeface originating from drawn rather than scripted letter forms. (2) A general term describing any illustration or design.

Guides In some applications, visible but non-printing horizontal and vertical lines that help you to position items with greater accuracy.

Half-title (1) The title of a book as printed on the recto of the leaf preceding the title page. (2) The page on which the half-title appears.

Halftone (1 *rep*) The process by which a continuous tone image is simulated by a pattern of dots of varying sizes. (2 *rep*) An image reproduced by the halftone process.

Halftone screen Conventionally, a sheet of glass or film cross-hatched with opaque lines. Also called a crossline screen or contact screen, it is used to translate a continuous tone image into halftone dots so that it can be printed.

House style (1) The style of spelling, punctuation, and spacing used by a publishing house to maintain a consistent standard and treatment of text throughout its publications. (2) Corporate identity.

Hyphenation and justification (H&J) The routines of an application that distributes spaces correctly in a line of type to achieve the desired measure in justified text.

Imprint page The page of a book carrying details of the edition, such as the printer's imprint, copyright owner, ISBN, catalog number, etc.

JPEG *abb:* Joint Photographic Experts Group, a data compression standard.

Justification The spacing of words and letters so that the beginning and end of each line of text share the same vertical left and right edges.

K *abb:* key, used to describe the process color black, deriving from the key, or black, printing plate in four-color process printing. Using the letter K rather than the initial B avoids confusion with blue, even though the abbreviation for process blue is C (cyan).

Kerning Adjusting the space (usually reducing it) between a pair of type characters to optimize their appearance.

Layer In some applications, a level to which you can consign an element of the design you are working on.

Layout Visualization which gives the general appearance of a design, indicating, for instance, the relationship between text and illustrations. The term is more properly used in the context of preparing a design for reproduction.

Lead(ing) Space between lines of type, originating from days when strips of lead were placed between lines of type to increase the space.

Light table/box A table or box with a translucent glass top lit from below, giving a color-balanced light suitable for viewing transparencies and for color-matching to proofs.

Linking In some frame based page layout applications, the facility for connecting two or more text boxes so that text flows from one box to another.

Logo-logotype Traditionally, any group of type characters (other than ligatures) such as company names or emblems cast together on one metal body. The term is now used to describe any design or symbol for a corporation or organization which forms the centerpiece of its corporate identity.

Manuscript (MS/MSS) An author's text submitted for publication.

Master page In some applications, the page to which certain attributes, such as the number of text columns, page numbers, type style, etc., can be given, which can then be applied to any other page in a document.

Original Any image, artwork, or text matter intended for reproduction.

Origination (*rep*) A term used to describe any or all of the reproduction processes that may occur between design and printing.

PANTONE Pantone, Inc.'s check-standard trademark for color standards, control, and quality requirements. It is a system in which each color bears a description of its formulation (in percentages) for subsequent use by the printer.

It is also a system that is used throughout the world, so that colors specified by any designer can be matched exactly by any printer.

Paste-up A layout of a page or pages incorporating all the design elements such as text, illustrations, and rules.

Proof (*typ*/*rep*/*pri*) A representation on paper, taken from a laser printer or imagesetter, inked plate, stone, screen, block, or type, in order to check the progress and accuracy of the work. Also called a "pull."

Recto The right-hand page of a book.

Register (*rep*/*pri*) The correct positioning of one color on top of another or of the pages on one side of a sheet relative to the other (called "backing up") during printing. As distinct from "fit."

Repro(duction) (*rep*) The entire printing process from the completion of artwork or imagesetter output to printing. Also called origination.

Resolution The degree of precision—the quality, definition, or clarity—with which an image is represented or displayed, such as by a scanner, monitor, printer, or other output device.

Retouching (*pho*/*rep*) Altering or correcting an image, artwork, or film to make modifications or remove imperfections.

Runaround Text that fits around a shape, like an illustration. Also called "text wrap."

Scanned image (*rep*) An image that has been converted by a scanner to a suitable file format that you can import into an application. To designers, the size of the file is important, since a single high resolution four-color scan for high

quality reproduction may create a file of many megabytes, thus reducing the practicality of working with any quantity of scanned images. On jobs containing multiple images, it is more usual for designers to work with low resolution scans and use them for position only.

Spec(ification) A detailed description of the components, characteristics and procedures of a particular job, product, or activity.

Specimen page A proof of a page as an example of a proposed style of design, paper quality, printing, etc.

Spot color (*rep*/*pri*) The term used to describe any printing color that is a special mix of colors, and not one of the four process colors.

Style (sheets) In some applications, the facility for applying a range of frequently used attributes, such as typographic and paragraph formats, to elements in a document by using specially assigned commands.

TIFF *abb*: tagged image file format, a standard and popular graphics file format used for scanned, high-resolution, bitmapped images.

Title page The page, normally a right-hand page, at the front of a book which bears the title, name(s) of the author(s), the publisher, and any other relevant information.

Verso The left-hand page of a book or, more precisely, the other side of a leaf from a recto (right-hand page).

Bibliography

Apeloig, Philippe, *Au Coeur du Mot* (Inside the Word), Lars Muller, 2001

Blackwell, Lewis, *20th-Century Type: Remix*, Gingko Press, 1999

Carter, Rob; Day, Ben; and Meggs, Philip, *Typographic Design: Form and Communication*, John Wiley & Sons, 2nd edition, 1993.

Craig, James, *Production for the Graphic Designer*, Watson-Guptill, 2000

Dabner, David, *Design and Layout*, Chrysalis Books, 2003

Dowding, Geoffrey, *Finer Points in the Spacing and Arrangement of Type* (Classic Typography Series), Hartley and Marks, 1997

Friedl, Friedrich; Ott, Nicolaus; and Stein, Bernard, *Typography: Who, When, How*, Konemann, 1998

Gordon, Bob, *Making Digital Type Look Good*, Watson-Guptill, 2001

Gutman, Laura, *Macromedia Dreamweaver MX 2004 Demystified*, Pearson Education, 2003

Hochuli, Jost, and Kinross, Robert, *Designing Books: Practice and Theory*, Princeton, 2004

Hollis, Richard, *Graphic Design: A Concise History* (World of Art series), Thames and Hudson, 1994

Kunz, Willi, *Typography: Macro- and Microaesthetics*, Ram Publications, 1998

Muller-Brockmann, Josef, *Grid Systems in Graphic Design*, Ram Publications, 2001

Muller-Brockmann, Josef, *Pioneer of Swiss Graphic Design*, Lars Muller, 2nd edition, 2001

Roberts, Lucien, and Thrift, Julia, *The Designer and the Grid*, Rockport, 2002

Spiekermann, Erik, and Ginger, E.M., *Stop Stealing Sheep and Find Out How Type Works*, Adobe Press, 2nd edition, 2002.

Towers, J. Tarin, *Macromedia Dreamweaver MX 2004 for Windows and Macintosh* (Visual Quickstart Guides), Pearson Education, 2004

Tufte, Edward, *Visual Explanations: Images and Quantities, Evidence and Narrative*, Graphics Press, 1997.

Wilber, Peter, and Burke, Michael, *Information Graphics: Innovative Solutions in Contemporary Design*, Thames and Hudson, 1999.

Index

Page numbers in *italic* refer to captions

Credits

Wendy Chapple (pp 14–15, 20–21) is a practicing printmaker and illustrator. She teaches within the graphic design schools at both the London College of Communication and Central St. Martin's School of Art and Design.

Moira Clinch (pp 122–125) completed an MA in Information Graphics at Central St Martin's School of Art and Design in London. She is Art Director of Quarto Publishing plc.

David Dabner (pp 16–19, 26–51, 56–57, 78–91, 94–109) is currently course director for the Foundation Degree in Design for Graphic Communication at the London College of Communication, and a member of the International Society of Typographic Designers. He is experienced at designing advertising typography, and has worked for both Ogilvy and Mather, and Young and Rubican.

Eugenie Dodd FCSD MSTD (pp 92–93, 136–147) runs a design practice in London that specializes in creative communication. Her studio's work has been exhibited and is widely published in professional literature. She is a visiting lecturer at Kingston University and the London College of Communication, and also runs typography workshops in Denmark and Israel. She is co-author of *Decorative Typography*, published by Phaidon Press.

Robin Dodd FCSD (pp 10–13, 52–55, 58–59) studied graphic design specializing in typography at the London College of Printing. He now practices as a freelance design consultant, and is an associate lecturer at the London College of Communication concentrating on design history and visual theory.

Graham Goldwater (pp 22–25, 64–65) is a London-based photographer who has spent many years working in the industry and in education. He is currently involved in researching "old" photographic methods and combining them with new technological advances in computer software.

David Gressingham (pp 158–165) is a senior lecturer in information design at the London College of Communication. He has many years of industry experience in the area of identity design and has worked for a number of leading design consultants.

Nick Jeeves (pp 52–55, 116–121, 148–157) has been a freelance graphic designer and writer for ten years. He also lectures at a number of colleges, including Cambridge School of Art.

Malcolm Jobling (pp 148–157) has spent over 20 years in advertising. He now teaches Design for Advertising at Dunstable College in southern England in conjunction with continuing freelance work.

Chris Jones (pp 72–73, 132–133, 166–173) completed his MA at the Royal College of Art in 1995. Since then he has worked on a wide variety of arts and communication design projects, many of which are web-related. He now lectures at Central St. Martin's School of Art and Design, and the Royal College of Art in London.

Chris Patmore (pp 74–77) is a London-based writer specializing in creative technology. He is the author of *The Complete Animation Course* and runs a website for animators. Chris has worked internationally as a graphic designer and photographer.

Benedict Richards (pp 112–115, 126–129) studied typographic design at the London College of Communication. He has been a busy graphic designer for the past 15 years. He teaches typography and print production at the London College of Communication.

Catherine Smith (pp 110–111) currently teaches Personal and Professional Development in the School of Graphic Design at the London College of Communication. She is the author of *Design and Layout: Understanding and Using Graphics*.

Bill Stewart (pp 174–181) has worked as Packaging Manager at 3M UK plc, and as Technical Director with the London-based design consultancy, Siebert Head. He is currently Senior Research Fellow at the Art & Design Research Centre, Sheffield Hallam University in the north of England, and has published many books and articles on packaging design.

Shaun Wilkinson (pp 60–63, 66–71 developed the Computer Graphics facilities in the London College of Communication's School of Graphic Design and has written a number of software packages. He has been a senior lecturer in Computer Graphics since 1983.

Picture Credits
With special thanks to the contributing students from the London College of Communication.

Quarto would like to thank and acknowledge the following for supplying illustrations and photographs reproduced in this book:

Key: l left, r right, c center, t top, b bottom, b/g background

10l, 47t, 62b, 63bl, 63br, 93t, 95br Design: Igor Masnjak Design
42 Design: Happy F & B, Gothenburg, Sweden www.fb.se. Client: Röhsska Museum, Sweden
51t Design: Pepe Gimeno, SL www.pepegimeno.com. Client: Feria Internacional del Mueble de Valencia
53t Caroline Tatham
64 Canon Inc. www.canon.com
72t Design: Simon Mellor. Client: Virgile and Stone www.virgileandstone.com
73t Pete King. Client: Knofler Clothing Ltd. www.knofler.co.uk
80 Agfa Monotype Ltd. www.customfonts.com and www.agfamonotype.co.uk
92tl Design: Rubin Coraro Design www.rubincordaro.com
92tr Design: Starling Design, London

92r Howard Lawrence
116tl Photolibrary.com www.photolibrary.com
116tr Image Source www.imagesource.com
118t The New York Times Co. Reprinted with permission. Copyright © 2004 International Herald Tribune. All Rights Reserved
120 Design: Hannah Firmin. Author: Alexander McCall Smith. Abacus
121t Design: Richard Ogle. Author: Carl Hiaasen. Macmillan, London.
126l, 127b Design: Sweden Graphics www.swedengraphics.com
129b Design: Vibeke Nodskov, LEO Pharma www.leo-pharma.com Client: Pondocillin®
158 Design: Rick Eiber Design (RED). Client: On The Wall
159 Design: David Carter Design. Client: Zen Floral Design Studio
166 Giraffecards www.giraffecards.com
167, 171br Artupdate.com www.artupdate.com
168 Google Inc. www.google.com
170l, 171cl American Airlines www.aa.com
170r Apple www.apple.com
171t Amazon www.amazon.com
171bl Cable News Network LP, LLLP. www.cnn.com
174l Design: Sandstrom Design. Brand: Miller Lite
174r, 175t Photographer: Ivan Jones www.ivan-jones.co.uk
175b Design: Design Bridge www.designbridge.com. Client: Rieber & Son

All other illustrations and photographs are the copyright of Quarto Publishing plc.

Quarto Publishing plc has made every effort to contact contributors and credit them appropriately. We apologize in advance for any omissions or errors in the above list; we will gladly correct this information in future editions of the book.

The publishers and copyright holders acknowledge all trademarks used in this book as the property of their owners.

Conceived, designed, and produced by
Quarto Publishing plc
The Old Brewery
6 Blundell Street
London N7 9BH

Editor: Damian Thompson
Art Editor: Anna Knight
Designer: James Lawrence
Assistant Art Director: Penny Cobb
Editorial Assistants: Kate Martin, Mary Groom

Publisher Piers Spence
Art Director Moira Clinch

$45.0

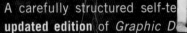

graphic

design school

A carefully structured self-te...
updated edition of *Graphic D*...
information on computer-aided design and the use of
software applications in all aspects of design, including the
creation of successful corporate logos, advertisements, and
magazine design solutions.

Graphic Design School is packed with **practical guidance** for
graphic designers working in both print and digital
media—from newspapers, magazines, and books, to packaging, advertising,
corporate work, and web design.

This interactive guide contains targeted assignments that give the reader tasks
and exercises to sharpen their skills, and includes a wealth of **full-color**
illustrations to inspire artistic expression and individual interpretation, as well
as professional tips and hints from leading design practitioners.

Throughout, real examples of students' work from designing logos and websites
to product packaging are highlighted, providing points of reference so you
can continually compare your own progress and enhance your potential in
what can be a very competitive field. *Graphic Design School* is a must-buy,
all-encompassing guide to this fast-evolving subject.

THE AUTHOR

After working in the print and design industry for several
years as a typographer, Dave Dabner returned to academic
life as a lecturer in design. He teaches at the renowned
London College of Printing and is Course Director of the
Better Internum Diploma in Typographic Design. He is the
author of *Design Media Handbook* and its sister

A FOUNDATION COURSE IN THE PRINCIPLES
AND PRACTICES OF GRAPHIC DESIGN

⊕**WILEY**